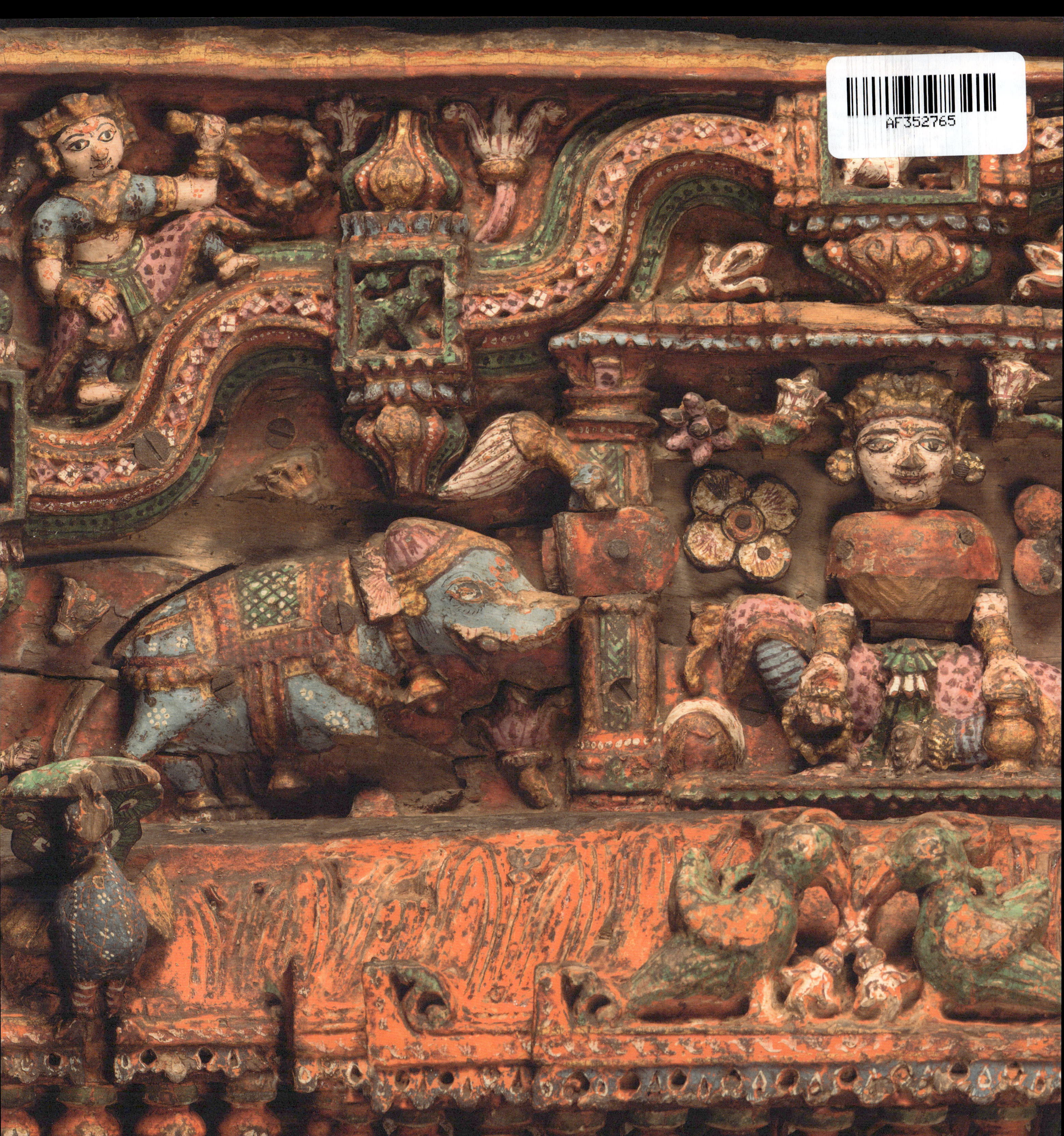
AF352765

Masterworks from India and Southeast Asia

THE NELSON-ATKINS
MUSEUM OF ART

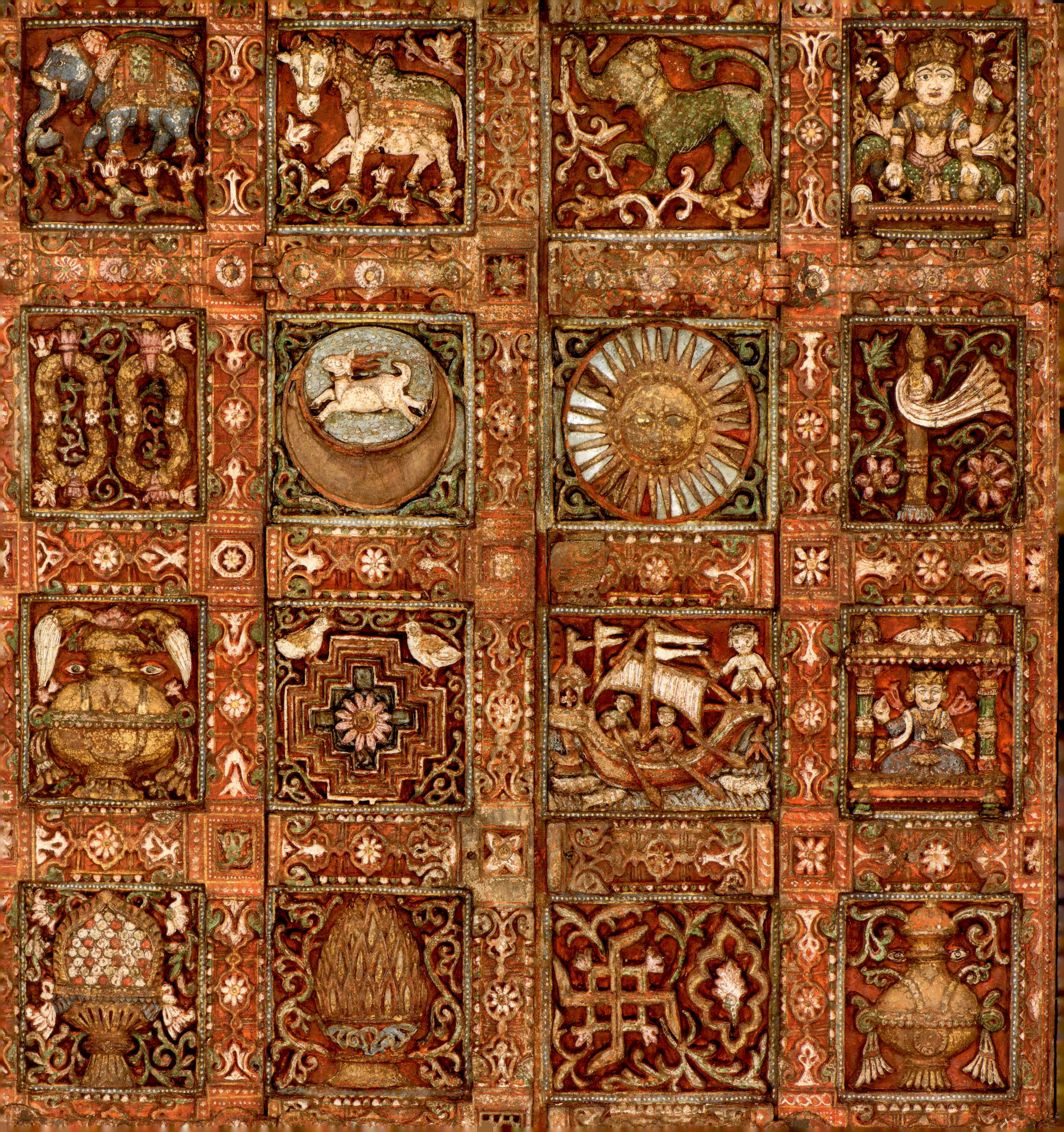

Masterworks from India and Southeast Asia

THE NELSON-ATKINS MUSEUM OF ART

KIMBERLY MASTELLER
JEANNE MCCRAY BEALS CURATOR
OF SOUTH AND SOUTHEAST ASIAN ART

THE NELSON-ATKINS MUSEUM OF ART   KANSAS CITY, MISSOURI
IN ASSOCIATION WITH UNIVERSITY OF WASHINGTON PRESS   SEATTLE AND LONDON

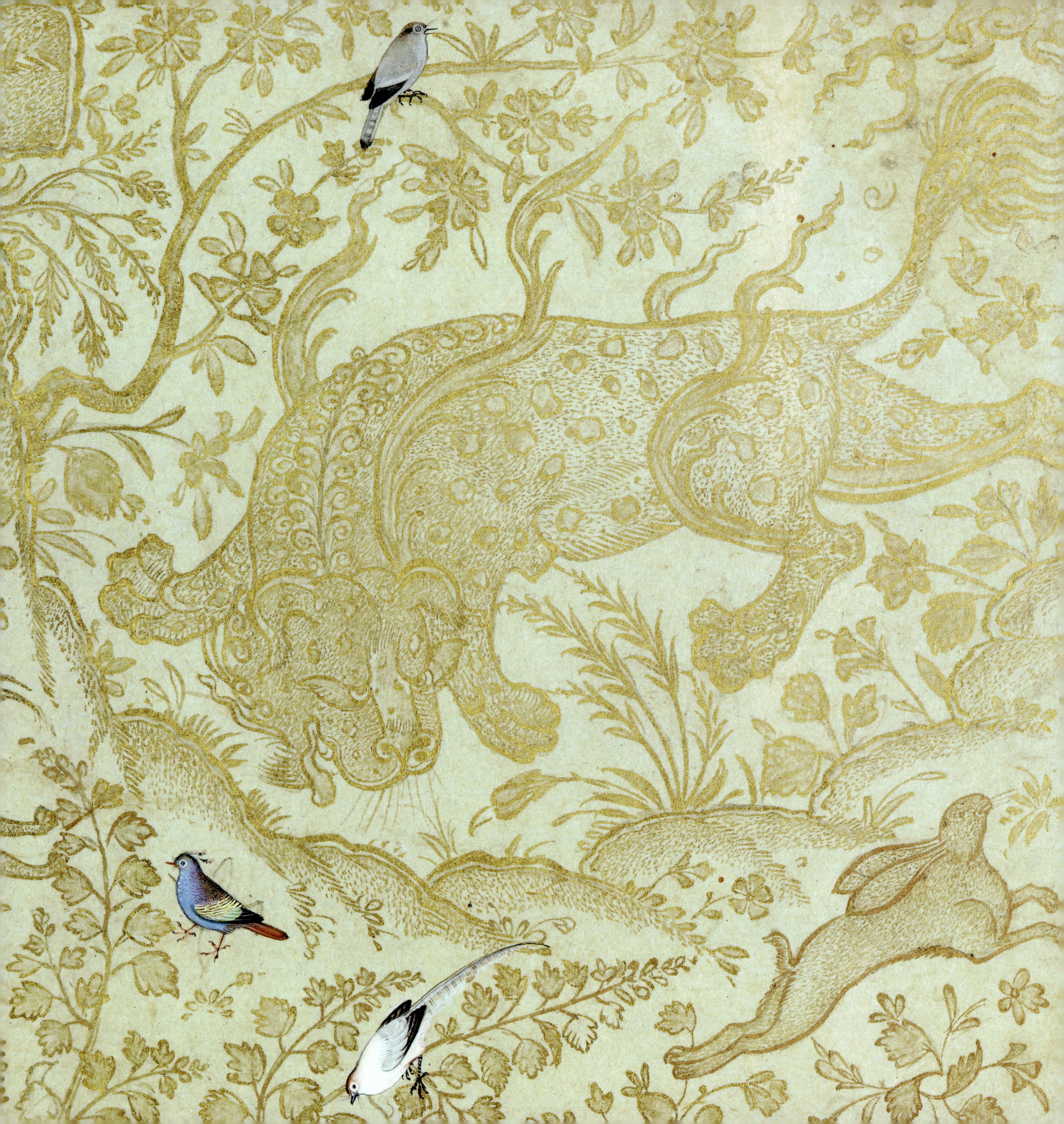

CONTENTS

DIRECTOR'S FOREWORD

One of the joys of working at the Nelson-Atkins Museum of Art is strolling through its Asian galleries. The Museum's Asian collections are internationally renowned, and the beautiful Indian and Southeast Asian works illustrated in this volume demonstrate why. This volume enables readers to engage deeply with a small selection of the masterworks from the rich South and Southeast Asian collections. Each beautifully illustrated work is accompanied by a detailed essay that locates it within its aesthetic and cultural context. The essays follow a prologue that provides both a rich history of the Indian and Southeast Asian collections at the Nelson-Atkins and a general introduction to the meaning, function, and aesthetics of South and Southeast Asian Art. Endnote citations and a complete bibliography are provided for the benefit of students, scholars, and those who wish to learn more. This book follows upon our recent volume *Masterworks of Chinese Art: The Nelson-Atkins Museum of Art,* by Senior Curator of Chinese Art, Colin Mackenzie (2011), also funded by the Estelle S. and Robert A. Long Ellis Foundation. Together, these publications attest to the high achievement of Asian artists and to the important role Asian art plays in the history of world art and civilization.

I would like to thank the Estelle S. and Robert A. Long Ellis Foundation and its directors, James H. Bernard Sr., James H. Bernard Jr., and Jean McGreevey Green for their generous grant in support of this publication. I especially want to acknowledge Jean Green's deep interest in the Nelson-Atkins Asian collections in general and in this project in particular. A publication devoted to these collections was a long-standing goal of the Museum. The support of these benefactors has made this goal a reality. Recently, the South and Southeast Asian Department and collections have also benefitted from the generosity of the Jeanne McCray Beals Trust, Dr. Bipin and Rita Avashia, and Dr. Roopa Bansal, who have provided department funding, supported programs, and gifted superlative works of art.

I would also like to thank Kimberly Masteller, Jeanne McCray Beals Curator of South and Southeast Asian Art, for her research on the collections and their history and her contribution of the essays and introduction of this book. It is my hope that this volume will inspire more curiosity, more looking, and more visits to these beloved collections in the Nelson-Atkins.

Julián Zugazagoitia
Menefee D. and Mary Louise Blackwell Director and CEO

ACKNOWLEDGMENTS

It is a great privilege to work with the outstanding collections of South and Southeast Asian Art at The Nelson-Atkins Museum of Art. These objects are not silent; they have the ability to tell stories, transmit cultural knowledge, and engage the viewer through their beauty, power, and presentation. I hope that this volume with enable readers to engage with these works of art as well. When I was hired by Marc Wilson, now Director Emeritus, one of our goals was to publish the collections and I hope that by sharing a selection of masterworks with students, scholars, and the public this work will be a good 'first step' towards this goal. Marc's knowledge of these collections is vast, and he contributed to the publication through conversations, cited in the introduction, and through his passion for the objects, which has served as an inspiration.

My thanks to Julián Zugazagoitia, the Menefee D. and Mary-Louis Blackwell Director and CEO of the museum. Julián has been an unwavering supporter of the department and of this publication. He is committed to sharing our collections with the public and making the museum an active center for dialogue and engagement. I would also like to thank Michele Valentine, Department Assistant, for her hard work in helping to prepare copy, format text, and create the bibliography. One could not ask for a better assistant and colleague than Michele. Colin Mackenzie, Senior Curator of Chinese Art, provided an excellent model with his publication of *Masterworks of Chinese Art: The Nelson-Atkins Museum of Art* (2011) and has been a great colleague with whom to share ideas during this process. Two Directors of Curatorial Affairs, Antonia Boström and Catherine Futter, have previewed various drafts of this volume and offered very helpful suggestions. I thank you both for your input. I am indebted to and generally in awe of our Objects Conservation team, Kate Garland, Paul Benson, and Joe Rogers, and of the outstanding research and analysis conducted by our Mellon Consulting Conservation Scientist, John Twilley. Conservation intern James Gleason did excellent work assisting with the cleaning and consolidation of the Jain Shrine. I also wish to acknowledge the former Director of Conservation and Collections, Elisabeth Batchelor, for her support of this endeavor and her passion for Indian art and culture. Outside the museum, these essays were enriched by conversations with John and Susan Huntington, Robert Linrothe, and Marilyn Stockstadt, who shared their knowledge and opinions about individual objects and about the history of the collection

Karen Christiansen, Chief Operating Officer of the museum, has been extremely helpful in negotiating our contracts and making this publication a reality. I also wish to thank Ann Friedman, the museum's Manager of Grants and Foundations, for helping to secure funding for the project. In the department of Imaging Services, staff photographers John Lamberton, Chris Bjuland, and Joshua Ferdinand did outstanding work, creating photographs that bring these elegant forms and detailed surfaces to light. Likewise, Mona Vassos, Matt Pearson, and Stacey Sherman worked hard in preparing the photography for the publication. I also wish to thank Doug Allen, Chief Information Officer of the museum, for making the photography of this publication a priority. I received excellent assistance and access to materials from Holly Wright, Museum Archivist, Roberta Wagener, Library Assistant, and Marilyn Carbonell, Head of Library Services at the Spencer Art Reference Library.

I am indebted to the expert editing and deep knowledge of John Stevenson, editor of the publication. John was quick, accurate, astute, and a joy to work with. At Lucia | Marquand, this volume benefited from the elegant vision of designers Jeff Wincapaw and Zach Hooker, the excellent management of Melissa Duffes, Editorial Director, the prompt service of Kestrel Rundle, Editorial Assistant, and the wise leadership of Adrian Lucia, Partner, who gave advice on the content and direction of the volume during his visits to the museum and the collection. Thanks also to our copublisher, University of Washington Press.

I extend my deepest gratitude to the Estelle S. and Robert A. Long Ellis Foundation and in particular, to Jean McGreevey Green, for their generous support of and interest in this project. Finally, I wish to thank my predecessors, former South Asian curators, Doris Srinivasan and Dorothy Fickle. Their hard work, research, and affection for these objects abound throughout the cabinets of green folders, boxes of old labels, and files of typed and hand-written notes. I hope this volume will go some way to honor their work and to share these wonderful collections with the public.

On a personal note, I wish to thank Donovan, Lois, and Louis. This work is for you.

Kimberly Masteller
Jeanne McCray Beals Curator of South and Southeast Asian Art

INTRODUCTION

KIMBERLY MASTELLER

The Nelson-Atkins Museum of Art is recognized around the world for its outstanding collections of Asian art objects. Nearly one thousand objects come from South and Southeast Asia, lands that created some of the greatest traditions in the history of art. The collections span over two thousand years, from the third century BCE to the present, and were produced across a wide geography: from the rugged hills of Afghanistan, through the vast Indian subcontinent from the Himalayas to the Indian Ocean, and throughout the plains and jungles of peninsular and island Southeast Asia, with contemporary works created by local and diaspora artists living in Asia and elsewhere. Much of the art featured in this volume was patronized by local rulers and elites. Regional kingdoms flourished in India and Southeast Asia, providing generations of patrons who supported both religious and courtly art. This volume includes works created during major dynasties, such as the Kushan (first–third century CE), Gupta (300–599), and Chola (850–1278) dynasties in India, and the Southeast Asian kingdoms of Dvaravati (500–900), Bagan (849–1287), and Khmer (902–1431). These objects demonstrate the high level of artistic skills and resources that were directed to the arts in these kingdoms.

This volume presents the collections of South and Southeast Asian Art at the Nelson-Atkins through a detailed exploration of thirty-seven masterworks. These were created in various media: sculptures and carvings in stone, bronze, and wood, paintings on paper, and jewelry, decorative objects, and furniture created from luxurious materials such as silver, gold, and gemstones. They represent some of the highest artistic achievements of the cultures that produced them, and illustrate the strengths and range of the Nelson-Atkins holdings.

This essay provides an introduction to the collections and the artistic traditions that they represent. It begins with a brief history and addresses the key figures involved in the development of the collections. The discussion also highlights recent research and conservation efforts on South Asian works. The second half of the essay introduces the general reader to the major art forms of South and Southeast Asia, addressing their meanings and functions within their original cultural settings. Two important categories of ancient to pre-modern art are identified: art created for religious use, and courtly art and luxurious objects. The essay concludes with an exploration of the concepts of secular use and sacrality and the fluidity between these categories, and of hybridity as a useful interpretative strategy for understanding the roles of South and Southeast Asian art within their cultural contexts.

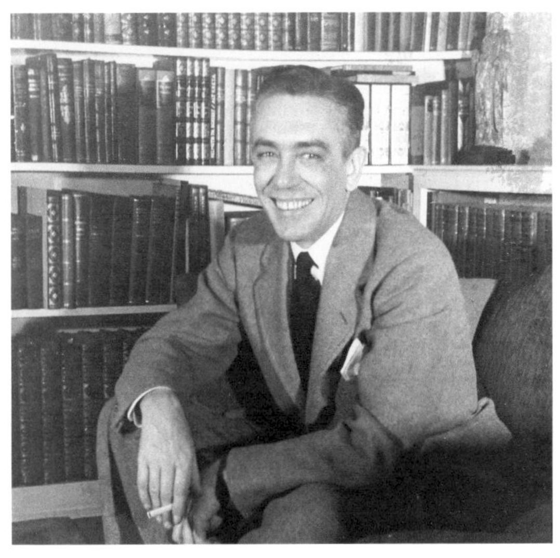

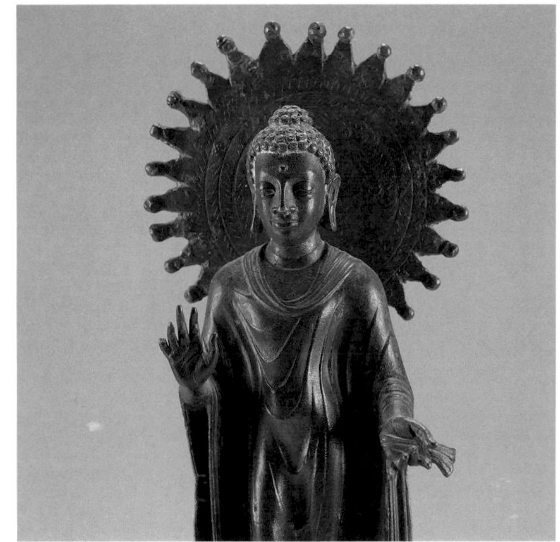

Collecting South and Southeast Asian Art at the Nelson-Atkins

Art from South and Southeast Asia has been a priority for the Nelson-Atkins since the museum first began to assemble a collection. Two sculptures from Cambodia purchased in 1930 were among the first objects acquired by the museum, which opened to the public in 1933 under the name the William Rockhill Nelson Gallery of Art and Mary Atkins Museum of Fine Arts.[1] The early South and Southeast Asian collections were significant enough to warrant their own subsection in the Asian collections, designated as the "Department of Persian and Indian Art" in the museum's first handbook of 1933.[2] In the early years, between 1930 and 1935, the museum did not have a curator of Asian art. Collecting was done by the museum's trustees, J. C. Nichols, William Volker, and Herbert V. Jones, who sought the advice of expert consultants.

In 1931, the Nelson trustees engaged the renowned Harvard professor and curator Langdon Warner (1881–1955; Asian Art Advisor 1931–1935) to help identify Asian works of art for sale and recommend purchases for the collection. On a buying trip in China Warner connected with his former Harvard student, Laurence Sickman (1907–1988; Asian Art Advisor, 1931–1935, Curator of Oriental Art, 1935–1973,

Director 1953–1977) (fig. 1), and the pair traveled and met with dealers together. Warner was impressed with his student's knowledge of art and soon proposed that Sickman, who was in China on a Yenching Fellowship, was perfectly suited to the task of finding high-quality works of art appropriate for the museum under an arrangement in which Warner reviewed and approved Sickman's recommendations. The Nelson-Atkins was on its way to employing its first curator devoted to the acquisition, research, and presentation of Asian Art, which it achieved in the hiring of Sickman full time in 1935.

Though Sickman was a Sinologist he also spent time in India, traveling there on his return from China in 1935 and while serving with the U.S. Army Air Corps in World War II. Sickman purchased nine Indian works for the collection during his 1935 visit and made further Indian purchases with dealers in London and Delhi in 1944 and 1945. Two of the most important works in the Asian collection came from Sickman's focus on India during wartime. The Gupta-period bronze sculpture of a *Standing Buddha* (Cat. 7) (fig. 2) was purchased from Spink and Sons in London after it was offered for sale by Dr. J. T. S. Hoey, son of the original owner.[3] Along with its exceptional aesthetic appeal, this sculpture is regarded as one of

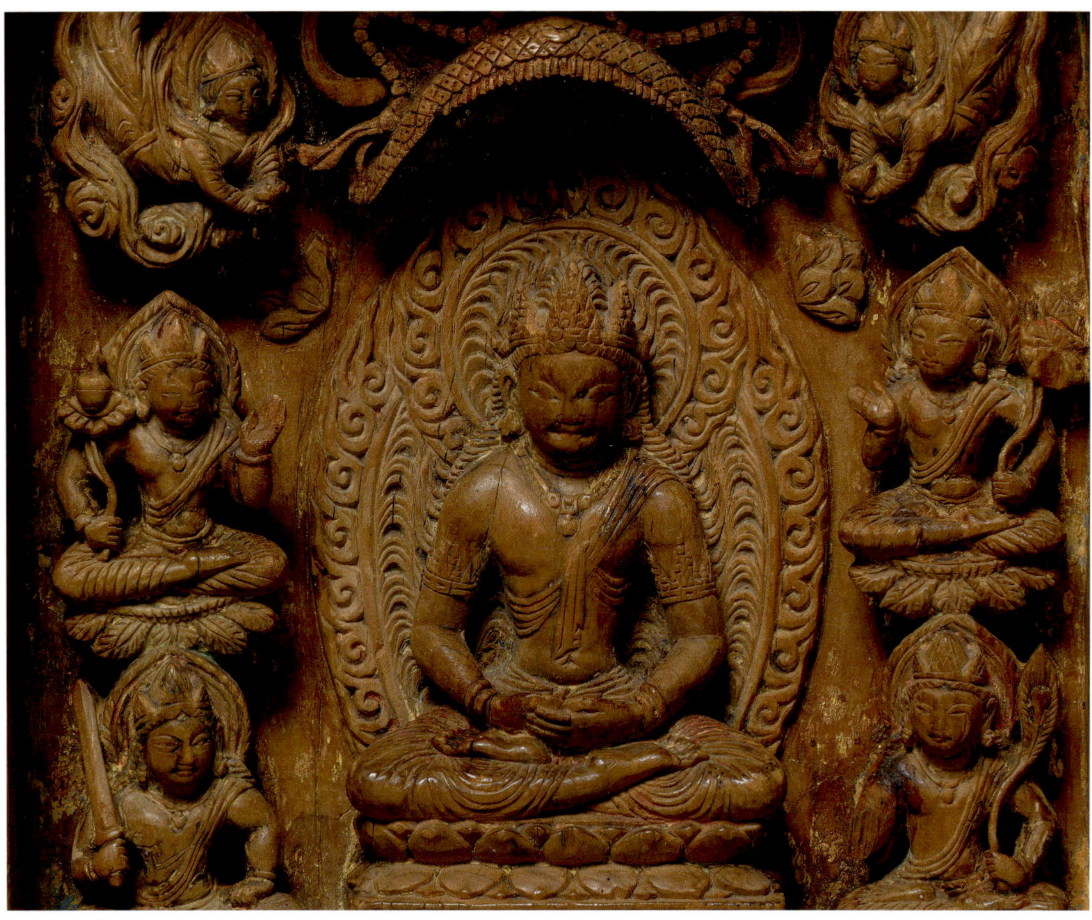

the few bronzes that can be dated confidently to the high point of the Gupta dynasty, the early fifth century.

The other treasure is an enigmatic wooden triptych depicting Buddhist imagery (Cat. 11) (fig. 3). Sickman first saw this work in a New Delhi art gallery during a stopover in 1935. The work caught his attention, but he was unsure whether to acquire it for the museum. He visited the same dealer when he returned to New Delhi during his army posting in 1944, by which time he had extended his studies of Buddhist art from beyond China's borders. According to museum docent Lee Pentecost, who interviewed Sickman, the little triptych "was in the same place in the back of the shop. It had sat there in the same spot for eleven years as if waiting for him."[4]

The object was a traveling shrine made either in Kashmir, India, or in a Kashmiri style. It is now considered to be one of the most historically important examples of its kind.

Sickman corresponded with the trustees about other potential acquisitions and even more works might have been acquired in India for the museum. For example, the notes from a meeting of the Board of Trustees dated March 28, 1944, state that the trustees would approve expenditures up to $10,000–$15,000 for "examples of Indian Decorative Arts and Mughal jewelry typical of 18th century Indian court life" that could be allowed to be exported from the country.[5] The minutes from the next board meeting indicate that while the museum had tried to cable $20,000 to Sickman in New Delhi, "the transfer was never consummated."[6] The trustees were able to send Sickman only five hundred dollars through a post office money order to acquire art at that time.[7] It is clear from this exchange that the museum intended to expand the South Asian collections with more works that represented later courtly and decorative arts, in addition to religious art. Sickman continued to acquire Indian and Southeast Asia works in later years, working with dealers in Europe and America.

Lindsay Hughes Cooper (1908–1997; staff member 1933–42, acting Curator of Oriental Art 1942–45) was another important figure for this early period of the museum's collection.[8] After studying at Mills College and Lindenwood College and earning a degree in art history from the University of Missouri, Hughes first served as an administrator of the Asian department. She was the acting curator of Asian art during Sickman's absence due to his service in World War II. During this time, she shepherded Sickman's acquisitions and added Indian and Persian textiles and Persian paintings to the collection.[9] After the war, Hughes received a scholarship from the Chinese Government to study at the University of Chicago. When she returned in 1946, Sickman was back at his post and she relocated to New York.[10]

Later curators also helped to shape the collection and presentation of South and Southeast Asian Art at the Nelson-Atkins. Marc F. Wilson (b. 1941) first held a research fellowship at the museum between 1967 and 1969, beginning his tenure as a curator of Chinese Art in 1971 and later becoming Director. Wilson was a specialist in Chinese art, following his graduate studies at Yale, however, like Sickman, he took an interest in the South and Southeast Asian collections. Wilson also shared Sickman's emphasis on quality and connoisseurship. Wilson became director of the museum in 1982, a position he held until 2010. During his tenures as curator and director, Wilson helped the museum acquire important South Asian and Himalayan works, including a gift of 141 Tibetan and Nepalese objects from the Bequest of Joseph H. Heil. In the early 1980s Wilson led efforts to redesign the galleries, transforming the old Persian Room into a suite of three galleries to present the expanding South and Southeast Asian collections. Working with the renowned designer Charles Lewis Forberg (1919–2013), Wilson created rooms with a series of projections and recesses to accommodate more works of art in a compressed space. He also oversaw the insertion of wall cases into the wooden Hindu Temple Room to create a unique display space for the museum's outstanding collection of Indian bronze sculptures. The resulting suite of four galleries currently displays over ninety sculptures, including several of the works presented here.

In 1983, Dorothy Fickle (1924–2005), who had been a research fellow at the museum from 1979 to 1983, was appointed as the first dedicated curator of South and Southeast Asian Art. With degrees from Boston University and the University of Pennsylvania, Fickle was a specialist in Thai Buddhist art. Fickle's major assignment was to research the collection and write a catalogue,[11] and the department files are filled with evidence of her scholarship. She wrote several articles on the collection, including an important study of the Gupta bronze standing Buddha (Cat. 7) (fig. 2). In late 1993, the last year that Fickle served as curator, the museum co-organized and hosted the exhibition *Gods, Guardians, and Lovers: Temple Sculptures from North India A.D. 70–1200* with the Asia Society.

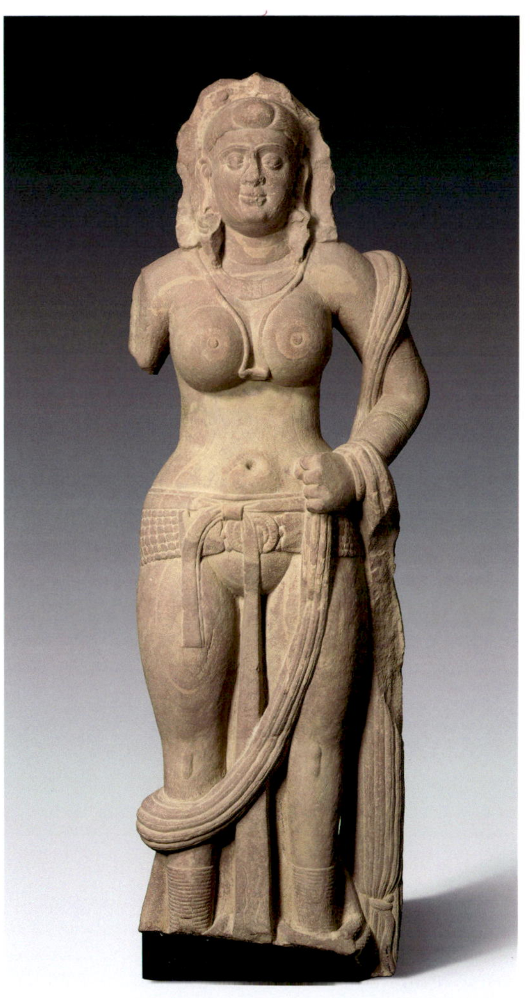

Fig. 4 *A Nagini,* 1st century BCE (79-21)

Doris Meth Srinivasan (b. 1940), an eminent scholar of ancient Indian art, was appointed curator of South and Southeast Asian Art in 1994.[12] During her first year as curator, Srinivasan helped organize the creation of a Tibetan sand mandala in the museum.[13] Srinivasan devoted her efforts to collections research, most notably on the pre-Kushan–period sculpture of a Nagini (snake goddess) (fig. 4), which led to a conservation study, discussed below, and to the focused exhibition *Snake Goddesses of Ancient India* in 2000. This exhibition included international loans of related Nagini sculptures, a major scholarly symposium, and

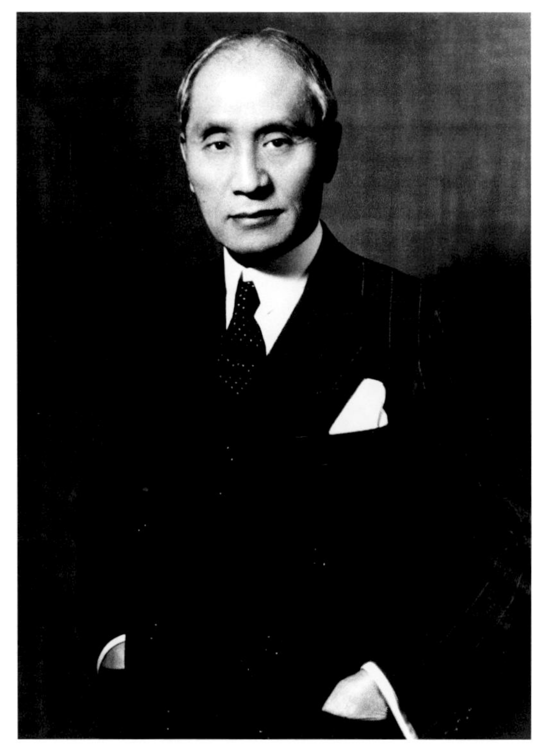

Fig. 5 C.T. Loo, photographer and date unknown, Nelson-Atkins Museum of Art Archives, copyright The Nelson-Atkins Museum of Art

the permanent collection. Current projects include a scholarly and conservation study of the domestic Jain Shrine (Cat. 26), discussed below. Recently, the department has expanded the scope of the collection to include later works from West and South Asia and contemporary twenty-first-century works. The museum is also focusing upon South Asian programming, and has instituted an annual family cultural festival titled *Passport to India*, which features South Asian art, music, food, and dance.

A number of other people outside the museum helped to shape the Indian and Southeast Asian collections in the early years of the museum. The Nelson Gallery worked with several prominent dealers in the early twentieth century, including the Heeramaneck Galleries, Hagop Kevokian, Ching Tsai Loo (C.T. Loo), and Paul Mallon. Of these figures, C.T. Loo (fig. 5) was most actively involved in contributing to the collection and how it is experienced at the Nelson-Atkins.

C.T. Loo (1880–1957) was the preeminent international dealer of Chinese Art in the first half of the twentieth century. Based in Paris with branches in China, Hong Kong, and New York, Loo's gallery was the source of some of the greatest masterworks in the Nelson-Atkins collections. In January of 1931, Loo was engaged by the Nelson Trustees to help find architectural elements to create a Chinese period room for the new museum.[15] It appears that the trustees decided to develop an Indian period room as well, as references to the creation and costs of an Indian room appear in the trustees' meeting notes throughout 1932.[16] Loo was also the source of an Indian room with carved doorways, moldings, friezes, and ceiling, described as a "Hindoo Room"; the woodwork was purchased in 1933.[17]

Loo's assistance with the Indian collection and galleries continued right up to the opening of the museum in December 1933. Although the Indian gallery was installed, Loo was reportedly concerned that the small collection of Indian and Southeast art was not substantial enough in terms of numbers or quality to create a suitable display.[18] As late as November, Loo

publication of the papers. Srinivasan also worked on building the collection and organizing an Indian festival with the local community to celebrate fifty years of India's independence.

After Srinivasan's tenure, the museum secured an endowment to support the Department of South and Southeast Asian Art through gifts from the Jeanne McCray Beals Trust and the Pauline A. MacNeven Trust in combination with a matching grant received in 2006 and 2007 from the National Endowment for the Humanities.

Kimberly Masteller (b. 1969) joined the museum in 2008.[14] Masteller has curated three exhibitions at the museum: as venue curator for *From the Land of the Taj Mahal: Paintings of India's Mughal Emperors in the Chester Beatty Library*; as curator of *Echoes: Islamic Art and Contemporary Artists;* and as venue co-curator for *Roads of Arabia: Archaeology and History of the Kingdom of Saudi Arabia*. She has also organized focused installations based upon loans and

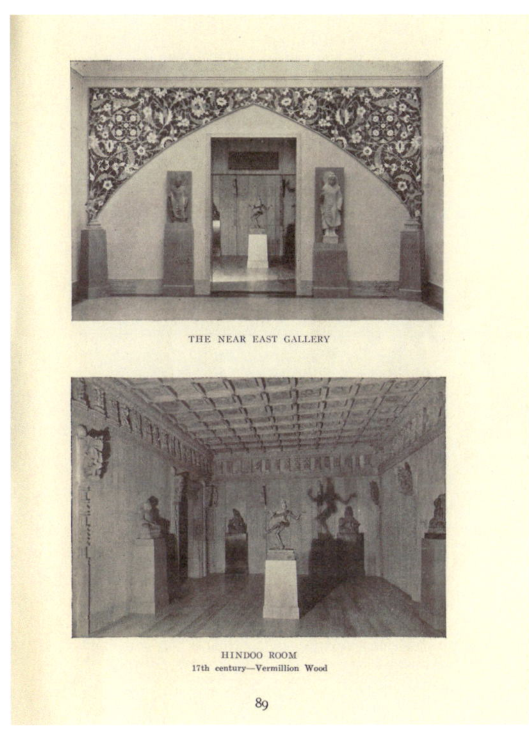

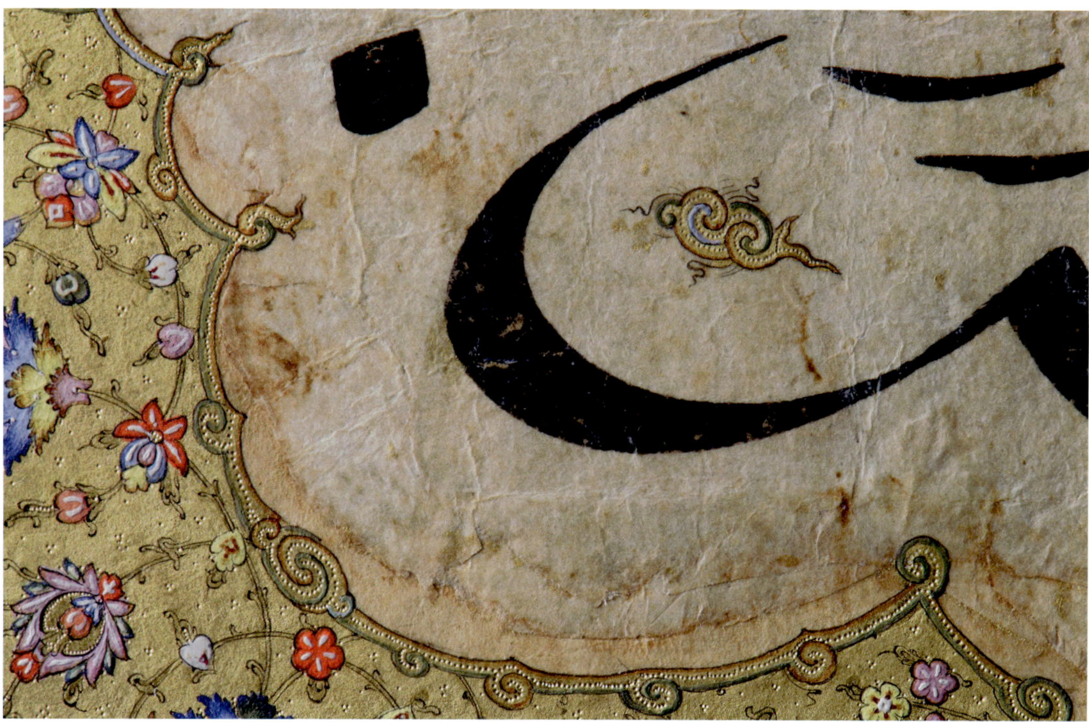

was trying to remedy this problem. Just eleven days before the opening, seven Indian sculptures arrived as a loan to the museum, along with additional important works of Chinese art.[19] These arrived in time to be installed in the Indian Temple Room for the grand opening (fig. 6). The museum's trustees agreed on the importance of the contribution made by these Indian sculptures, and they were among the works purchased by the Nelson Gallery in January of 1934. These works helped form the museum's core collection of South and Southeast Asian art, and include the great Chola bronze sculptures of Shiva Nataraja (Cat. 22) and Sambandar (Cat. 23), and a stone sculpture of Durga Mahishasuramardini (Cat. 24). While these efforts were certainly financially advantageous for Loo as a businessman, Marc Wilson believes that Loo also took a very personal interest in the success of the Nelson Gallery and its potential to become an important public institution for Asian art.[20]

Research and Conservation of South and Southeast Asian Art at the Nelson-Atkins Museum

Recent conservation efforts on works in the South and Southeast Asian collections have produced fascinating discoveries. Conservators begin each project with a careful visual inspection; analysis can be as simple as the close visual examination of a work of art in different lighting conditions. For example, the examination of a folio from the Mughal *Gulshan Album* (Cat. 28) under raking light reveals the different components of the work, including where separate pieces of paper were attached, to incorporate examples of earlier calligraphy on a new sheet of paper with new illumination featuring scrolling arabesque designs (fig. 7). Notice how the raking light also highlights the textured pattern of the design, revealing tiny indentations made by a stylus into the gold. The use of ultraviolet light helped conservator Paul Benson determine that the red carbochans set

Fig. 6 Photograph of the Indian Temple Room (lower), including the sculpture of *Shiva Nataraja* (34-7), published in *Handbook of the William Rockhill Nelson Gallery of Art, 1933,* p. 89

Fig. 7 Detail in raking light of calligraphy by Mir Ali al-Katib al-Sultani, set in a page with new illumination on *Folio from the Muraqqa Gulshan,* ca. 1600 (48-12/1 verso). Photographed by Conservation Associate Joe Rogers on February 2, 2015

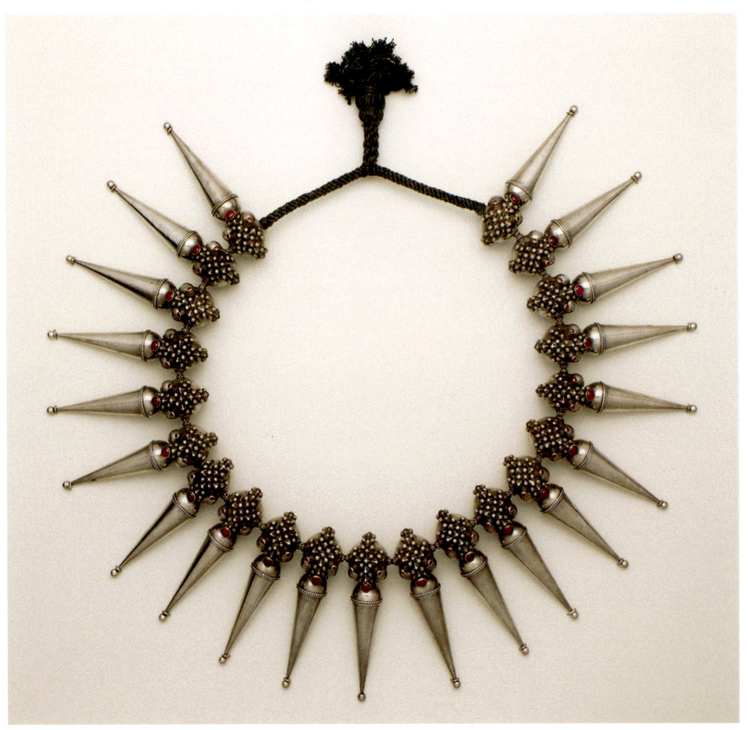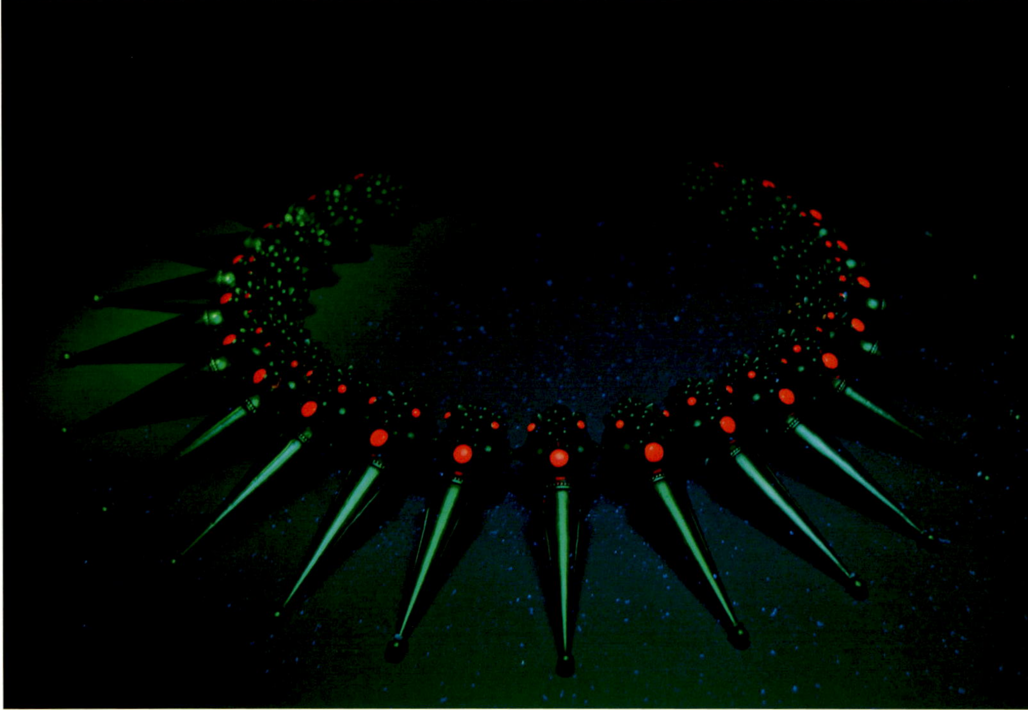

Fig. 8 *Ceremonial Necklace for Nandi Sculpture,* 19th century (2010-24), shown in studio lighting (left) and with rubies fluorescing in ultraviolet light (right), photograph taken by Objects Conservator Paul Benson on May 6, 2010

into a silver ceremonial necklace were actually rubies, rather than glass (fig. 8).[21]

A large research project in the 1990s on the Nagini in the collection involved both comparative analysis of the work with two related Nagini sculptures in Indian and Japanese collections and scientific analysis of its stone and patina.[22] This project included field research in India: curator Doris Meth Srinivasan and conservation scientist John Twilley traveled to the village where the sculpture is believed to have originated and were shown the broken feet and ankles of another sculpture. Through precise measurements, they determined that the feet *in situ* did not to belong to any of the three known sculptures, and that there may have been a group of four Nagini sculptures at this site.[23]

Carved and polychrome wooden objects in the collection have been the recipients of recent treatment and analysis, thanks in part to the support of the Andrew W. Mellon Foundation endowment for conservation science at the Nelson-Atkins Museum

of Art. In 2013–2014, conservators treated the *Traveling Shrine* (Cat. 11), removing later regilding to reveal traces of the original gold and polychrome decoration (fig. 3). In early 2016, the shrine was scientifically dated by carbon-14 testing to 727–888, supporting its art historical attribution.[24] The *Domestic Jain Shrine,* or *ghar derasar,* from Gujarat in Western India, has also received extensive conservation treatment and scientific study (Cat. 26). Though the shrine is illustrated in the 1933 handbook of the museum, by all accounts it appears to have lived most of its life at the Nelson-Atkins in storage. This was likely due to condition issues as well as space limitations. The components of the shrine had fragile layers of polychrome under a heavy coating of varnish and grime. Efforts were made in 2010 to do test cleanings with new gel-based solvents, and the promising results prompted a full consolidation and cleaning of the shrine (figs. 9, 10). During this process, Kate Garland, Senior Objects Conservator, observed at least two paint layers on

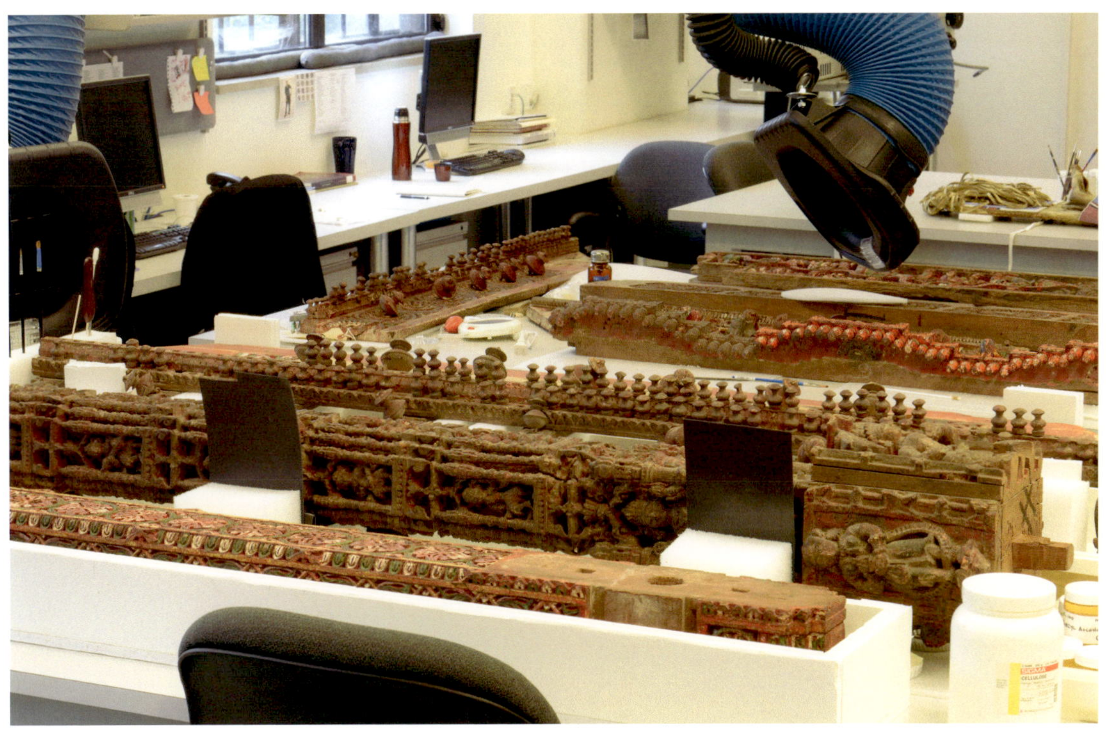

Fig. 9 Components of the *Domestic Jain Shrine*, 16th to early 17th century (32-136), in Objects Conservation for treatment (photograph taken April 16, 2013)

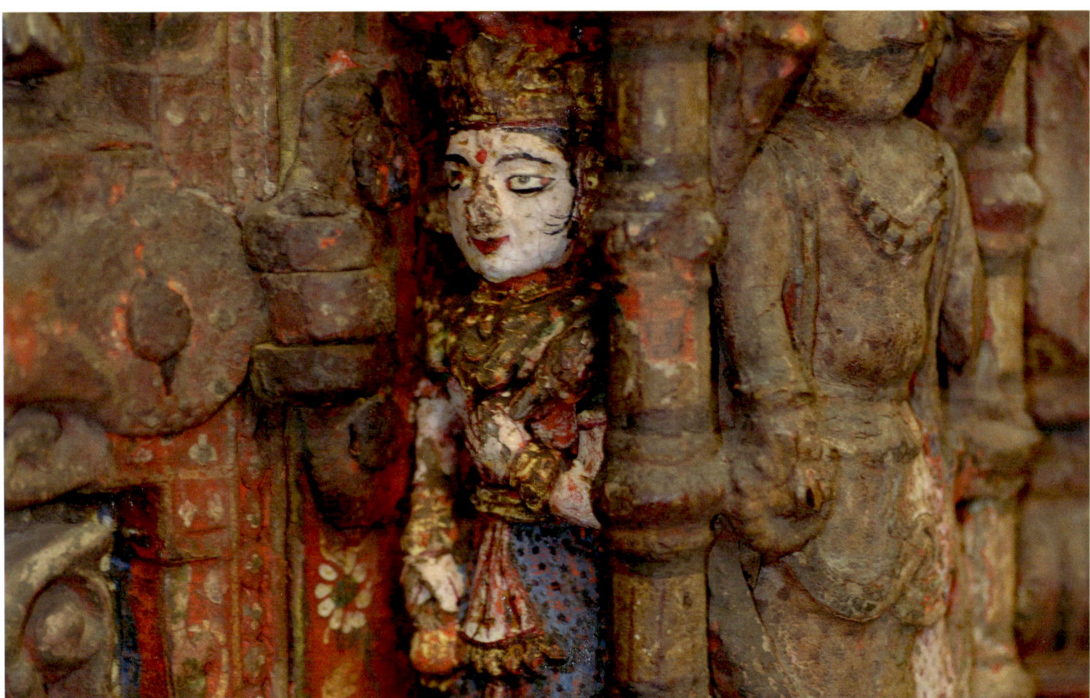

Fig. 10 Detail of the *Domestic Jain Shrine*, 16th to early 17th century (32-136), during cleaning (photograph taken in Conservation on December 14, 2012)

the carved surfaces. John Twilley, now a consulting Mellon Conservation Scientist for the Nelson-Atkins, analyzed samples from the shrine to determine the pigments used and to study cross sections of paint layers. Twilley reported that the shrine appears to have two paint layers, separated by a layer of red primer. The original paint included the use of expensive lapis lazuli in areas of blue paint, suggesting that the shrine was a very expensive and luxurious commission. Later paint layers included the use of "Emerald Green," the name of a chemical pigment developed in the nineteenth century, which helped to date the shrine's refurbishment. The Jain Shrine was also dated by carbon-14 analysis to the sixteenth or early seventeenth century,[25] placing its creation in the late medieval period when Gujarat was under Sultanate and Mughal control. In 2014, the focused exhibition *Revealing a Hidden Treasure: A Jain Shrine from India* was installed in the Asian galleries, which showcased the shrine and its treatment and analysis.

Understanding the Collection
Art in the Service of Religion
Works of art from India and Southeast Asia in the Nelson-Atkins generally fall into two categories: religious art or courtly art and luxury objects. The majority of the sculptures in the collection belong to the first category and are associated with religious beliefs and practices. These include examples of temple sculptures, icons and processional images, and narrative reliefs. The religious traditions represented in the collection include three of the major world religions that developed in India—Buddhism, Jainism, and Hinduism—as well as works made in Muslim courts and communities. The indigenous Indian religions all developed in response to the ancient Indian worldview, which presupposes that time is cyclic and life is eternal. Beings are constantly experiencing the cycle of *samsara,* with recurring life, death, and rebirth into various forms. These ancient religions also shared a kind of existential concern about the prospect of perennial rebirth. The goal of each tradition is to navigate life following belief systems and

practices that promote spiritual development and the elimination of *karma*, with an end goal of achieving *moksha* (release), or *nirvana* (meaning to "blow out" or "stillness") and removal from the cycle of *samsara.* Buddhism and Jainism are ascetic traditions based upon the knowledge and practices transmitted by a spiritually advanced teacher, who serves as a role model for practitioners. These two religions were propagated by nearly contemporaneous teachers in the sixth to fifth century BCE: Buddhism by Prince Siddharta Gautama, later known as Shakyamuni, and Jainism by Prince Mahavira. Both religions recognize these men as teachers, not as founders. They were the last earthly manifestations from lineages of enlightened teachers who taught the *dharma* (meaning in Buddhism and Jainism the sacred knowledge and practices) of each faith to their contemporaries before achieving *nirvana*. Both religions consist of monastic and lay communities who support each another, the former through providing teachings and observing rituals, the latter through their patronage and charity.

Buddhism is represented in the collection by many works from South and Southeast Asia, including stone and metal sculptures that served as the focus for worship in shrines, altars, or architectural niches, and narrative relief sculptures that decorated Buddhist architectural monuments. A small twelfth-century stele from Myanmar (Burma) (Cat. 10) (fig. 11) presents a lively combination of Buddhist iconography and art forms. In the stele, a large image of Shakyamuni is surrounded by small buddha figures representing various scenes from his life. This kind of imagery was often spread across multiple sculptures in individual niches on a temple or *stupa*. In this tightly packed composition based upon sculptures from the Pala–Sena dynasties in India, the artist created a composite narrative, with individual figures serving as reminders of key miracles and moments after enlightenment that were important to Burmese Buddhists.[26] All the figures sit or stand on lotus platforms, and the entire composition rests atop a projecting platform that replicates architectural forms. The various elements are

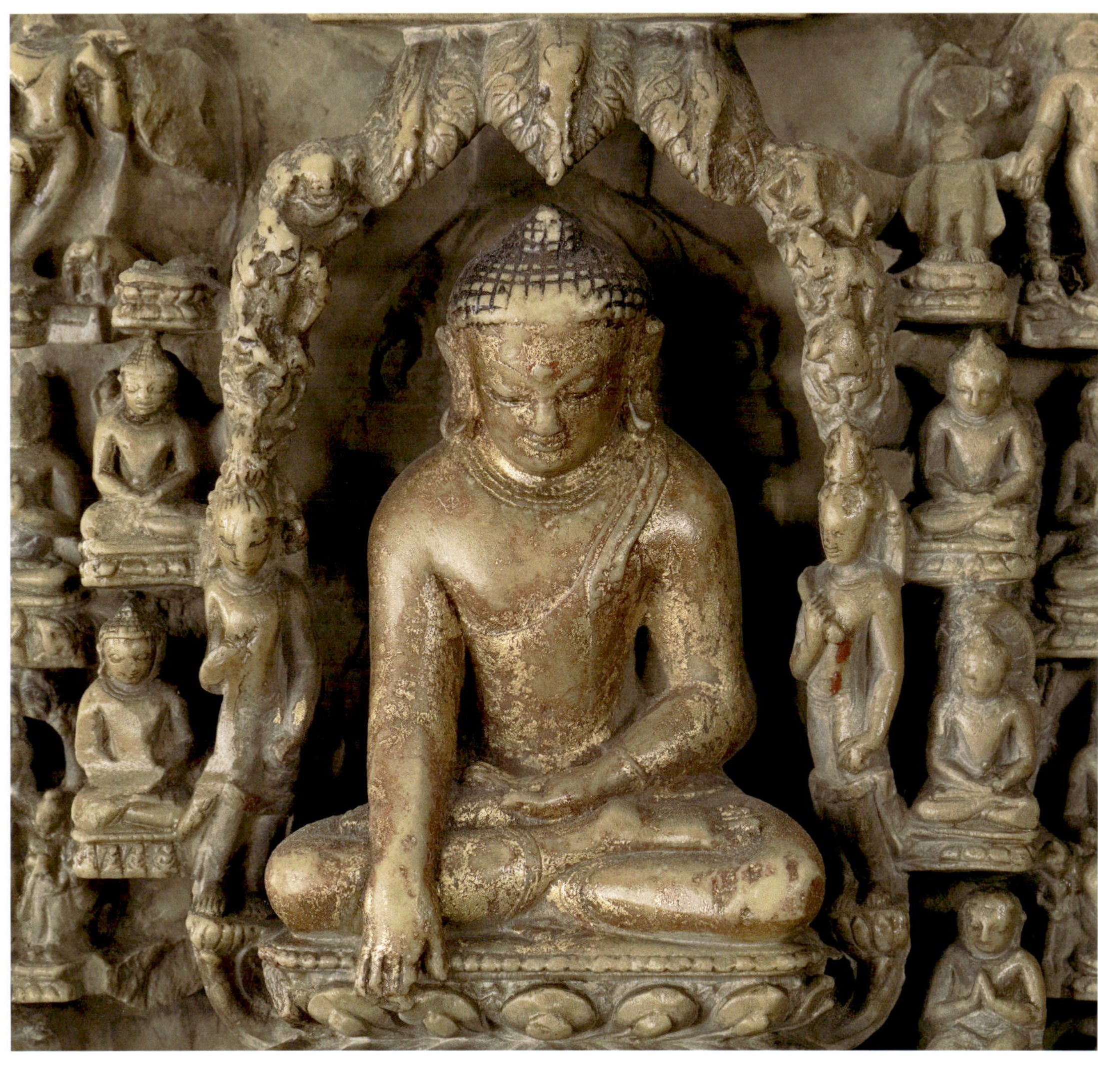

brought together in a portable stele that was intended for personal devotion; the entire work can be cradled in a worshipper's hands. Jain works in the collection comprise sculptures, architecture, and paintings, and include works created for temple, monastic, and personal use. Notable are the manuscript of the *Kalpasutra* and *Kalakacharyakantha* (Cat. 25) and the ornately carved and painted domestic shrine, discussed above. (Cat. 26).

The other great Indic religion represented by sculptures in the collection is Hinduism. Hinduism is an umbrella term that is used to define the religions of "Hindustan," the lands beyond the Indus River, which constitute India. By its very definition Hinduism refers to multiple religious traditions that coexisted in India. That said, many of these traditions share common beliefs and practices, including belief in the Vedas, an ancient body of Sanskrit literature that outlines core beliefs and divinities and prescribes the ritual veneration of the latter. Hinduism promotes the concept that the divine can be manifest and experienced on earth, at sacred sites, in an invoked image,

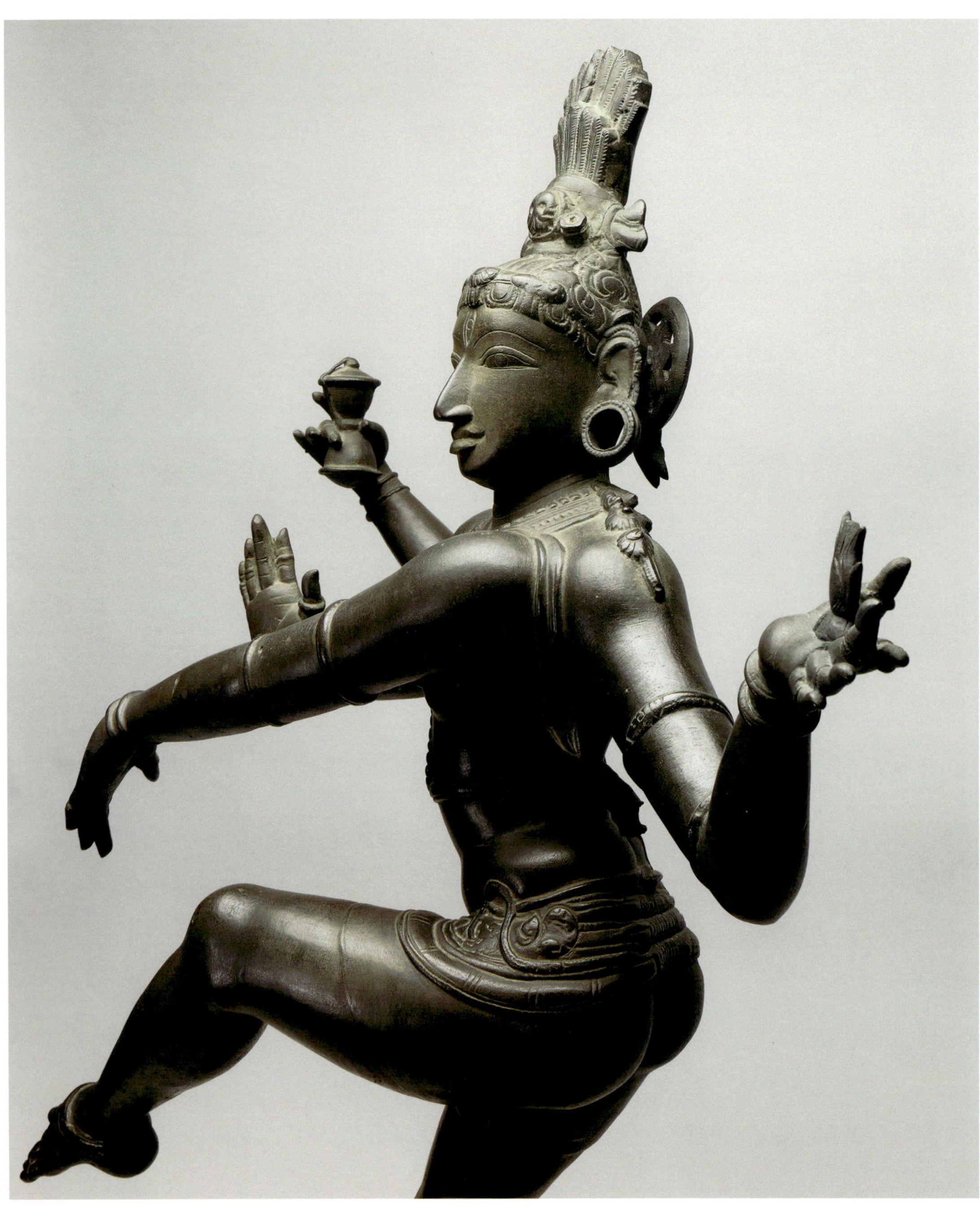

Fig. 12 Detail, left side, of *Shiva Nataraja,* early 13th century (34-7)

and in transient ritual moments, and that experience of the divine aids spiritual development. Hindu practitioners recognize a group of major deities and their stories as central to their beliefs and practices, particularly the 'Great Gods': Brahma the creator, Vishnu the preserver, Shiva the creator and destroyer, and the Great Goddess in forms such as Durga, Saraswati, Lakshmi, and Parvati; and other major figures such as Ganesha, the elephant-headed god, and Hanuman, the monkey god. Throughout the centuries, many local deities were 'Sanskritized' and recognized as forms of one of these major gods and goddesses, thus integrating local sites, divinities, and beliefs into a pan-Indic 'Great Tradition.' For example, the bronze sculpture of Shiva as Nataraja in the Nelson-Atkins (Cat. 22) (fig. 12) is a form of Shiva based on his cult in Cidambaram, India, where local tradition holds that Shiva resided and danced in the city's groves and cremation grounds. Many of the Hindu sculptures in the collection would have functioned as icons, placed in temple niches or at a central altar as a focus of veneration. Most orthodox forms of Hinduism promote the possibility of *moksha,* the release of an individual soul from *samsara* through the reduction of *karma* over many lifetimes by following the social order and doing *dharma* (in Hinduism this refers to "duty," in the sense of living a proper and ethical life within one's societal role). However, Hinduism offers many methodologies, from prayer and rituals moderated by priests to strict forms of monasticism and asceticism taught by lineages of *guru*s, following a similar model demonstrated in the life histories of Shakyamuni and Mahavira.

Another form of Hinduism demonstrated by works in the Nelson-Atkins Collection is Tantrism. Tantric practices involved esoteric teachings passed from *guru* to disciple that dictated specific meditations, visualizations, and rituals, including heterodox and polluting activities, that were believed to give the practitioner immediate access to divine power. The *Yogini* (Cat. 20) from Tamil Nadu is a deity associated with tantric practices, and her wild appearance demonstrates the intense power she was believed to embody.

The religious art of these cultures may function as icons hosting divine presence and as semiotic vessels presenting the abstract concepts, narrative stories, and personal and communal interpretations and experiences of the divinities. As Susan Huntington has described in her discussion of ancient Indian art, "The art works, then, are not just aesthetic expressions or exercises in color or form but are visualizations of the transcendent, brought into the range of human understanding."[27]

Courtly Arts and Luxurious Objects

Courtly arts and luxury objects from South and Southeast Asia in the Nelson-Atkins collection include examples of paintings, textiles, decorative arts, and furniture. Unlike temple sculptures, many of these works have primarily aesthetic functions. Like the temple arts, these art forms have benefited from the support of royal and wealthy patrons. Indian courts have long patronized manuscript and album painting. The impact of court patronage upon Indian painting is so profound that the dominant art historical approach to the study of the medium has focused on associating paintings and their distinct styles and content with the schools of individual kingdoms.[28] This is certainly the case with the study of Mughal painting, which benefits from rich historical documentation of individual painters and their patrons, such as the Mughal emperor Jahangir, a connoisseur who commissioned an album from which the Nelson-Atkins owns two beautiful pages (Cats. 28, 29). The Mughal court, in particular, had a great influence upon the art, architecture, and courtly culture of other Indian kingdoms, regardless of whether the rulers were Hindu or Muslim.

Mughal influence can be seen in this detail from an eighteenth-century Deccan painting of *Dhanasri Ragini* (Cat. 31) (fig. 13) in the architectural forms, costumes, and decorative objects depicted, besides the overall style of the painting, with its emphasis on naturalism. What is most striking is the painting's depiction of courtly life and activities. We see a high-ranking court lady, perhaps a queen or princess,

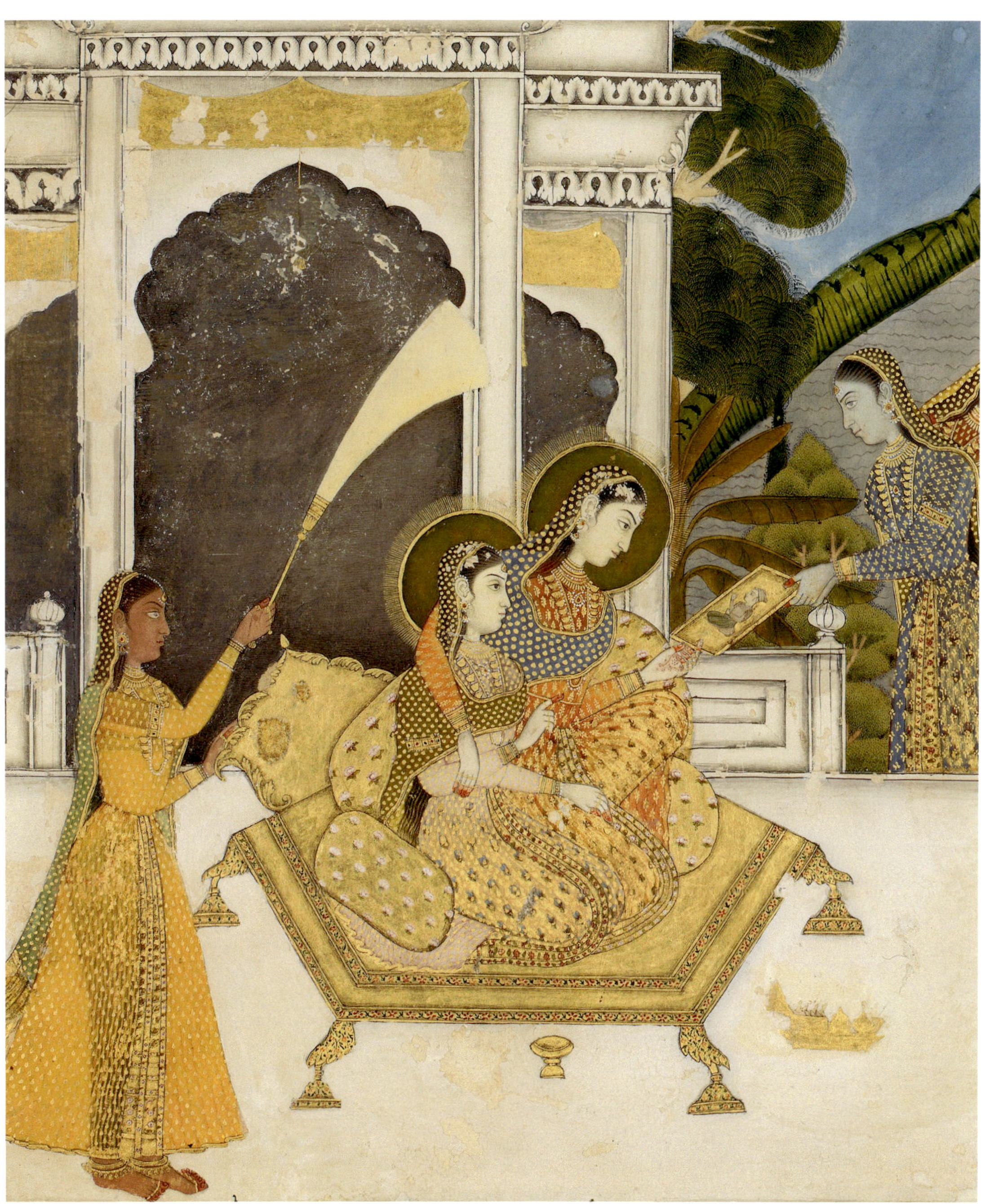

Fig. 13 Detail of *Dhanasri Ragini,* first quarter of the 18th century (31-131/7)

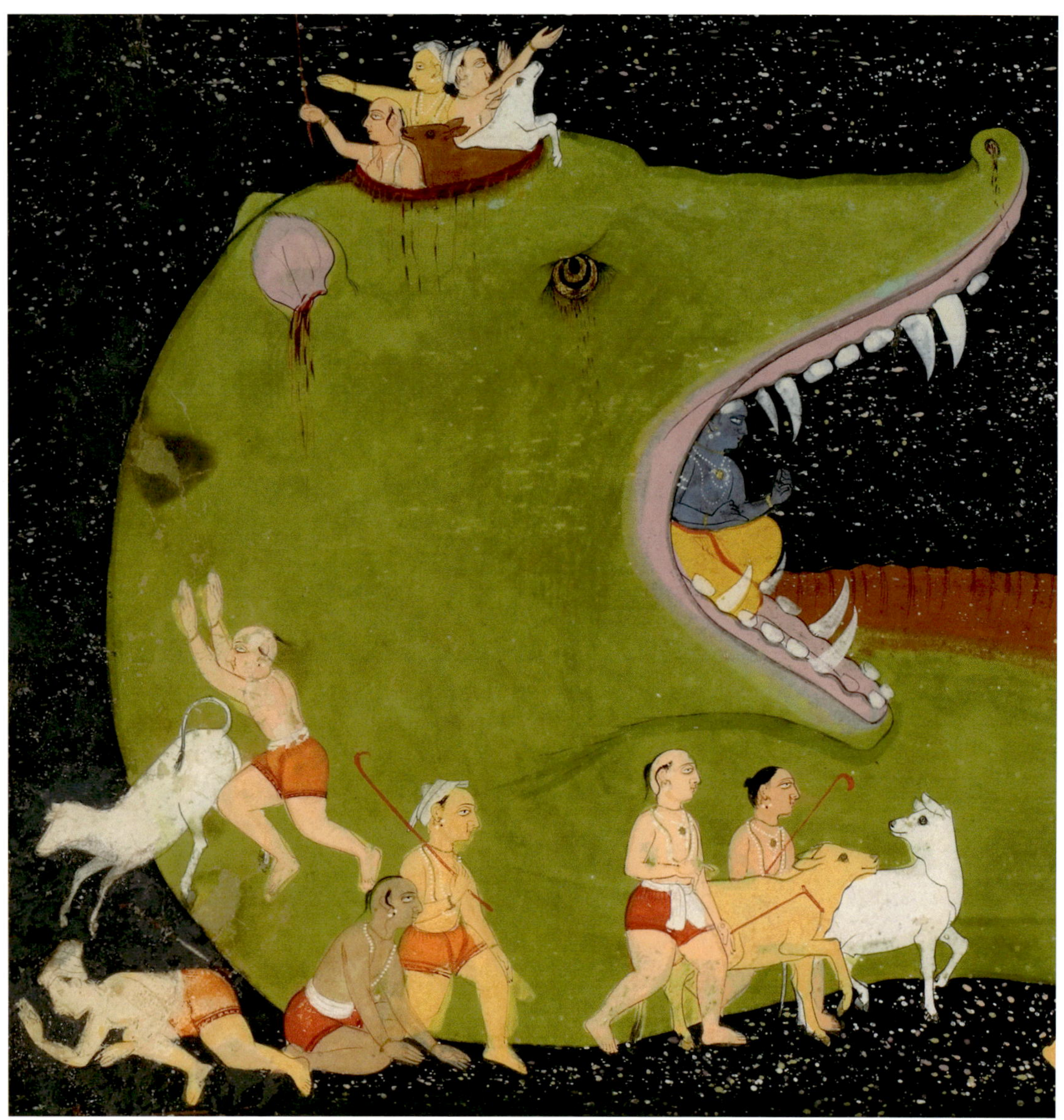

Fig. 14 Detail of *Krishna's Victory over Aghasura,*
early 18th century (60-34)

these paintings were commissioned, collected, and enjoyed. A number of depictions of this scene depict women gazing at paintings, with some versions even depicting the heroine in the act of painting her lover's portrait,[29] hinting at a wide participation in the consumption of, and perhaps even the courtly creation of, Indian paintings.

Fluidity between Sacred and Secular Art in India and Southeast Asia

In considering the categories of religious and courtly art, it should be noted that there was not always a clear divide between sacred and secular subjects in Asian cultures and that many works of art have multivalent associations. For example, the painting of Krishna slaying the demon Aghasura (Cat. 35) (fig. 14) depicts an event associated with Krishna, an *avatar* of the Hindu god Vishnu. The painting was once part of a series of narrative paintings devoted to stories of Krishna. While the series depicted a divine subject based upon a traditional text, viewing these paintings was not only a religious experience. An eighteenth-century viewer would immediately recall the fantastical story illustrated in the painting. He or she could pick out the iconographic elements and appreciate the novel way in which they are presented. A viewer might also spend time looking at fine details and taking pleasure in the bold rendering of the mythical beast or the expressiveness of the men and animals. Likewise, sculptures ornamenting a sacred temple may invoke a range of very mundane human responses, as evident in the poem *The Hundred Verses on King Kumarapala's Temple,* by the twelfth-century monk Ramacandragani. Ramacandragani describes a sculpture of a celestial goddess adorning a Jain temple that is very similar to the *Apsara* from Khajuraho in the Nelson-Atkins collection (Cat. 18) (fig. 15). The poet's verses provide a window into the rich and varied nature of medieval visitors' experiences:

> There, in that temple, the statue of a lady who
> struggled to hold fast to her girdle as a monkey
> untied its knot made young gallants feel desire

seated with her companion on a golden throne in a palace courtyard. Propped on cushions, she intently examines the painting of a seated prince that her attendant hands to her. While this clearly carries a narrative associated with the subject of its particular *ragini*, in which the heroine is longing for her absent lover, it also illustrates its subject within a contemporary court environment. This is the context in which and confirm the steadfast in their rejection of sensual delights; it disgusted the pious and made old ladies feel embarrassed; while it made young men laugh and young girls wonder.[30]

It is this juxtaposition of spiritual and human experience that led A. L. Basham, one of the leading Indologists of the twentieth century, to conclude that the people of India "delighted both in the things of the senses and the things of the spirit."[31] While this is a broad generalization, it seems to hold true for the pre-Modern cultures of India and in some ways for the cultures of Southeast Asia, where the interplay between human and divine, the mundane and spiritual, play out in their forms of visual art.

Influence and Synthesis

Another broad observation about Indian and Southeast Asian art frequently noted by scholars is how it demonstrates both the influence and synthesis of foreign styles, forms, and materials. India experienced multiple invasions during its history, particularly from the northwest, where foreign armies entered through Himalayan passes or across the Punjab plains. However, the indigenous civilizations of South Asia were strong enough to maintain much of their ancient culture and local traditions, such as Hinduism, while actively adopting useful influences from the foreign sources, synthesizing them, and making them their own. In the visual arts, this synthesis is evident in ancient art from Gandhara, which applies the muscular naturalism of Hellenistic and Roman art to present depictions of Shakyamuni and scenes from his past and present life in bold detail. Vestiges of Roman influence are still apparent in the Nelson-Atkins *Standing Buddha* from the Gupta dynasty (Cat. 7) (fig. 2). Often considered the 'Classical' or 'Golden Age' of India, no other ancient period conjures up such a wealth of examples of indigenous Indian creativity and discovery. This is the era of the poetry and plays of Kalidasa, scientific treatises on medicine and astronomy, the discovery of the concept of zero and the place values system in mathematics, and the creation

of the artistic canon responsible for the beautiful figures in Gupta art. Though the Gupta bronze in the Nelson-Atkins exhibits the smooth body and proportions of the Gupta canon, he wears a loose two-shouldered cowl-necked robe and holds the edge of the fabric in his left hand. This garment and pose are based on the wearing of the Roman toga, a holdover from Gandharan art and an indexical reference to

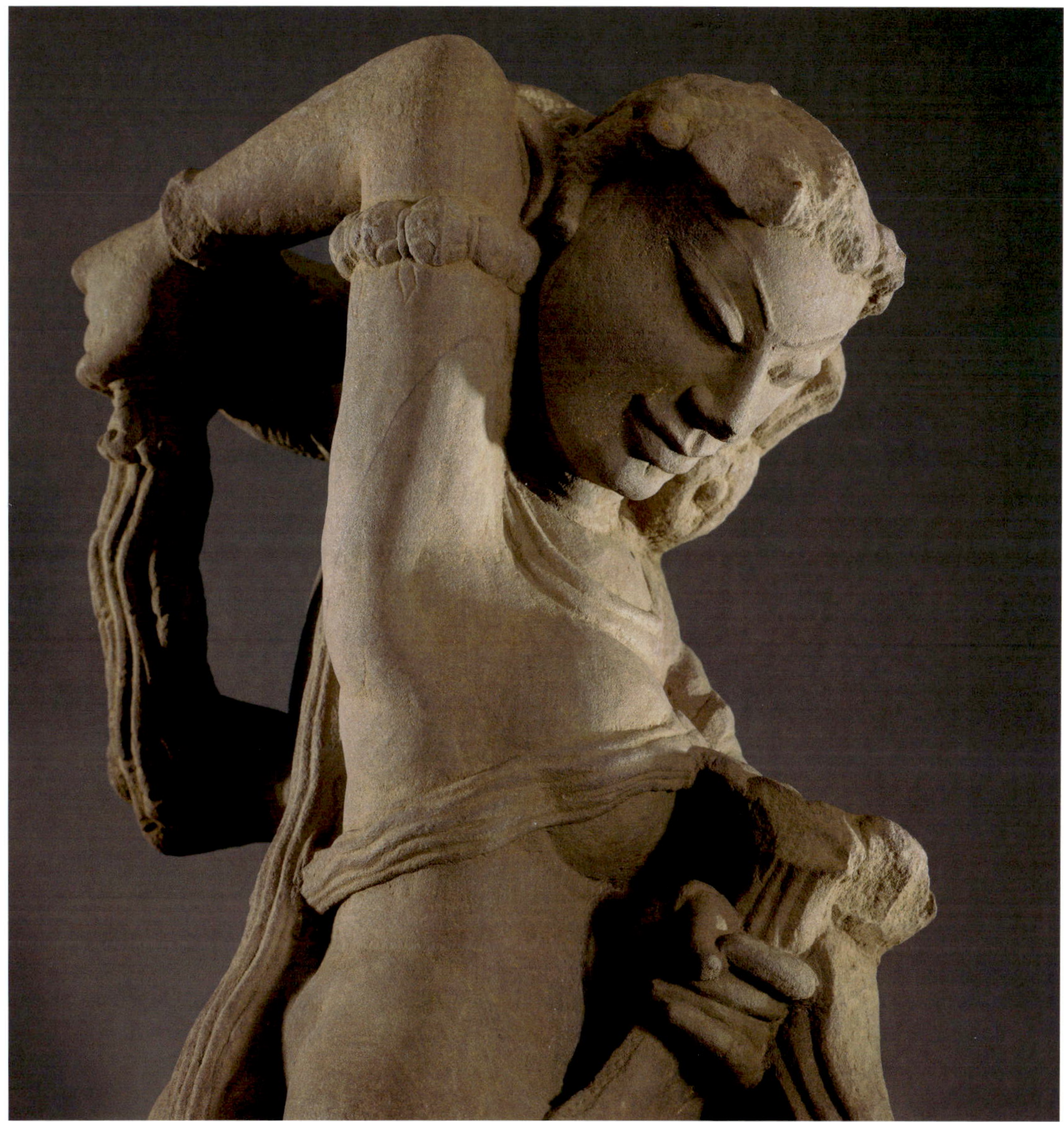

Fig. 15 Detail of *A Celestial Nymph,* or *Apsara,* ca. 1000 (81-27/26)

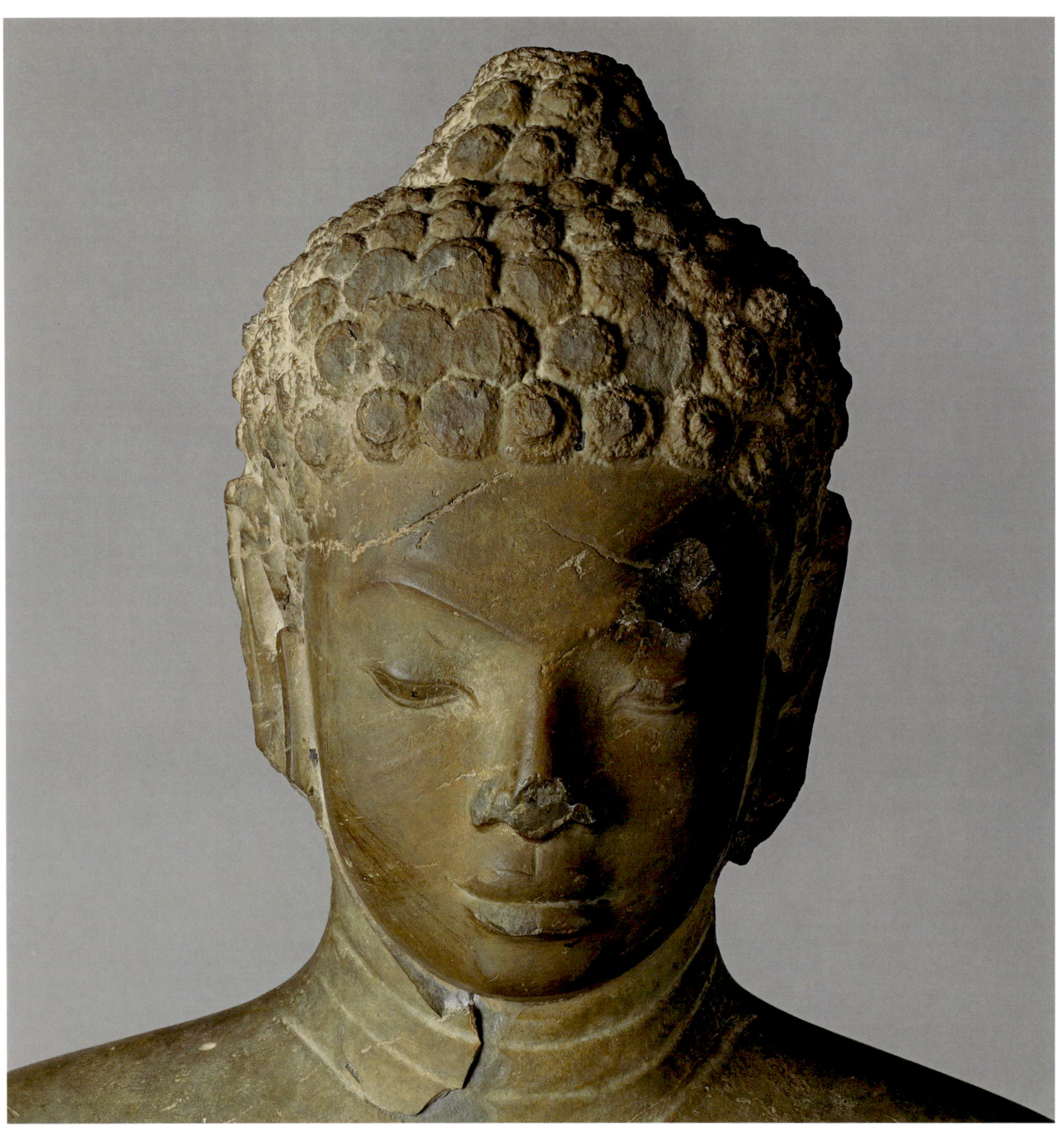

language, Indian epic literature, and the mandalic system of government. India's influence was so strong that the historian and translator George Coedès named his groundbreaking study of the region *The Indianized States of Southeast Asia.*[32] This political history accounts for the widespread adoption of Hinduism and Buddhism in the region and the production of vast, elite-funded monuments. Yet, the visual record of Southeast Asia reveals that it was not blindly reproducing Indian art, but synthesizing it into something new. The *Standing Buddha* from Dvaravati (Cat. 8) presents an excellent example of this (fig. 16). The Dvaravati artists were looking to Gupta Indian art as a model. One sees evidence of this in the figure's wide shoulders, narrow waist, and quiet, downcast expression. It is clear, however, that this is not an Indian sculpture, nor is this an idealized Gupta-style face. Over time, Southeast Asian sculpture moved even further away from Indian models, as in the Khmer sculpture of a standing male deity in the collection (Cat. 15). While the figure can be identified as Hindu, one feels the pull of the local aesthetic in his compact body and broad smile. Regardless of his foreign iconography, this figure is wholly Khmer.

Hybridity and synthesis are most evident when there is a direct political or economic presence of one culture over, or within, another. This can be seen in art produced in, or contemporary with, the Mughal and Sultanate empires in India and during the era of European colonialism in South and Southeast Asia. A pair of royal silver-wrapped thrones from the state of Dungarpur in Rajasthan were created during the period of British Rule in India (Cat. 37). They are dated to 1911, which was the year when the British King George V traveled to Delhi to be crowned Emperor of India. The thrones present a tour-de-force of cross-cultural forms and imagery, from the sitting lions that form the legs and arms of these Rococo-style chairs to the deities embossed on their backs (fig. 17). As in other works from South and Southeast Asia, the makers of these thrones have appropriated the form of a European-style chair and transformed it, creating works that are unmistakably Indian.

Rome and its presence in South Asia. Even this most Indian of sculptures is, in some ways, a hybrid.

Hybridity is also evident in the works from Southeast Asia in the Nelson-Atkins collection. This vast region, with its riverine cities and maritime kingdoms, was shaped by both regional and foreign influences. The impact of India was great, giving the kingdoms of Southeast Asia their state religions, the Sanskrit

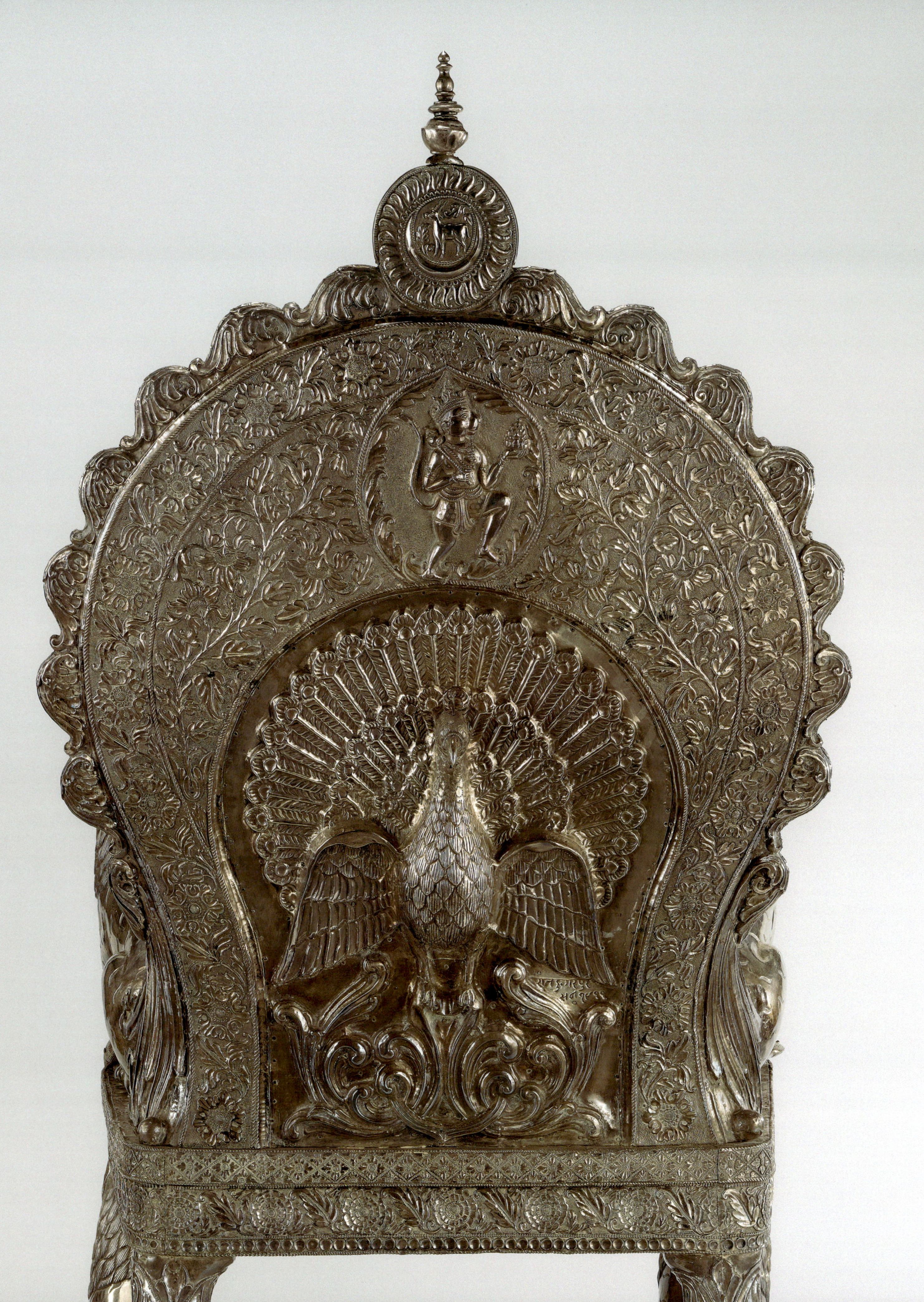

NOTES

1. The works are *Buddha Sheltered by the Serpent King Muchalinda,* eleventh century (30-26), and *Head of the Bodhisattva Avalokiteshvara,* late twelfth to early thirteenth century (30-34), purchased from Robert Rousset and Paul Mallon, respectively.

2. William Rockhill Nelson Gallery of Art and Mary Atkins Museum of Fine Arts, *Handbook of the William Rockhill Nelson Gallery of Art* (Kansas City: The Gallery, 1933), 82–89. The department holdings also include Himalayan art from Tibet and Nepal and Islamic Art, primarily from West Asia. These areas of the collection may be addressed in future publications.

3. For the provenance of this sculpture, see Sheila E. Hoey Middleton, "The Quest for the Third Buddha, A Sequel," in *South Asian Studies* (Vol. 26, No. 2, September 2010), 119–24, Registration records and Department Object File.

4. Sickman's version is retold in Lee Pentecost, "Making a Masterpiece: 75 Years of the Nelson-Atkins Museum," essay based upon 2008 lecture, http://volunteer.nelson-atkins.org/documents/MusGuide/Research%2075th%20Anniversary%20by%20Lee%20Pentecost.pdf

5. Board of Trustees minutes, March 28, 1944, Archives of the Nelson-Atkins Museum of Art.

6. Board of Trustees minutes, April 28, 1944, Archives of the Nelson-Atkins Museum of Art.

7. Ibid.

8. For an excellent biographical article on Lindsay Hughes Cooper, see Chelsea Schlievert and Jason Steuber, "Collecting Asian art, defining gender roles: World War II, women curators and the politics of Asian art collections in the United States," *Journal of the History of Collections* (20: 2), 2008, 291–303.

9. Ibid., 297–98.

10. Hughes resigned after returning to the Museum after the war and married Frank Morrow Cooper. She was offered a position at The Metropolitan Museum of Art, but turned it down to work with C. T. Loo at his gallery. Ibid., 300.

11. Interview with Marc Wilson, October 13, 2015.

12. Born in Germany, Srinivasan received her BA from Hunter College, State University of New York, and her PhD from the University of Pennsylvania. Before and after serving as a curator at the Nelson-Atkins, Srinivasan held distinguished teaching and research appointments at a number of colleges and universities, most recently at Stony Brook University. Biographical information on Srinivasan and her outstanding career is cited from the Stony Brook University website, http://www.stonybrook.edu/commcms/india/people/dorissrinivasan.html

13. *The Wheel of Compassion Sand Mandala,* on exhibition from April 4 through May 15, 1995.

14. Masteller joined the Nelson-Atkins after serving as Assistant Curator of Islamic and Later Indian Art at the Harvard (University) Art Museums. Masteller received her BA from Muskingum College and did her graduate work in South Asian Art History at Ohio University and The Ohio State University.

15. "Quite a discussion was had with Mr. Loo in reference to building a Chinese Room or part of a Chinese Temple into the new museum and Dr. Loo stated he would be on the lookout for such a room." Board of Trustees minutes, January 27, 1931, Archives of the Nelson-Atkins Museum of Art.

16. For example, see Board of Trustees minutes of May 16, which discusses creating a larger room; August 8, which discusses the cost of the rooms and casework; and December 19, which discusses the efforts Mr. Gardner and Mr. Warner put into the planning of the Persian and Indian Rooms, Archives of the Nelson-Atkins Museum of Art.

17. Board of Trustees minutes, May 2, 1933, Archives of the Nelson-Atkins Museum of Art.

18. Opinions about C. T. Loo's concerns and motivations must have been passed down through the museum staff. These opinions were expressed by Marc Wilson, personal interview, October 13, 2015.

19. Ibid.

20. According to Wilson, C. T. Loo took the Nelson Gallery under his wing and "was very favorable to the Nelson-Atkins, perhaps more so than to any other institution at that time." Ibid.

21. Examination of the necklace under ultraviolet light by Objects Conservator Paul Benson, May 6, 2010.

22. The related Naginis are in the collections of the National Museum, New Delhi, and the Katolec Corporation Collection, Tokyo. For a full discussion of this work and the stylistic and scientific study of it and its related sculptures, see Doris Meth Srinivasan, "Monumental Nāginīs from Mathura," *On the Cusp of an Era: Art in the Pre-Kuṣāṇa World* (Leiden: Konninklijke Brill's Inner Asian Library 18, 2007), 351–84.

23. Ibid., 357–65.

24. Calibrated radiocarbon date of the central panel: 727–888, University of Arizona AMS laboratory number AA106919, report date January 8, 2016, on material sampled by John Twilley, October 26, 2015.

25. Twilley, John, "Polychrome Materials from a 16th century Jain Shrine (#32-137)," unpublished scientific report to the Nelson-Atkins Museum of Art, on file, April 10, 2012.

26. For a discussion of the narrative imagery in these stele from Myanmar, see Vidya Dehejia, *Discourse in Early Buddhist Art: Visual Narratives in India* (New Delhi: Munshiran Manoharlal Publishers Pvt. Ltd., 1997), 251–54.

27. Susan L. Huntington and John C. Huntington, *The Art of Ancient India: Hindu, Buddhist, Jain* (New York and Tokyo: John Weatherhill, Inc. 1985), xxiii.

28. Scholars who have taken a non-regional approach include B. N. Goswamy and Eberhard Fischer, who have attempted to associate stylistic developments in paintings from the hill kingdoms of North India to a lineage of painters who traveled to different courts. Tryna Lyons provides a further example of this approach in her study of recent painting lineages among the living painters of Nathadwara. See B. N. Goswamy and Eberhard Fischer, *Pahari Masters: Court Painters of Northern India* (Zurich: Artibus Asiae Publishers, 1992), and Tryna Lyons, *The Artists of Nathadwara: the Practice of Painting in Rajasthan* (Bloomington, IN: University of Indiana Press, 2004).

29. http://artgallery.yale.edu/collections/objects/83943

http://www.artic.edu/aic/collections/artwork/49229

http://www.britishmuseum.org/research/collection_online/collection_object_details.aspx?objectId=1607792&partId=1&people=138196&peoA=138196-1-7&page=1

https://www.kimbellart.org/collection-object/ragamala-painting-dhanasri-ragini

30. Ramacandragani, *Kumaraviharasataka,* verse 112. Published in the Jaina Atmananda Sabha in Bhavnagar, 1909, cited in Phyllis Granoff, "Halayudha's Prism: The Experience of Religion in Medieval Hymns and Stories," *Gods, Guardians, and Lovers: Temple Sculptures from North India A.D. 700–1200,* edited by Vishakha N. Desai and Darielle Mason (New York and Ahmedabad: The Asia Society Galleries, New York, in association with Mapin Publishing Pvt. Ltd., 1993), 66–93, 90.

31. A.L. Basham, *The Wonder that was India: A Survey of the Culture of the Indian Sub-Continent Before the Coming of the Muslims* (London: Sidwick and Jackson, 1954), 9.

32. George Coedès, *The Indianized States of Southeast Asia,* original French edition (Paris: Editions E. de Boccard 1964); English edition, translated by Susan Brown Cowing (Honolulu: East-West Center Press, The University of Hawai'i Press, 1968). While commending his work, some contemporary scholars suggest that Coedès overemphasized India's impact on the region and propose a history that reflects a greater role of local traditions and politics in the formation of Southeast Asian culture.

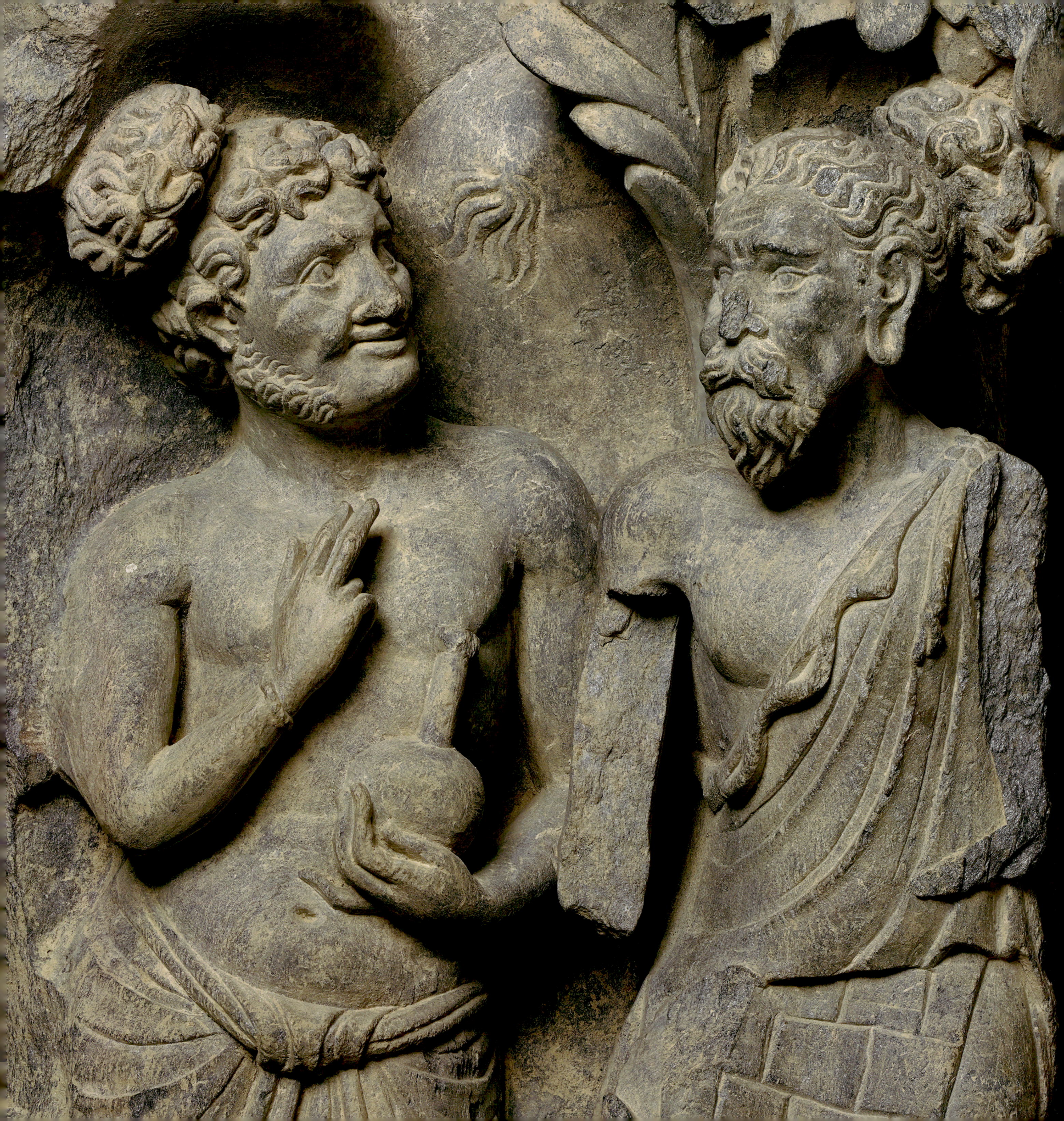

Plates & Commentaries

1 *A Scene from the Past Lives of the Buddha, from the* Dipankara Jataka

Late 2nd–early 3rd century CE
Pakistan, Swat Valley, ancient Gandhara
Kushan dynasty (1st–3rd century)
Phyllite
22½ × 36 inches (57.15 × 91.44 cm)
PURCHASE: William Rockhill Nelson Trust, 55-105

This deeply sculpted and modeled relief represents a narrative scene associated with the Buddhist religion. The visual focus is a figure of a buddha standing to the right of a curving river that bisects the scene. He is being honored by a kneeling figure to the left, as others offer him food. Monks and men in princely dress stand to either side, displaying powerful emotional reactions to the buddha's arrival.

This relief would have been part of a program of Buddhist scenes that decorated a Buddhist *stupa,* or reliquary mound. Stupas were essential features of Buddhist sites and monastic complexes. Stupas enshrined physical relics and objects belonging to Buddhist teachers, besides other items, which were invested into the mound to endow them with life. In the Gandharan regions, these structures were richly ornamented with bands of reliefs and niche sculptures featuring Buddhist scenes. These often depicted events in the life of Shakyamuni, the historical Buddha, and *Jataka* scenes, which narrated events from the past lives of Shakaymuni.

Though this relief has previously been identified as an unspecified life scene of Shakyamuni Buddha, the event depicted here bears similarities to Gandharan scenes of the *Dipankara Jataka.* In Buddhist art different earthly buddhas are depicted identically, symbolizing their perfected and non-differentiated state. Therefore, it is not the buddha but the other figures in the scene that enables this attribution. The story of Dipankara is told in two important early Buddhist texts, the *Jatakamala* (second century CE) and the *Mahavastu Avadana* (compiled between the second century BCE and the fourth century CE). In these versions Shakyamuni was born into the life of a Brahmin turned ascetic named either Sumedha, in the *Jataka*

tales, or Megha, in the *Mahavastu*. In the pivotal event of the story, Sumedha went to venerate Dipankara, a buddha of the past. Here, the ascetic is shown prostrating before Dipankara, offering his matted locks for the Buddha to walk on so he does not have to touch the muddy ground. During this important encounter Dipankara makes the prediction that he will achieve enlightenment in a future rebirth and become a buddha. This story is also significant because it represents one of the earliest of the *Jataka*s and lays a foundation for the concept of a *bodhisattva,* an enlightened being on the path toward Buddhahood.

Sumedha's prophetic meeting with Dipankara was depicted with some frequency in Gandharan art. Kurt Behrendt attributes this to the belief that the event occurred locally, and its site was said to be marked by a stupa near Hadda, Afghanistan.[1] Similar groupings of figures are depicted in a relief of the *Dipankara Jataka* in the collection of The Metropolitan Museum of Art.[2] In this example, the ascetic kneels at the feet of the Dipankara Buddha, who stands to the right with his proper right hand raised in *abhaya mudra* as his left hand grasps his robe. In the Metropolitan relief, the ascetic who will become Shakyamuni is depicted three times, creating a continuous narrative. Notably, the ascetic is shown offering lotus flowers to Dipankara, above the figure of him kneeling. There are no less than five Gandharan reliefs of *Dipankara Jataka* in The British Museum collections.[3] In a detailed relief from the stupa at Sikri, now in the Lahore Museum, four moments in the Sumedha story are present.[4] All these sculptures depict the young Brahmin's offering of flowers as he kneels to spread his hair before Dipankara in the same composition. While there is only one clearly recognizable depiction of the ascetic in the Nelson-Atkins relief—the figure with ascetic garments and matted coiffeur prostrating in the foreground of the scene—it is possible that the broken figure at the top left of the composition, next to what appear to be round bunches of flowers, was originally another depiction of Sumedha making his offering.

While this sculpture depicts Indian subject matter, it is strongly influenced by Hellenistic and Roman art. This is evident in the standing Buddha, who wears a two-shouldered robe with a cowl neck, a garment derived from a Roman toga that was popularized in Gandharan art. The influence of Roman dress and imagery upon this sculpture is evident in the way Dipankara grasps the corner of his robe in his left hand, similar to the way a Roman toga was held. Another feature directly borrowed from Roman sources is the depiction of the muscular sword-bearing warrior who accompanies the Buddha. In Buddhist iconography, this figure is known as Vajrapani, the *bodhisattva* attendant of a buddha who holds a diamond-shaped weapon known as a *vajra*. In ancient Gandhara, artists found their model for this strong, protective *bodhisattva* in a heroic classical equivalent and based the figure's form upon imagery of Hercules. Indeed, ancient Gandhara was a crossroads of cultures, beliefs, and visual models, providing rich material for the inventive artists who created masterworks like this sculpture.

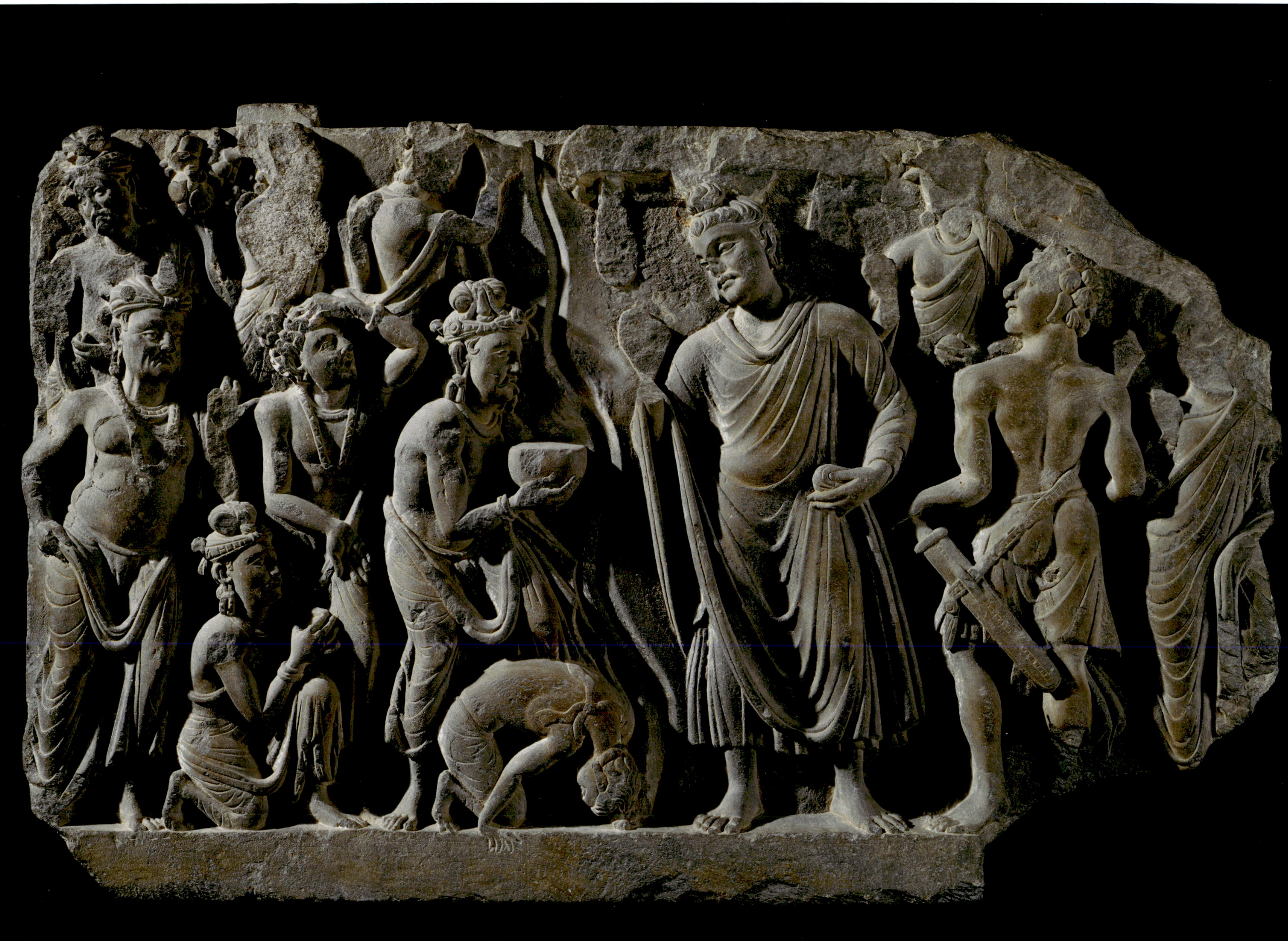

2nd–3rd century
Pakistan, ancient Gandhara
Kushan dynasty (1st–3rd century)
Schist
27¼ × 11 × 7¾ inches (69.22 × 27.94 × 19.69 cm)
PURCHASE: the Asian Art Acquisition Fund in memory
of Laurence Sickman, F99-2

Three ascetics and a princely devotee inhabit a rugged landscape in this fragment of an ancient relief sculpture from Pakistan. The group once belonged to a larger scene, and the leftward orientation of the figures suggests that they were located to the right side of a larger composition, looking toward the center. From the position of this group of figures we can guess that they were part of a narrative scene, most likely a depiction of Indra's visit to Indrashala Cave.

In the story of Indrashala Cave, Shakyamuni has traveled to the city of Rajagriha (Rajgir) after his enlightenment to meditate in a cave on top of Vediyaka Hill. While there, Indra, the king of the Vedic gods, descends from the heavens to speak with Shakyamuni. Indra engages Pancasikha, the lute-playing *gandharva* (a low-ranking male nature deity) assigned to accompany him on his visit. They find the Buddha deep in meditation in the center of the cave with the entire hilltop ablaze from the power of his yogic energy. This is likely referenced by the small whorls of flame that are depicted on the rocks between the figures in the sculpture. With his lute, Pancasikha performs a song to rouse Shakyamuni from his meditation. Indra then asks Shakyamuni a series of theological questions that lead ultimately to Indra's conversion to Buddhism. This is a highly significant and propagandistic moment in the Buddhist tradition, as the highest of the Vedic gods, associated with the dominant pre-existing religion, which Buddhism rejects, relinquishes his beliefs and adopts the Buddhist *Dharma*.

Though incomplete, the fragmentary relief in the Nelson-Atkins collection tells much of the story. The mountainous landscape of Rajgir was populated by ascetics, such as the partially draped figures with matted hair depicted here. Also in attendance is a kneeling figure in a princely crown and garb. The feet of two additional figures are visible at the top of the fragment, suggesting that in the original work these four were part of a larger group of attendants. The specific identities of these figures are unknown. In fact, the main characters in this story, Shakyamuni, Indra, and Pancasikha, would have been placed in the center and lower portions of the composition, as they appear in the well-known example from the site of Mamane Dheri, now in the Peshawar Museum. The current fragment, however, does not represent this part of the composition. The group of figures in the Nelson-Atkins sculpture can be identified, then, as part of a multitude of people who came to the mountain to meditate, to be blessed, and to be in the presence of the living Buddha.

This fragment reveals the great skill of the Gandharan artist who created it. Together with its naturalism, a characteristic of Gandharan sculpture, this example demonstrates exceptional care in the rendering of these figures. Various types of garments, from animal skins to an armor apron, are easily distinguishable. The figures' bodies are well proportioned and display naturalistic musculature and movements. Notice, for example, the bare-chested male ascetic to the lower left. His body gently bends in a *contrapposto* pose that, like some of the garments of the figures, is likely derived from Roman models. Most striking, however, is the expressive rendering of the figures. They look at the Buddha and each other with wide eyes, open mouths, and deeply chiseled cheeks. Curator Doris Meth Srinivasan noticed how these elements created a sense of psychological intensity that is clearly evident even now, 1,800 years after the creation of the work.[5]

The visit to Indrashala Cave became part of the codified program of life scenes of the historical Buddha Shakyamuni that were frequently illustrated in Gandharan art. However, the visit of Indra did not feature prominently in the Pali Canon, the earliest authoritative body of Buddhist texts, which raises questions about the reasons for its local popularity in Gandhara. Certainly, the scene of a Buddha meditating in a rugged mountainous landscape may have resonated with Buddhist communities living in the valleys of the Hindu Kush. However, the most likely source for interest in this subject was found in Gandharan monasteries, which by the Kushan era (first to third centuries) were dominated by the Sarvastivada sect of Buddhism. It is likely that the Sarvastivada sect embraced this event with its emphasis on meditation, and Sarvastivadan monks would have guided the selection of scenes that were created to decorate the *stupa*s associated with their monasteries.[6] The fierce realism and emotive depictions of the figures in this fragment, however, are the result of the skill and inventiveness of Gandharan artists.

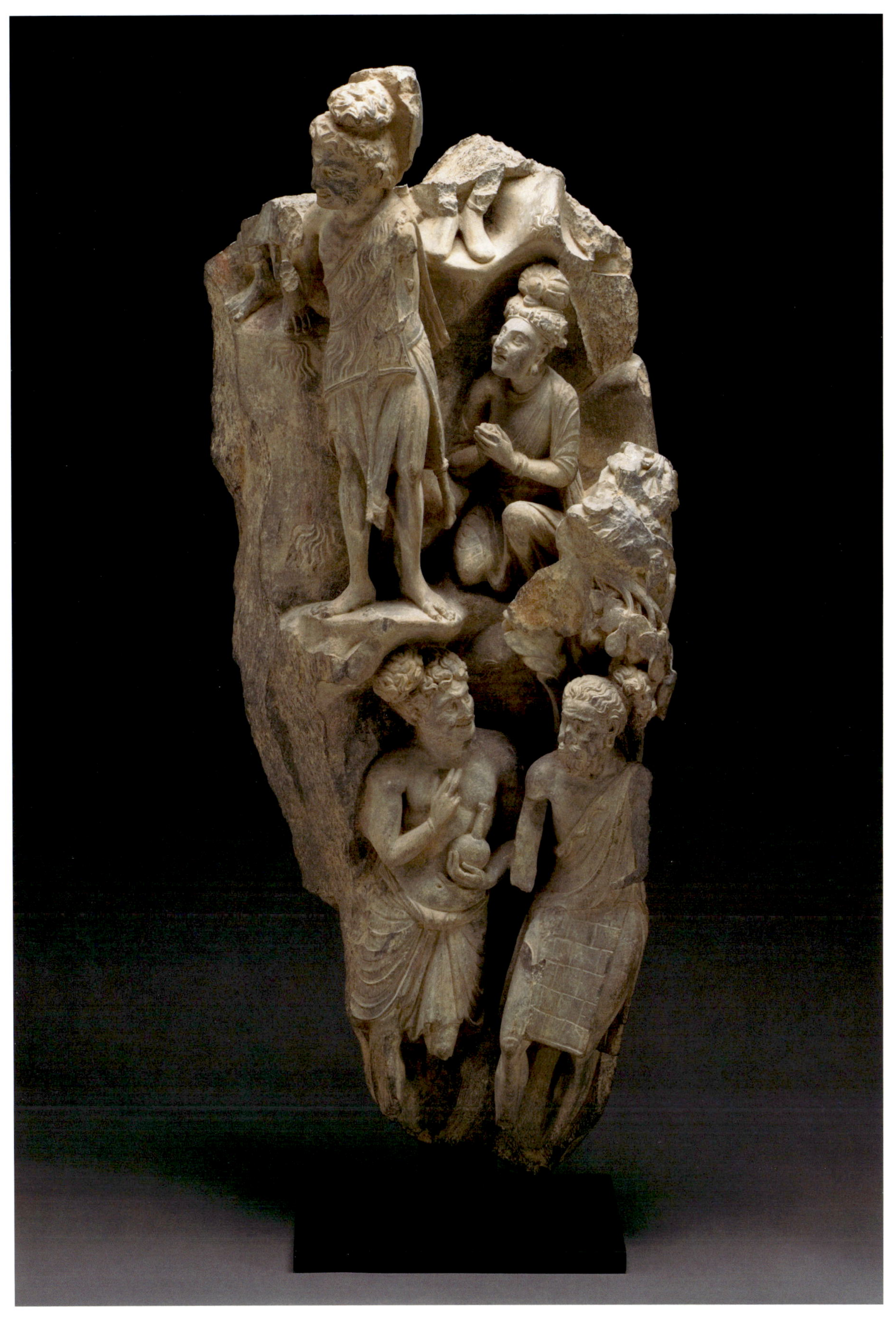

200–299
Pakistan, possibly Swat region, ancient Gandhara
Kushan dynasty (1st–3rd century)
Phyllite with paint
55 × 17½ × 10½ inches (139.7 × 44.45 × 26.67 cm)
PURCHASE: William Rockhill Nelson Trust, 35-32

8th century
Pakistan, Gilgit or Swat, or India, Kashmir
(Karkota dynasty, 627–855, or Patola Shahi dynasty,
6th–8th century)
Brass with silver inlay, gilding, and traces of paint
9⅞ × 5¾ × 3¾ inches (25.0825 × 14.605 × 9.525 cm)
PURCHASE: William Rockhill Nelson Trust, 66-22

Two elegant young men greet us, one rendered in stone, the other cast in brass. Both are dressed in a fine waistcloth known as a *dhoti*, drawn up in tiered folds. The standing youth on the left also wears an *uttariya,* a loose cloth draped over his left shoulder and across his body. Adorned with crowns, necklaces, earrings, and cascades of curly hair drawn up into elegant coiffures, our subjects could easily be mistaken for earthly princes. However, the riches associated with them are spiritual rather than material. They are *bodhisattva*s, "enlightened beings" who are on the path toward Buddhahood. Both of these sculptures depict Maitreya Bodhisattva, one of the key figures associated with the Buddhist religion in the early centuries of the Common Era. Maitreya can frequently be identified by the flask or water pot he holds in his left hand. A tall slender flask is evident hanging from the left hand of the seated *bodhisattva*, and one was likely held in the now-broken left hand of the standing stone sculpture.

Maitreya figures prominently in both the Theravada and Mahayana schools of Buddhism, where he is recognized as the future successor to Shakyamuni, the historical Buddha. Filling a messianic role, tradition holds that Maitreya will be born on earth to become a fully enlightened Buddha and re-educate humanity on the path to enlightenment. Until that time, Maitreya is still a *bodhisattva* and serves as the Lord of Tushita Heaven, a palatial celestial abode where he offers Buddhist teachings to its heavenly inhabitants. Maitreya served multiple functions for early Buddhists: as the last of the earthly (*manushi*) buddhas (the Buddha-to-Be), as an exemplar for Mahayana practitioners who adopted the *bodhisattva* model as the guiding

principle in their own religious development, and as the ruler of a heavenly world into which practitioners could hope to be reborn after their death.

Though separated by centuries, these two sculptures of Maitreya may share the same birthplace of northwest Pakistan. These lands formed the heart of the ancient Himalayan culture known as Gandhara. During the first through the third century of the Common Era, when the standing Maitreya sculpture was created, Gandhara was under the control of the Kushans, a Central Asian dynasty that grew in power and prestige through their control of the central and southern Silk Routes. Numerous Buddhist art works and structures were created during the Kushan era, which incorporated large devotional sculptures of buddhas and *bodhisattva*s. The round youthful face of the standing Maitreya in the Nelson-Atkins collection looks especially similar to sculptures from the Swat Valley. Greco-Roman influence is evident in the naturalistic musculature and drapery of this sculpture, a result of the Greek and Roman trading colonies established in Gandhara before the Kushans arrived. While the Kushans adopted the Buddhist religion, their art developed in a syncretic style based upon existing Hellenistic and Roman models in the region.

The later sculpture of seated Maitreya was created in the regions that formed eastern Gandhara. This small metal image, perhaps created for a personal shrine, can be dated stylistically to the eighth century. By this time, the region was under the cultural influence of Kashmir, and the artistic styles of the region had shifted away from Mediterranean-influenced naturalism toward a more schematic, Indian-inspired ideal. The broad round shoulders and narrow waist of

the seated Maitreya are found also on sculptures produced during the Gupta dynasty (third to fifth century) in central India. The use of brass as a medium with inlaid silver and the sculpting of figures with full, round-jawed faces and wide slanting eyes are common to Kashmiri art of this period. However, the base of the sculpture, which depicts a throne supported by two lions with a wide swag of tasseled cloth draped over the center, is diagnostic of sculptures created in Pakistan, in both Gilgit, home of the Shahi Kingdom to the north, and in the Swat Valley to the west. Unlike the larger sculpture of Standing Maitreya, discussed above, which was likely created for veneration in a Buddhist temple, the small scale of this metal sculpture suggests that it could have been created for use in a more intimate environment, like a home. However, the traces of cold-gold gilding on the face, as Robert Linrothe notes, suggests that this sculpture, like many Indian and Himalayan metal sculptures, was once venerated and preserved in a Tibetan Monastery.[7]

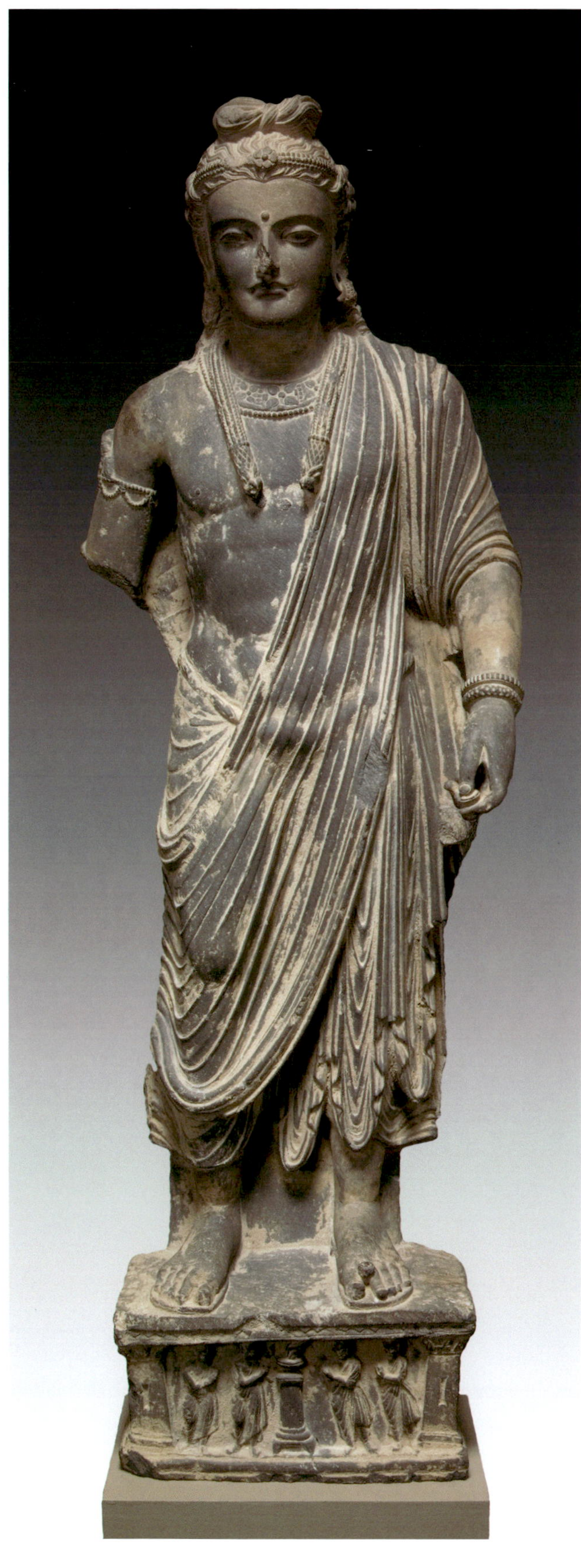

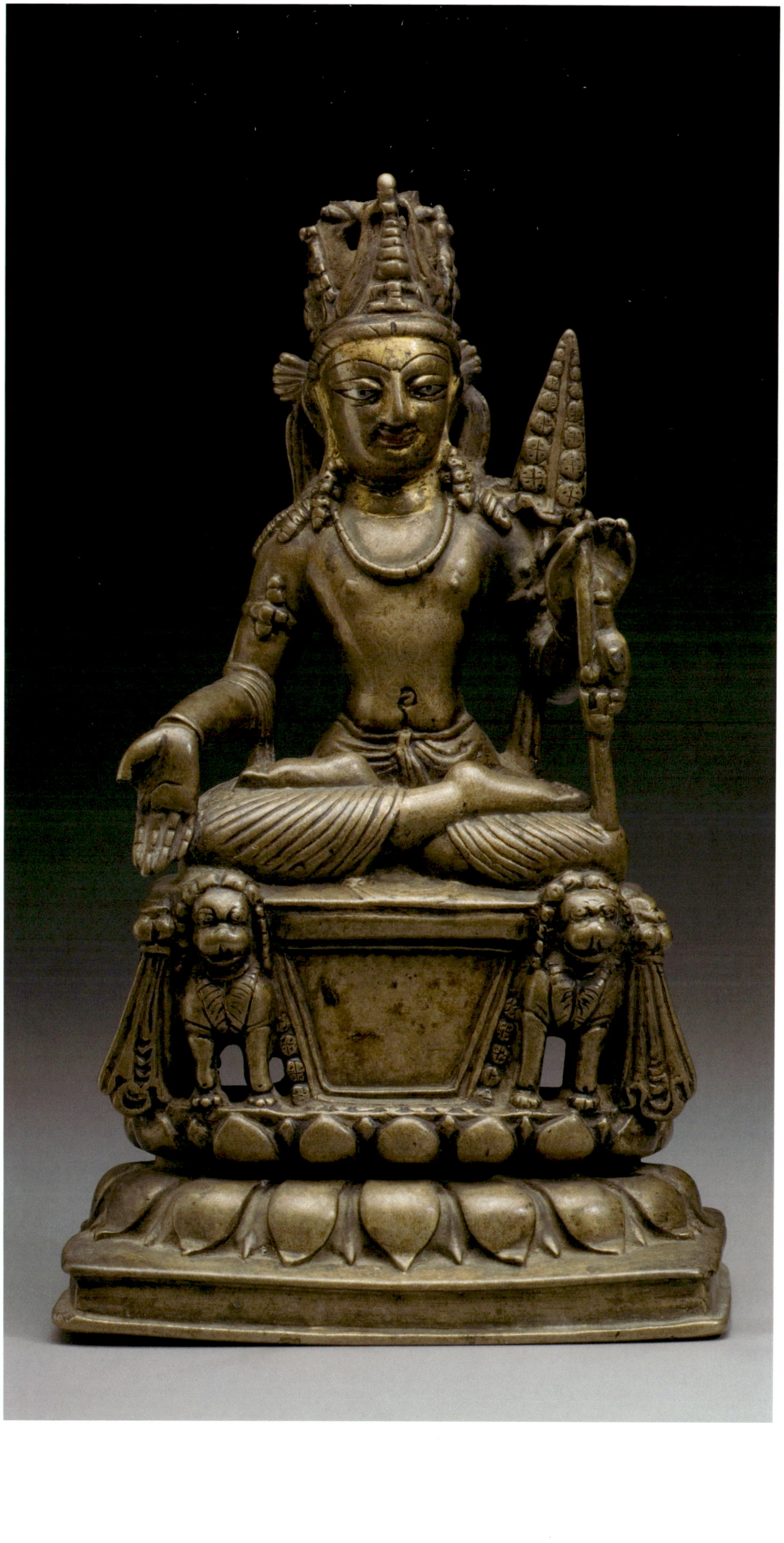

Torso of a Buddha, Torso of a Buddha, and *Standing Buddha*

Early 5th century
India, Mathura
Gupta dynasty (300–699)
Sandstone
45¼ × 20 ½ inches, 350 lb. (114.94 × 52.07 cm, 158.76 kg)
PURCHASE: William Rockhill Nelson Trust, 45-15

5th century
India, Sarnath
Gupta dynasty (300–699)
Sandstone
34 × 14½ × 7 inches (86.36 × 36.83 × 17.78 cm)
PURCHASE: William Rockhill Nelson Trust, 39-19

ca. 400
India, found at Dhanesar Khera
Gupta dynasty (300–699)
Bronze
14⅝ × 5¼ × 4¼ inches (37.15 × 13.34 × 10.8 cm)
PURCHASE: William Rockhill Nelson Trust, 44-13

A comparison of these three elegant sculptures of a standing Buddha, most likely Shakyamuni, in the Nelson-Atkins collection reveals striking similarities. Though each work is a different size and is created from different materials—mottled red *sikri* sandstone, buff sandstone, and bronze—they all share key visual features, such as broad, curving shoulders, narrow waists, long limbs, and slight bodies enhanced by a gentle bulge of flesh at their waists.

These similarities are intentional. Each sculpture was created following a similar stylistic canon, which developed during India's Gupta dynasty, a kingdom that ruled much of northern India from the fourth to the sixth century. At their height, the Guptas controlled a vast empire, with the territories defined by the Yamuna and Ganges Rivers as their heartland. During this time, India experienced an unprecedented flourishing of art, literature, and science, which historians have traditionally described as India's Classical Period or Golden Age.

The Guptas inherited the great ancient urban centers of northern India. Two of these cities served as the artistic capitals of the Guptas: Mathura, on the Yamuna River in central India, and Sarnath, near the Ganges River next to the ancient city of Varanasi. Both these cities were active centers of artistic production during the Gupta era, and each region developed a distinctive style, referred to by art historians as the Mathura and Sarnath "schools" of Gupta art. These schools flourished from a wealth of local patronage, as both cities had multiple Buddhist sites and monasteries that were endowed with shrines and imagery. The Mathura and Sarnath schools also influenced the style of art produced across India and internationally.

Sometime in the early reign of Chandragupta I (r. 320–ca. 330), the Guptas gained control of the city of Mathura, which was already an important religious site and art-making center during the Kushan era (first to third century). Mathura was still thriving in the early fifth century, when the Chinese monk Faxian (337–ca. 422) visited the city and reported seeing over twenty monasteries and three thousand monks.[8] The Gupta style appears to have primarily developed here, as is evident in a standing Buddha sculpture from the Katra Mound, dated 390.[9] The Katra Mound sculpture has the same broad shoulders and tubular limbs found in all three of the Nelson-Atkins sculptures. All these Buddha sculptures are depicted wearing a two-shouldered cowl-necked robe based on the monastic garments depicted in Gandharan art.

By the early to mid-fifth century, the elements of the Mathura style had become codified. These elements are clearly visible in the Nelson-Atkins sculpture of a *Standing Buddha.* Through its tall proportions, slightly relaxed frontal pose with bent knee, and lack of muscular definition, this stone Buddha embodies all the idealized qualities of the Mathura school from this remarkable period. These proportions, according to former curator and director Laurence Sickman, "are not those of mortal and imperfect humanity but are ideally conceived and set by iconic canons."[10] Still, hints of the Buddha's anatomy and undergarments are suggested as transparent, folding drapery arcs over the figure's swelling belly and around and between the recesses created by the arms, pelvis, and legs. The soft mottled red stone, weathered by nature and time, looks almost like flesh under light drapery. However, though this figure is at ease, it is not at rest. The Nelson-Atkins *Buddha* from Mathura stands alert,

lifelike, and life-size before us. If the sculpture's head were not broken, we would look into the face of a transcendent man.

The same pose and proportions are evident in a second sculpture of a *Torso of a Buddha* at the Nelson-Atkins. Carved in tan sandstone, this sculpture was created at Sarnath, the other great artistic center in the Gupta heartland. Sarnath lies on the outskirts of the ancient city of Varanasi, near the Ganges River. Though large-scale artistic production at Mathura under the Guptas preceded production at Sarnath by at least fifty years, scholar Joanna Williams speculates that the output of Buddhist sculpture at Sarnath may have surpassed that produced in Mathura.[11] Sarnath's rise as an artistic center is likely due to its direct connections with the historical Buddha Shakyamuni and Buddhist monastic communities. Sarnath is the location where Shakyamuni Buddha gave his First Sermon after achieving enlightenment. For many Buddhists, Sarnath is almost as sacred and significant as Bodh Gaya, the site of Shakyamuni's enlightenment. In the centuries after Shakyamuni lived, Sarnath became a vibrant Buddhist center and pilgrimage site, populated with *stupa*s (reliquary mounds), *vihara*s (monasteries), and thousands of practitioners. Indeed, by the seventh century, the Chinese pilgrim Xuanzang reported that Sarnath contained a large complex with a community of fifteen hundred monks.[12] The local need for sculpture and architecture to support these monastic communities was likely the major impetus for the development of the so-called "Sarnath School" of Gupta art. Sarnath sculpture appears as an important art form in the late fifth century, as is evident from a number of highly refined sculptures dated to the 470s. The Nelson-Atkins *Buddha* from Sarnath

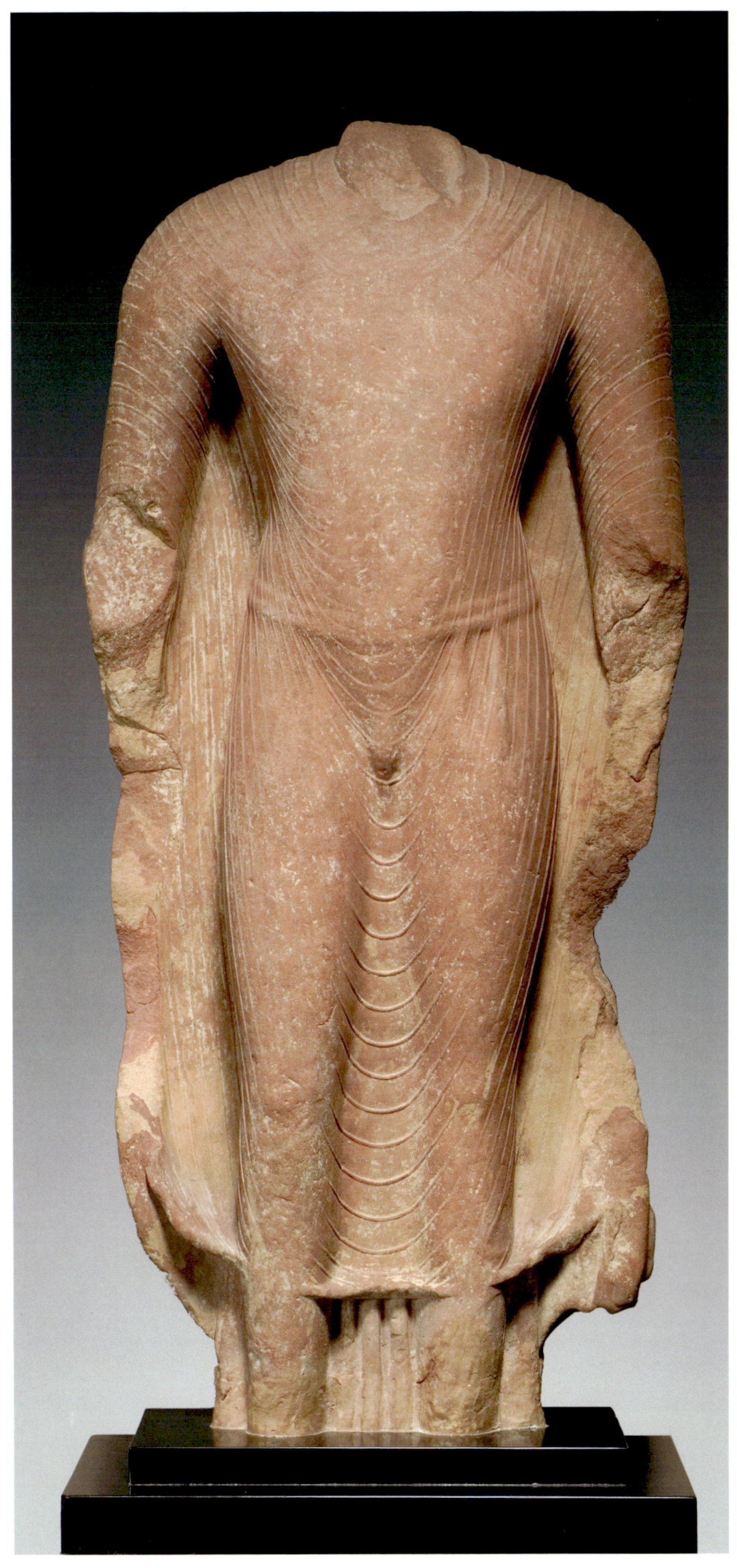
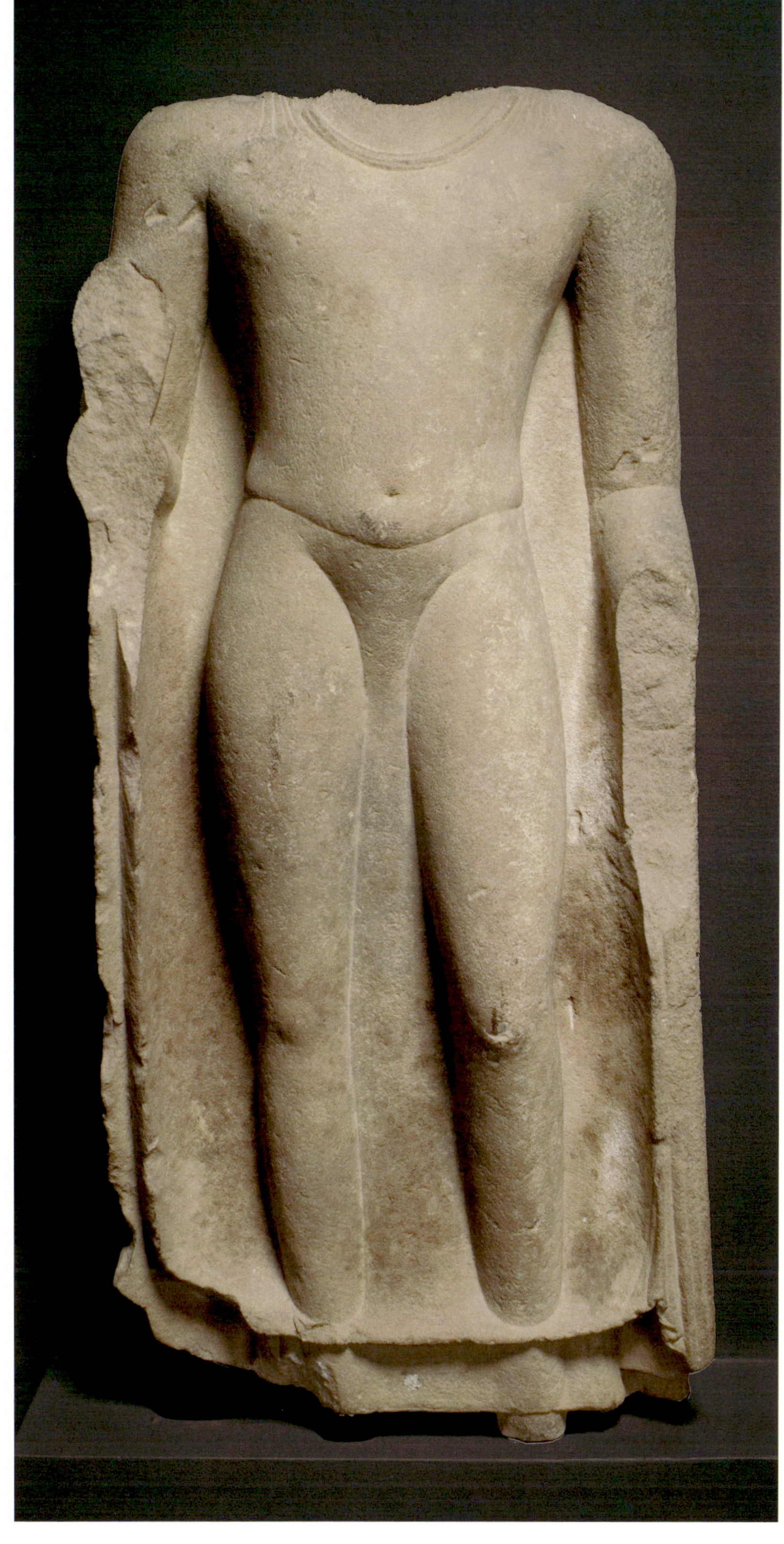

exhibits the same traits as these sculptures. It has the broad shoulders, narrow waist, and relaxed pose that are seen also in Mathura sculpture, discussed above. Its proportions are slightly compressed, with a shorter, wider torso. Unlike Mathura examples, the Sarnath *Buddha* sculptures wear transparent drapery with no folds, revealing itself only at the heavy edges of the garment. According to Williams, this treatment of drapery appears to draw from earlier Kushan styles from central India, which were copied in Sarnath until around 400. The effect of these smooth surfaces and nearly invisible clothing highlights the swells and contours of the Nelson-Atkins sculpture, revealing a youthful and somewhat genderless body, an ideal form for the depiction of a perfected being.

The most complete and rare sculpture in this group is the Gupta-era bronze Buddha in the Nelson-Atkins collection. This *Standing Buddha* shares the lean body, long legs, and wide shoulders of its stone companions. Its head, with its long, oval face crowned by tight curls of hair, is very similar in features and proportions to a stone *Standing Buddha* sculpture from Jamalpur (ca. 440–455), now in the Mathura Museum.[13] Indeed, the Nelson-Atkins sculpture bears such an affinity to early Gupta sculpture from Mathura that it remains one of the few "Gupta" bronzes whose fifth-century dating has not been challenged by scholars in recent years.[14] The properties of bronze and the techniques used to create bronze sculptures are evident in the Nelson-Atkins *Standing Buddha*. One can imagine the artist rolling the wax cylinders to craft the figure's long thin legs and oversize arms with their expressive gestures. Soft forms give way to crisply edged lines, marking the places where the artist's hands were replaced by sharp tools to delineate the lids of the Buddha's eyes, the creases in his neck, and the cascade of folds and pleats that roll down his body and around his contours. While we know that the Nelson-Atkins bronze was one of three bronze sculptures excavated at the village of Dhanesar Khera in eastern Uttar Pradesh in the late nineteenth century, we do not

know if it was created there. Neither do we know if there were bronze workshops in Mathura, though the Nelson-Atkins sculpture was certainly created within the Mathura stylistic canon. The style of the Buddha's robe and his stellate halo are elements found in some Gandharan bronzes, leading Pratapaditya Pal to suggest that the Nelson-Atkins sculpture could have been created in the greater Gandharan region in a hybrid style, or in Central India, but maintaining Gandharan elements.[15] Whatever the context of its production, this elegant work serves as a bridge across time and geography.

The Sanskrit inscription wrapping the base of this sculpture provides a window into its patronage and intended function in the fifth century. The inscription states that the sculpture was a gift from a lay woman named Bedika for the benefit of the attainment of wisdom for her parents and all sentient beings.[16] This sculpture would have been a very expensive gift, and the figure was likely intended to serve as an altar image in a Buddhist temple or monastery. It illustrates the ancient Indian concept of *dana*, the offering of a pious gift or charity that enabled the giver to accrue or transfer spiritual merit. This economy of merit connected the Buddhist lay and monastic communities and is likely responsible for the commission of many sculptures and structures during this period. Thus we see echoes in this exquisite bronze Buddha of how the Gupta stone sculptures in the collection would have appeared when they were complete, why they were created, and also how they were intended to be used.

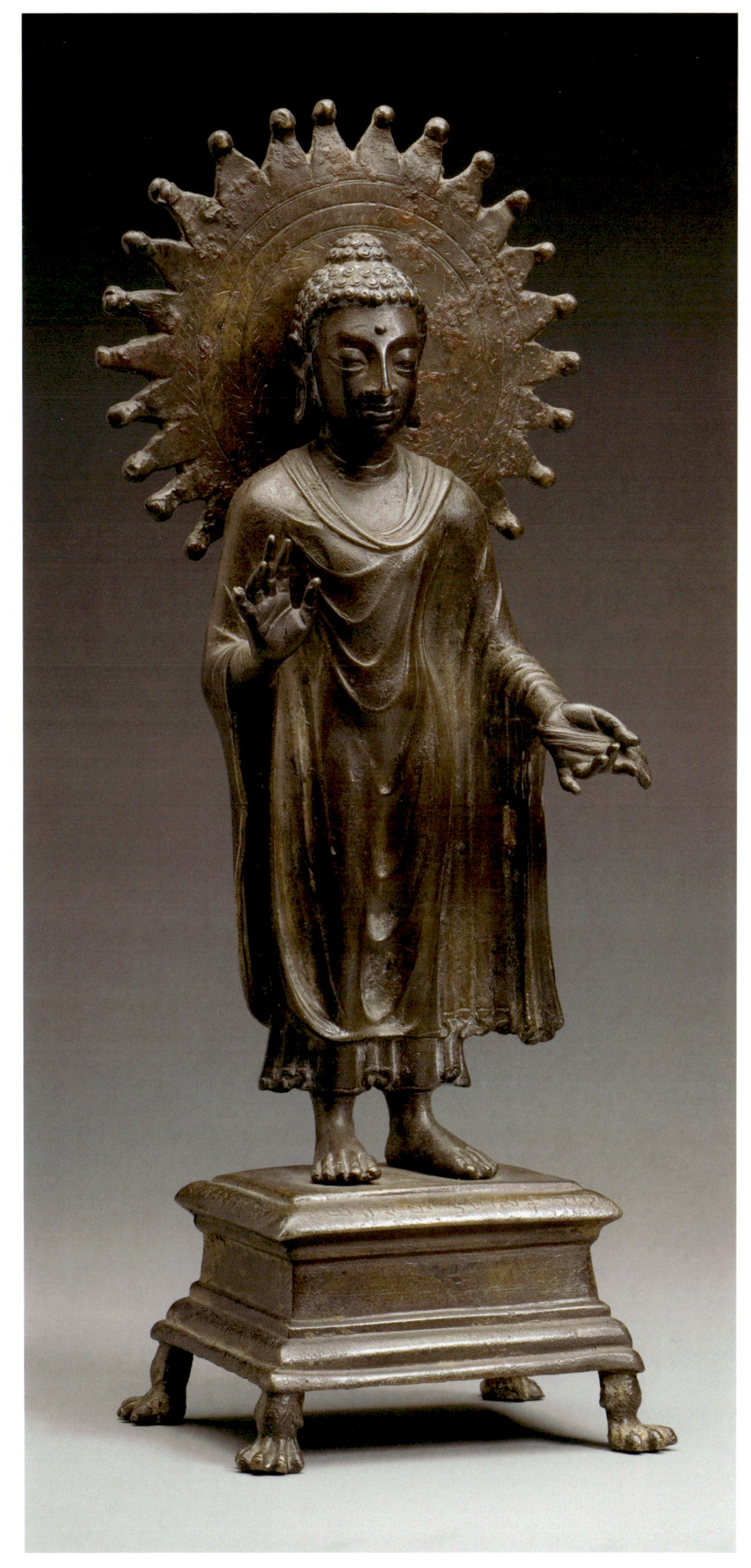

First half of the 7th century
Central Thailand, but discovered in Chiang Mai
Dvaravati culture, 6th–11th century
Limestone
51½ × 18 × 6 inches (130.81 × 45.72 × 15.24 cm)
PURCHASE: William Rockhill Nelson Trust, 35-33

During the sixth through the eleventh century, a riverine kingdom known as Dvaravati occupied central Thailand and parts of Burma and Laos. The Dvaravati people appear to have been the descendants of Mon peoples who migrated from western China into peninsular Southeast Asia. With direct access to the sea through the Cho Praya River Delta, the Dvaravati were able to exchange both goods and ideas with neighboring Southeast Asian kingdoms and also with India. Though the Dvaravati were weak politically, they participated in one of the greatest cultural transformations in the history of Southeast Asia, actively adopting and transmitting India's religions, social models, and artistic practices within the peninsula. Buddhism was perhaps the greatest cultural import that flourished in the Dvaravati kingdom.

Hundreds of archaeological finds from this era demonstrate that the Dvaravati had adopted the architectural forms and sculptural styles associated with the art produced in the region of Amaravati in southern India and Gupta-era art (fourth to seventh century) in northern India. The similarities between this standing Buddha, likely Shakyamuni, and other Gupta-era sculptures from India are striking. The broad, rounded shoulders and narrow waist of the Thai Buddha are clearly rooted in the Gupta artistic canon. The modeling of the figure's body and drapery reveal a direct connection to the sculptural school at Sarnath in eastern India, as evident in a comparison with the *Torso of a Buddha* from Sarnath in the Nelson-Atkins collection (Cat. 6), discussed in the previous essay. Slight subtle changes are also evident in this Southeast Asian translation of the Gupta idiom. The Dvaravati *Standing Buddha*'s figure is more slight than its Indian models and is rigidly frontal. His body is indicated only through gentle swells of flesh that push forward through a transparent Sarnath-style robe.

The most striking feature of the *Standing Buddha* is how well it illustrates the achievements of Dvaravati artists who, working over twelve hundred miles away across the Bay of Bengal, were able to capture the psychological state found in the best examples of Gupta Buddhist sculpture. The Nelson-Atkins *Standing Buddha* is withdrawn yet alert, quiet, and sublime. His features, pose, and mood are similar to those of a well-known sculpture of a *Standing Buddha* from Dvaravati in the collection of the National Museum in Bangkok.[17] His focus is inward, his eyes half open in meditation. Nevertheless, this Buddha engages with us directly, and if we meet his gaze we see how the Indian model has been transformed. In its shape and proportions, the Buddha's face is Mon, not Indian. This subtle but unmistakable change signals both the localization of Buddhist art and the widening and diversification of the Buddhist community, which by the first millennium CE had spread well beyond India's shores.

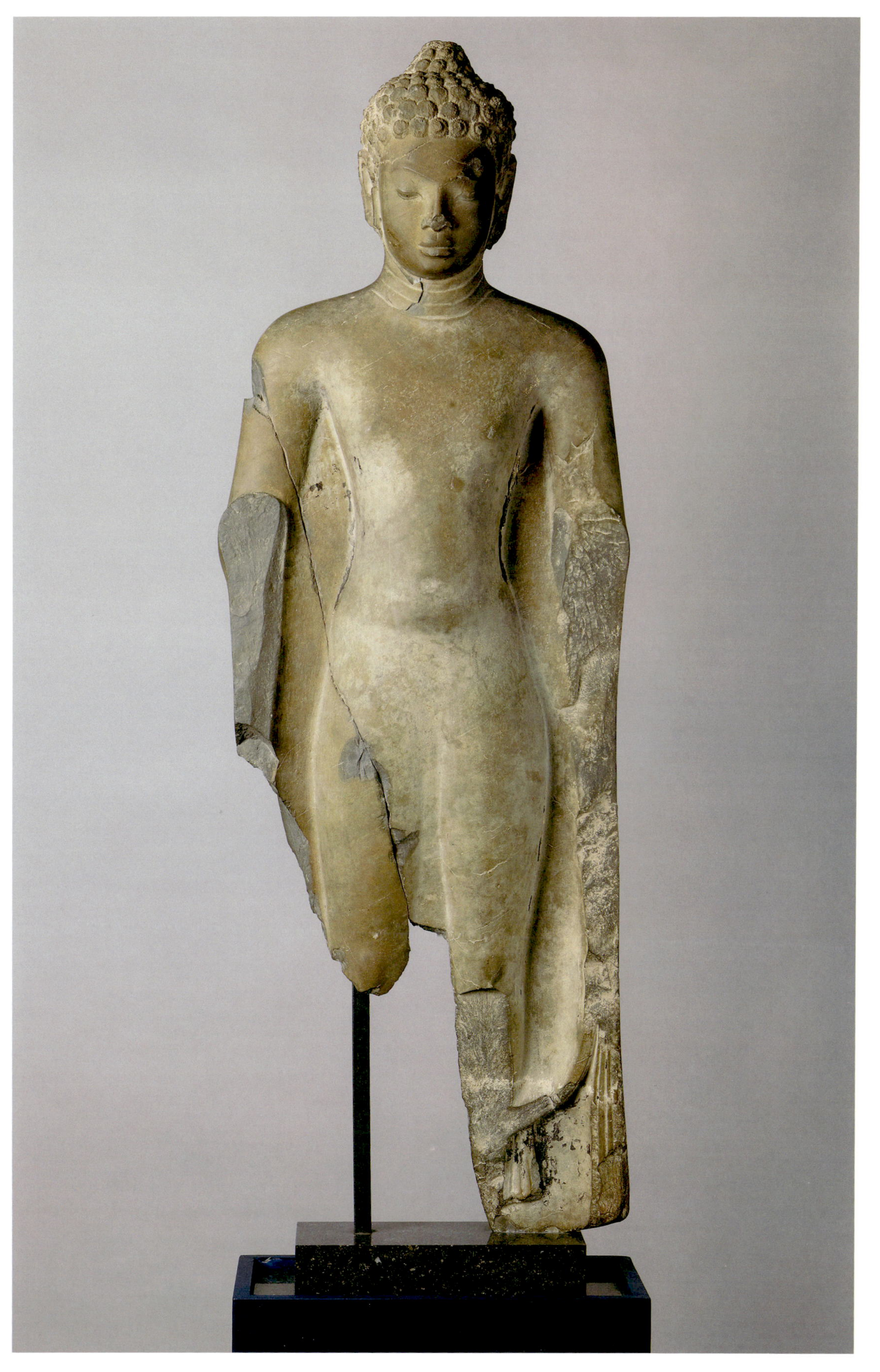

9 | *Seated Buddha*

Late 9th–10th century
Northeast India, Bihar
Pala–Sena dynasty (750–1100)
Schist
21½ × 14½ × 5½ inches (54.61 × 36.83 × 13.97 cm)
PURCHASE: William Rockhill Nelson Trust, 31-63

Five hundred years before the birth of Jesus of Nazareth, a wandering Indian ascetic sat down to meditate beneath a fig tree outside the ancient Indian city of Gaya. That man was Prince Siddhartha, also known as Shakyamuni ("sage of the Shakya clan"), and the religious enlightenment he experienced after forty days of intense meditation is the most important event in the history of the religion he propagated: Buddhism. Imagery depicting the moment of his enlightenment at Bodh Gaya first appeared in art from the Kushan era in India. The scene was frequently represented in sculptures created during the Pala dynasty (750s to the second half of the twelfth century) in eastern India. The Palas ruled over the eastern Gangetic Plain, where Shakyamuni traveled, became enlightened, and taught. This sacred landscape was populated by numerous Buddhist sites, none more important than the site of the enlightenment itself. Susan L. Huntington argues that Pala political control of this region as well as the religious significance of Bodh Gaya may have contributed to the popularity of depictions of the enlightenment scene during this period.[18]

The *Seated Buddha* in the Nelson-Atkins collection is an excellent example of the early Pala style of the late ninth to the early tenth century. Carved in a dark grey schist characteristic of the region, the stele features a large central figure of Shakyamuni seated on a double-lotus throne, flanked by two small buddha figures and rearing composite animals known as *vyalaka*. The Buddha sits in the *vajrasana* yogic position with legs crossed and holds his left hand in *dhyanamudra*, a meditation gesture. The key to the iconography is the position of his right hand, which touches the ground. This is *bhumisparsha mudra*, the earth-touching gesture, and signifies the moment

before Shakyamuni achieved enlightenment, as he called on the Earth Goddess to confirm and witness this great event. The figure's heart-shaped face, full-pursed lips, broad round shoulders, and thin waist are elements of the early Pala style and derive from earlier Gupta-era models.

The Sanskrit inscription on the base of the sculpture appears to be the Buddhist creed. This outlines that all phenomena result from causes (or suffering) that have been explained by the Buddha, who has proclaimed their cessation. This mantra was frequently inscribed on Buddhist images during the Pala period and is an appropriate subject for a depiction of the moment when the bonds created through causation are overcome through enlightenment.

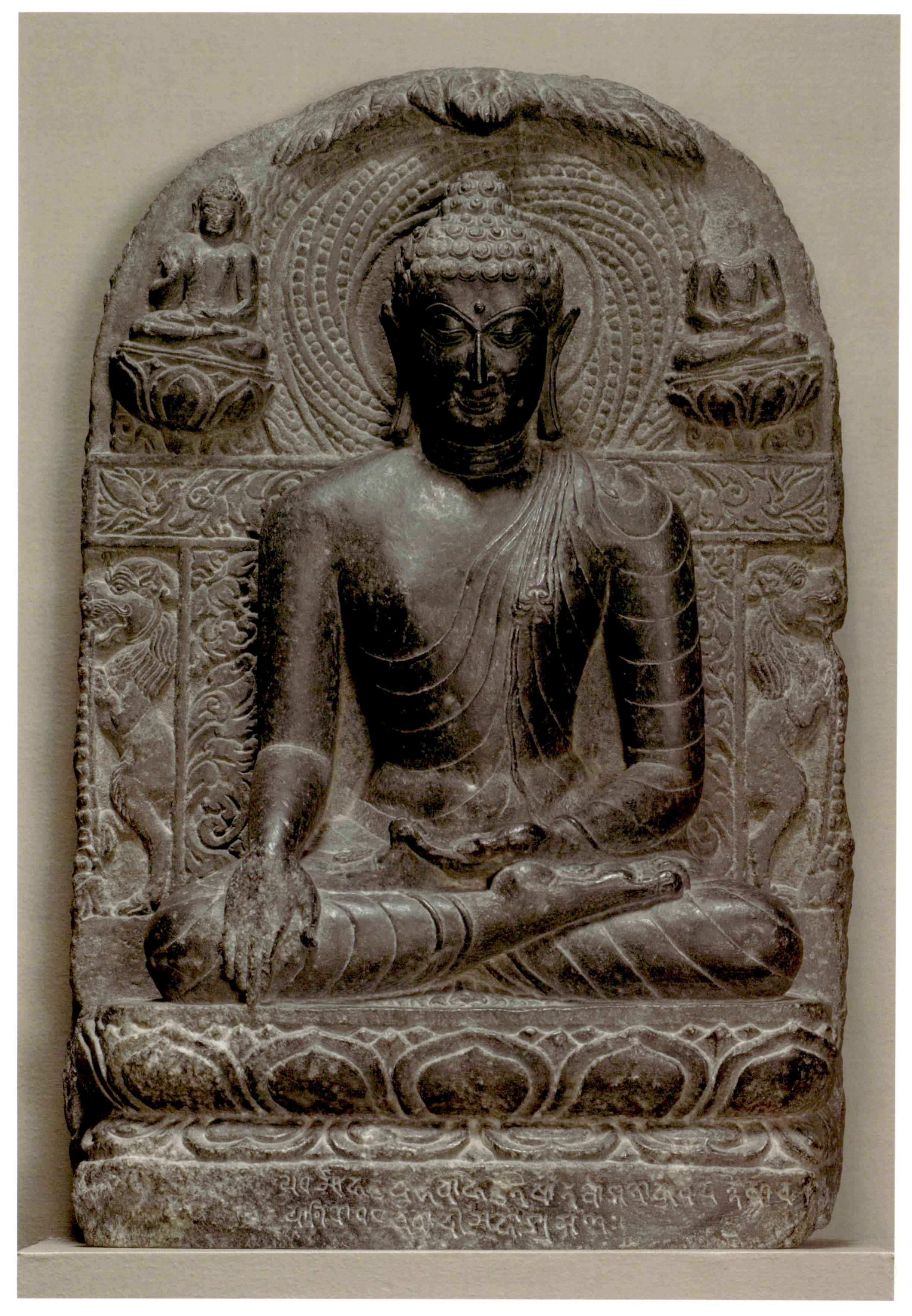

12th century
Myanmar, Bagan [Pagan]
Kingdom of Bagan (849–1287)
Stone with traces of pigment and gilding
5⁹⁄₁₆ × 3⁵⁄₈ inches (14.13 × 9.21 cm)
PURCHASE: acquired through the generosity of members
of the Asia Society, New York, F72-12

The most important city of the kingdom of Bagan lay along a vast bend in the great Irrawaddy River, which winds for over a thousand miles through central Myanmar (Burma). Bagan was founded in the ninth century as a Buddhist kingdom, and in just a few centuries its capital, of the same name, developed into one of the largest and grandest Buddhist sites in the world. Here, thousands of monuments ranging from small votive *stupa*s (reliquaries) to large monasteries and massive pyramidal temples stretch across forty square miles in the main archaeological zone. Besides commissioning monuments, local patrons were also interested in portable images. This Bagan-era stele in the Nelson-Atkins collection is one of a number of surviving examples of *andagu*, a small stone stele carved in dolomite that features scenes from the life of Shakyamuni Buddha.[19]

The central scene depicted on the Nelson-Atkins stele is the pivotal moment when Shakyamuni touches the earth and achieves enlightenment. This is the most important event in the life history of Shakyamuni and remains the most commonly depicted Buddhist image in Southeast Asia. This stele also incorporates representations of multiple life events of Shakyamuni in the columns of small figures that flank the central Buddha. The outer columns contain eight other significant life events that are frequently associated with his enlightenment. These can be identified from the lower left as: Shakyamuni's Meditation beneath Muchalinda, the Birth of Shakyamuni, the First Sermon, and the Taming of the Elephant Nalagiri. The life scenes continue down the outer right column and are most likely the Descent from Tryastrimsha Heaven, the Miracle at Shravasti, the Gift of the Monkey, and the

Emaciated Shakyamuni. The final life event, the Parinirvana, which occurred at the time of Shakyamuni's death, is prominently depicted at the top of the stele and is represented by the reclining Buddha beneath a bell-shaped *stupa*, surrounded by attendants. The inside columns originally depicted seven figures, six of which can be identified as buddhas. The buddha figures likely depict the seven events that occurred at Bodh Gaya shortly after Shakyamuni defeated Mara and became enlightened. According to John and Susan Huntington, this subject matter was of special interest in Bagan and is not found in Indian sculptures depicting multiple life scenes.[20] The Nelson-Atkins stele features two additional figures, willowy *bodhisattva*s that stand immediately to either side of the central Buddha.

Bagan looked to India in the development of its art, and Bagan sculpture and paintings reveal close connections with the contemporary art of the Pala dynasty in eastern India and Bengal. The format of the stele, with the central Enlightenment scene, is found in many examples of Pala Buddhist sculpture, like the *Seated Buddha* in the Nelson-Atkins collection discussed earlier (Cat. 9). Pala sculptures frequently depicted eight life scenes in a composition similar to this sculpture. Pala influence can also be seen in the postures of the figures, particularly the S-shaped sway of the standing ones. Moreover, the double-lotus platform, supported by curling leafy stems, and the tiered architectural-styled base are taken from Pala models. There are Burmese elements present here as well. Notice the wide, oversized head of the central Buddha, surmounted by a cone-like cap of tightly curled hair. The proportions of this Buddha's body have shifted away from the Pala canon, as evident in its thick neck, round shoulders, and wide, bulky arms. The style, composition, and complexity of the Nelson-Atkins sculpture are similar to those of a stele in the collection of the Harvard Art Museums, which has been dated to the twelfth century by the Huntingtons.[21]

Traces of the original pigment and gilding remain on the Nelson-Atkins stele, providing evidence of how the stele may have looked originally. The central Shakyamuni Buddha, the Parinirvana Buddha, and the *bodhisattva*s were all gilded, and traces of gold leaf and rich red ground are still visible. Black pigment was applied to the surface and has settled in carved lines and crevices, revealing fine details like the grid of lines that indicate individual curls of hair, the curving smiles of the *bodhisattva*s, and the veins in the lush cordate *pipal* leaves of the Bodhi Tree, above.

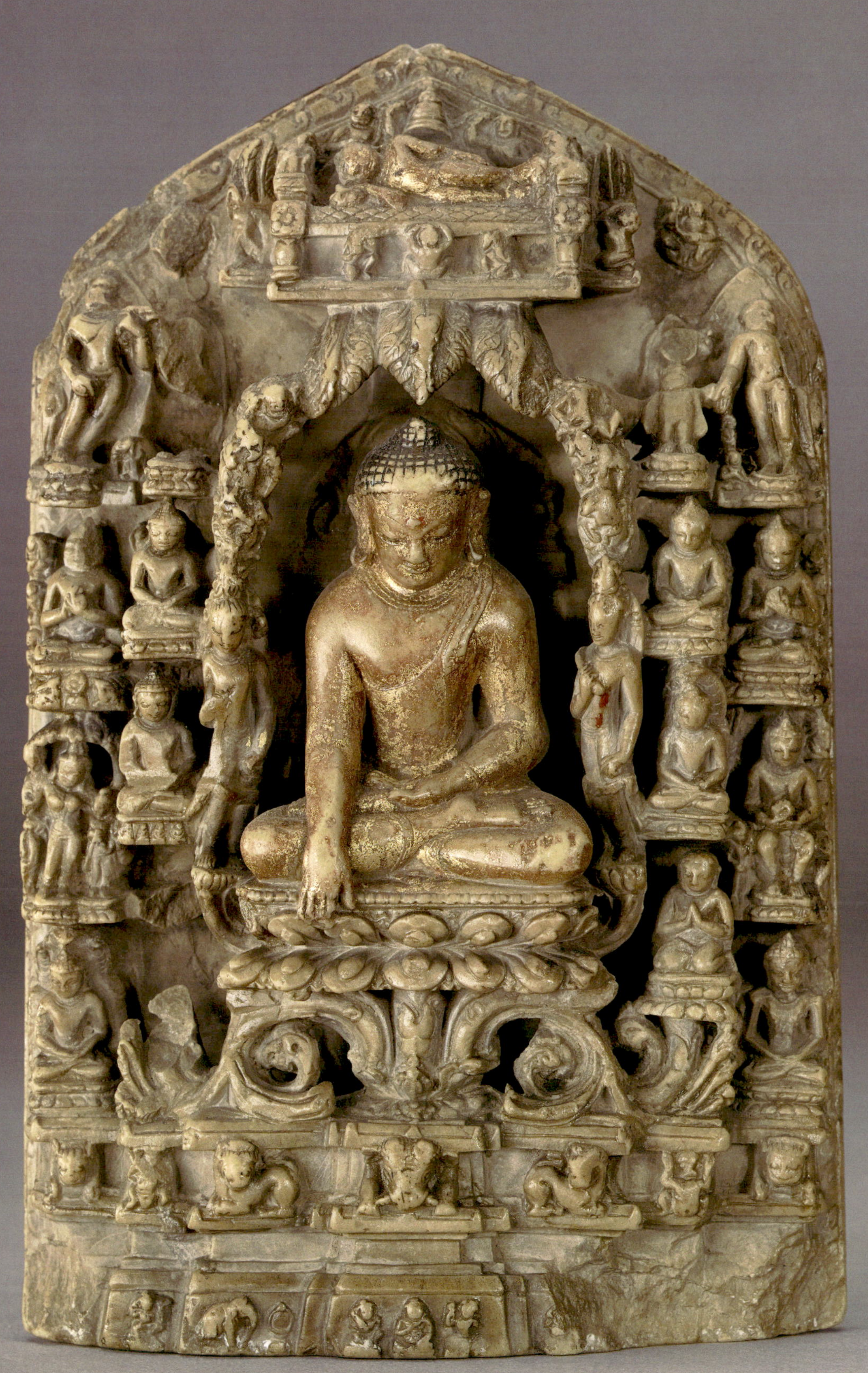

 Traveling Shrine with Vairocana and Eight Bodhisattvas

8th–9th century
Probably Chinese Central Asia, Xinjiang, Khotan,
or Kucha
Possibly India, Kashmir
Wood, with traces of polychrome and gold
12¼ × 14 inches (31.12 × 35.56 cm)
PURCHASE: William Rockhill Nelson Trust, 44-18

This rare, portable Buddhist shrine is one of the most significant works in the Asian collections of the Nelson-Atkins Museum of Art. The three-paneled shrine depicts complex multifigural imagery featuring a central Vairocana Buddha surrounded by other buddhas, *bodhisattva*s, celestial attendants, guardian figures, and a patron. As a work of art it demonstrates a strong link between the artistic traditions of Kashmir and those of the Tarim Basin. As a religious artifact, it demonstrates how the teachings and practices of later Buddhism were transmitted from India to Central Asia along the Silk Road. The shrine's deep connections with India, as regards to its artistic style, content, and materials, warrant its special consideration in this volume, placing it in dialogue with other Buddhist works from India and Southeast Asia in the Nelson-Atkins collections.

The origin of this shrine is unknown and is the subject of much scholarly debate. What we do know about the shrine's provenance is fascinating. It was purchased for the museum in New Delhi by former Nelson-Atkins curator and director Lawrence Sickman. It was reported to have been previously acquired in Nepal by the Austrian-born scholar Stella Kramrisch (1896–1993) while she was a professor in Calcutta (Kolkata). The shrine bears a Tibetan inscription on the back, *byan chub sems [dpah]*, which means *bodhisattva*. However, this work was not created in Delhi, Nepal, or Tibet.

The Nelson-Atkins shrine could have been created either in Kashmir or Central Asia. The shrine's use of Indian sandalwood and its overall style can be associated with the art of Kashmir in northwest India. In the

first millennium CE Greater Kashmir was an important region for artistic production, as evident in the Nelson-Atkins sculpture of a seated Maitreya (Cat. 4). Kashmir lies between the Indian subcontinent and Gandhara and is connected through multiple mountain passes to the Silk Road. During the eighth century Kashmir had an industry producing portable wooden and composite shrines, and several examples of carved wood and ivory portable shrines in the Kashmiri style have been found in India and in Central Asia. The Nelson-Atkins shrine demonstrates the Kashmiri style in the treatment of the bodies and features of many of the figures in the shrine, including the figures' triple-pointed triangular crowns, the elegantly posed *bodhisattva*s that surround the central Buddha in the center panel, and the two buddhas in cowl-necked robes depicted on the top of the side panels. Robert Linrothe has also associated the pointed flaming double halos that surround the figures' bodies and heads and the lion throne with a double-row of lotus petals as diagnostic of Kashmiri art.[22]

However, Linrothe, together with Phyllis Granoff and Pratapaditya Pal, also points out elements of the Nelson-Atkins shrine that appear to be Central Asian, such as the garments and armor worn by the four guardian kings depicted in the side panels and the round faces with wide narrow eyes of some of the figures.[23] These details led Granoff to conclude that the Nelson-Atkins shrine was created in Central Asia, most likely in Turpan, but possibly in Kucha, or Khotan.[24] Pal compares the Nelson-Atkins shrine to a very similar shrine, now in a private collection, that he assigns to Khotan or Kucha. Pal further suggests that both shrines likely came from the same artistic school, if not from the same artists' workshop.[25] Linrothe proposes that the shrine could have been made in Khotan in a Kashmiri style or that it was from Kashmir and incorporated visual influences from Central Asia.[26] While we may never be certain of the birthplace of this sculpture, its artistic ancestry points directly to Kashmir.

The iconography of the Nelson-Atkins shrine illustrates esoteric Buddhist deities and practices associated with Tantric Buddhism. The central figure of the shrine is Vairocana Buddha seated in *padma asana* with his hands in the meditative *dhyani mudra*. Vairocana sits upon a lion throne supported by a lotus stalk and underneath a canopy flanked by flying celestial attendants. Unlike the earthly historical Buddha, Shakyamuni, Vairocana is a conceptual cosmic buddha. In esoteric traditions, he is the greatest of the celestial buddhas, the primordial being of pure enlightenment who generates the universe filled with world systems and heavens governed by different buddhas. As a representative of this conceptual "bliss body" (*sambhogakaya*), the celestial Vairocana is dressed not as an earthly monk but in a crown and royal garb, which symbolize his attainments. Tantric literature devoted to Vairocana as a presiding deity was well known across Asia by the eighth century.

Surrounding Vairocana are eight *bodhisattva*s, enlightened beings who attend buddhas and assist humankind. They can be identified by their attributes as Maitreya, Samantabhadra, Avalokiteshvara, and Akashagarbha (left side, top to bottom), and Kshitigarbha, Sarvanivaranavishkambhi, Manjushri, and Vajrapani (right side, top to bottom). These known in Buddhist literature as the "Eight Great Bodhisattvas" (*ashtamahabodhisattvas)* and they were venerated as protective deities who intervened to save practitioners from earthly perils.[27] Indeed, we know that a group of eight *bodhisattva*s were particularly popular in Khotan, where they, along with the Buddhist Guardian King Vaishravana, were venerated as local protective deities.[28] Textual references to a set of eight *bodhisattva*s date back at least to the third century, and the group was canonized in Tantric literature in the *Ashtamandalaka Sutra* in the seventh century. Eight great *bodhisattva*s accompany Vairocana in the *garbhadhatu mandala* described in the *Mahavairocana Abhisambodhi Sutra*, also likely written in the seventh century.

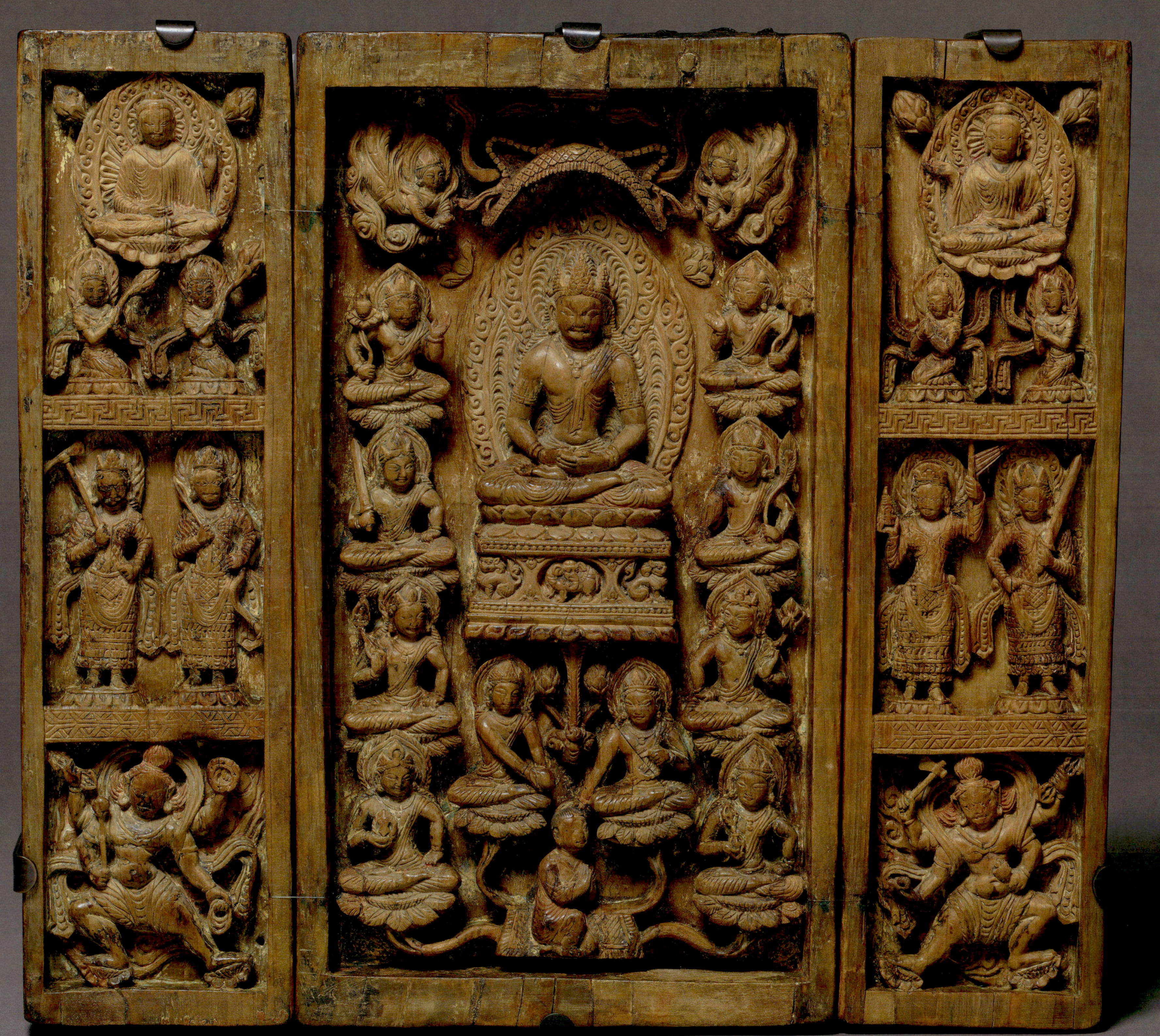

The side wings of the Nelson-Atkins traveling shrine each depict two meditating buddhas in monastic garb attended by two *bodhisattva*s (top), the four *lokapala*s, directional guardian kings: Virudhaka and Dhritarashtra on the left, and Vaishravana and Virupaksha on the right (center), and two fierce-looking protectors, the *vidyaraja*s, or wisdom kings (bottom), with Acala on the left and Mahakala on the right. The two meditating buddhas may represent the Buddhas of the Remote Past and the Future, Dipankara and Maitreya, respectively, who are sometimes shown attending Buddhist sermons.

The centrifugal composition of the shrine appears to represent the spatial arrangement of a mandala. While the Tantric texts associated with these deities and their worship in mandalas were generated in India, the texts traveled with monks on the trade routes to Tibet, Central Asia, and China, where they were translated into local languages. Therefore, the complex iconography of the shrine does not clearly indicate its place of origin, but points instead to the broad dispersal of esoteric Buddhist knowledge in the late first millennium.

Even if we cannot identify precisely where the Nelson-Atkins shrine was made, we can likely identify for whom it was made. Below Vairocana's throne, two additional *bodhisattva*s bestow blessings upon a man with hands raised in the respectful gesture of *anjali mudra,* as he kneels on a fringed carpet. Although his facial features are worn, delicate carving and traces of polychrome reveal his closely shorn black hair and red robes. The man appears to be a monk and he was likely the specific patron or recipient of the shrine, which he could have commissioned or received as a pious gift. The monk is attended by two crowned *bodhisattva*s. One *bodhisattva* holds a round object, perhaps a pot of water, over his head, as the other touches his head with one hand while holding a crown with the other. This gesture may indicate the bestowal of blessings on the monk.[29] These actions and gestures may also specifically reference an *abhisheka* ceremony,

an initiation that confers the realization of a religious attainment, such as an induction into a monastic order or confirmation of a specific esoteric teaching.

A final clue to the symbolism lies beneath the monk's carpet. Linrothe notes that the stems of the lotuses supporting the Buddhist deities appear to rise from the carpet.[30] Indeed, if we consider this shrine to be a mandala, then this is a most appropriate detail, as the initiated monk would generate the deities of this Tantric system internally, through visualization. Thus the composition demonstrates both the conceptual generation of a Budddhist world from Vairocana, in the center, and the earthly generation and veneration of these deities from the memory and practices of the monk at the base.

The Nelson-Atkins shrine would have been a highly treasured possession to its owner. It represented the deities and teachings associated with current developments in Buddhism from India. Its eight *bodhisattva*s could offer the worshipper protection from the dangers of the material world. And as a mandala, it provided the initiate with a tool to visualize and connect with the enlightened beings of the celestial realms. After worship, the monk who owned it, whether he was from Kashmir, Tibet, or Khotan, could fold the wings closed, wrap it in cloth to protect it, and set off along the Silk Road to encounter a whole new world.

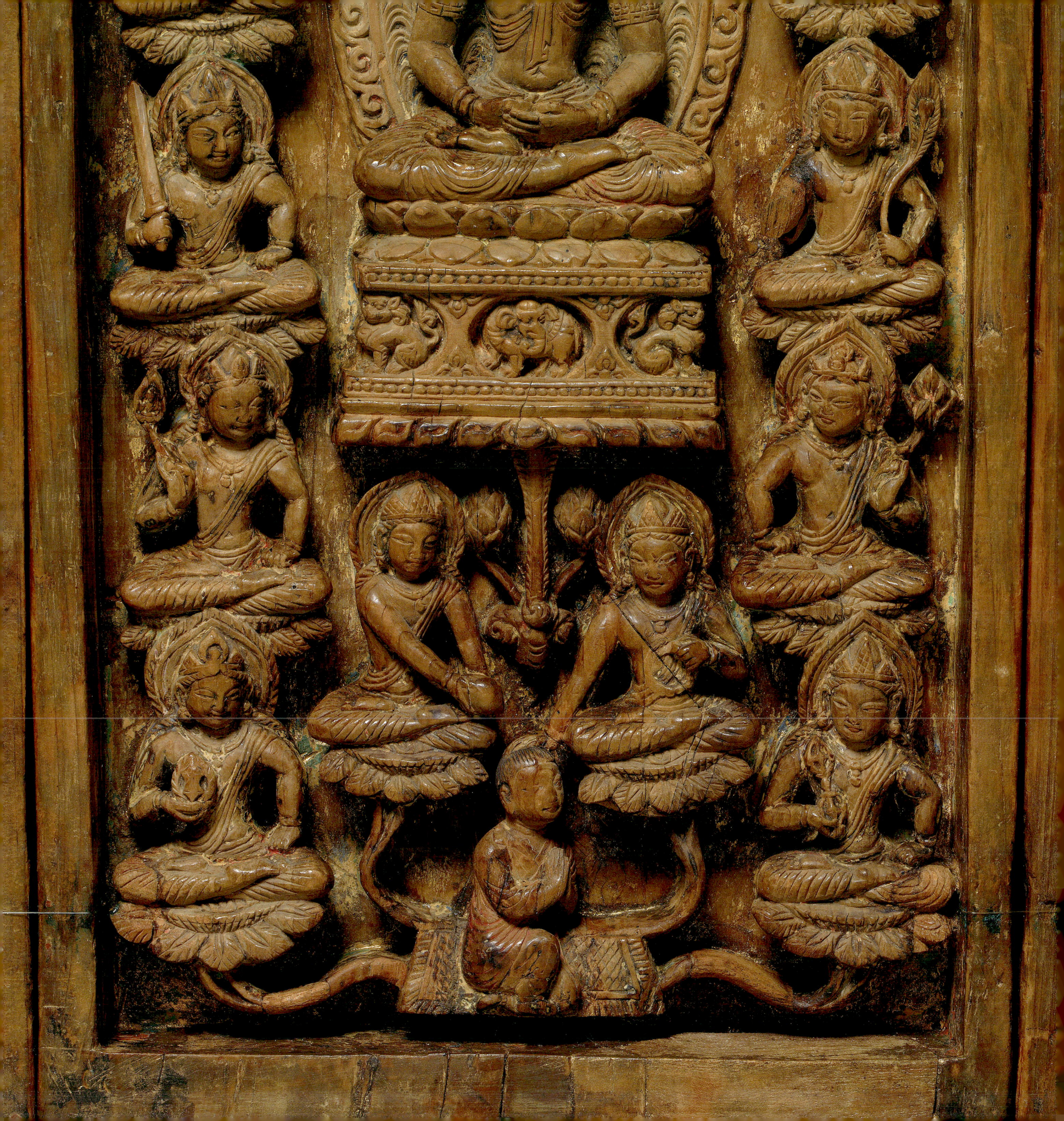

9th century
India, Malwa
Paramara dynasty (ca. 800–1327)
Light gray sandstone (argillaceous quartz arenite)
39 × 20¼ × 8¼ inches (99.06 × 51.44 × 20.96 cm)
PURCHASE: William Rockhill Nelson Trust, 70-45

Late 10th–early 11th century
India, Tamil Nadu
Chola dynasty (850–1279)
Bronze
23¾ × 11 × 7⅞ inches (60.33 × 27.94 × 20 cm)
PURCHASE: William Rockhill Nelson Trust, 62-14

Ganesha, the elephant-headed god, is one of the most beloved deities in the vast Hindu pantheon. He is also known as Ganapati and Vinayaka, and all three names refer to his role as the Lord of the *gana*s, a class of impish nature spirits. Ganesha is easily recognizable as a composite figure that joins an elephant head to a human body. He is frequently depicted with a squat, pudgy body and a full belly, which helps associate him with the form of a healthy child.

This youthful body accords with the best known identification of Ganesha as the child of the Hindu gods Shiva and Parvati. Various Puranic texts recount versions of how Ganesha became part of the divine family. One of the most popular versions of Ganesha's creation involves an unfortunate misunderstanding of his identity. Longing for a child, Parvati rubbed some skin from her body as she bathed, and brought it to life in the form of a young boy. She gave the miraculous child the task of guarding her bath so no one would enter. Shiva returned to join his wife and was stopped by this fiercely protective youth. Not knowing who the boy was, the angered Shiva cut off his head. Parvati was infuriated by the murder of their child and demanded that Shiva revive the boy by replacing his head with that of another living being. The first creature to approach the scene was an elephant, hence their son was given an elephant's head. In fact, the elephant-headed Ganesha appears to have been a deity in his own right during the early centuries of the Common Era, associated with both the *gana*s and as a protective attendant of the *matrka*s, a group of powerful and ambivalent mother goddesses. Sometime in the first half of the millennium he became identified with Shaivism. Ganesha also became an important deity in the tradition of Smarta Brahmanism, a

sect dedicated to the veneration of five great gods—Ganesha, Shiva, Vishnu, Surya, and a form of one of the Great Goddesses—that became popular in the ninth century.

While a few sculptures of Ganesha are known from the Kushan era (first to third century), he is depicted with some frequency during the Gupta era (300–699). Ganesha is shown as the first figure in the program of deities in Cave 6 at Udaygiri, dated 401. This is significant, as it demonstrates one of the key roles of Ganesha as *Vighneshvara,* "the lord of obstacles," the god one worships first when beginning a task or religious activity to overcome obstacles in one's path.[31]

These sculptures of Ganesha in the Nelson-Atkins Collection were created at the end of the first millennium, when the identity and function of the god were firmly established. The sculpture of Dancing Ganesha was created in central India to serve as a niche sculpture for a stone temple, most likely from Malwa in western Madhya Pradesh. Ganesha was frequently depicted in the central *bhadra* niche on the south exterior wall of a Hindu temple, regardless of the deity to which the temple was dedicated. As temples were usually oriented to open to the east, the south niche would be the first shrine a practitioner would encounter when he or she circumambulated the temple in a clockwise direction. In this way, one's worship would begin with Ganesha, then proceed with the symbolic attainments represented by the other deities enshrined on the temple walls. An original exterior location for the sculpture is suggested by the weathering of its sandstone surfaces, which appear like soft flesh and contribute to the lifelike appearance of the sculpture.

Nritta-Ganapati, or Dancing Ganesha, is frequently represented in central Indian temples. This example

has ten arms, which hold a range of attributes. They include a *pasha* (noose), *uttariya* (scarf), *ikshu* (sugarcane), *kuthara* (axe), the head and tail of a *naga* (serpent) stretched between two upper hands, a *gada* (mace), *modaka* (sweets), and what appears to be another *uttariya*. The god rests the curling fingers of a tenth hand jauntily on his proper left hip. The artist fully employs the medieval *tri-bhanga* (three-bend) pose to render the dynamic movement of Ganesha's dance. He is surrounded by attendants that include pairs of female and male musicians to his lower left and right, who provide the music to his performance. While the basic format of an image of Dancing Ganesha follows a canonical plan, there is room for variation. Artists and workshops from different regions may adjust details, such as the shape of Ganesha's head, the number of arms displayed, and the number and postures of his attendants. Features of the Nelson-Atkins sculpture, the god's wide flat head, bulbous forehead, and curving trunk that twists to the right as he grasps a sweet, are very similar to features depicted on a sculpture of Ganesha from Ashapuri in western Madhya Pradesh, dated to the ninth century, and now in the Birla State Museum in Bhopal, India. Other similarities include the cutting away of the stone behind Ganesha to accentuate his silhouette and the shape of the lotus platform supporting each deity, which has stylized petals that dip down to a point in the front. The close similarity of the details and overall styles of the Nelson-Atkins and Birla Museum sculptures suggest that they were created in the same region and time period, perhaps by the same workshop. During the ninth century, this region was under the control of the Paramara dynasty (ca. 800–1327). This was a royal house known for its patronage of literature, science, and architecture.

The second image of Ganesha features the god standing upright and alert. The dynamic bends of the Dancing Ganesha are transformed in this image into a gentle sway, suggesting a relaxed and naturalistic posture. This Ganesha has four arms and holds

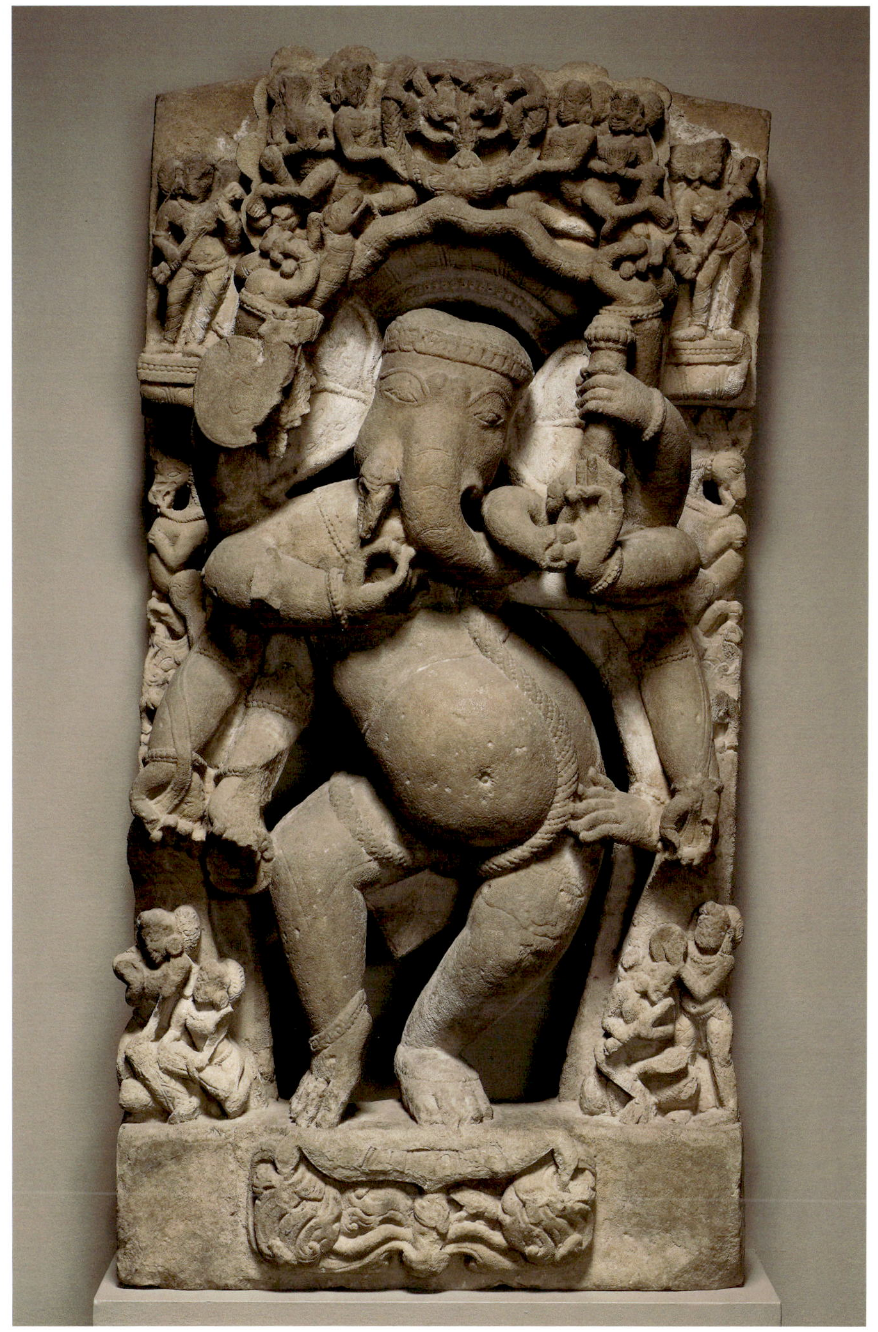

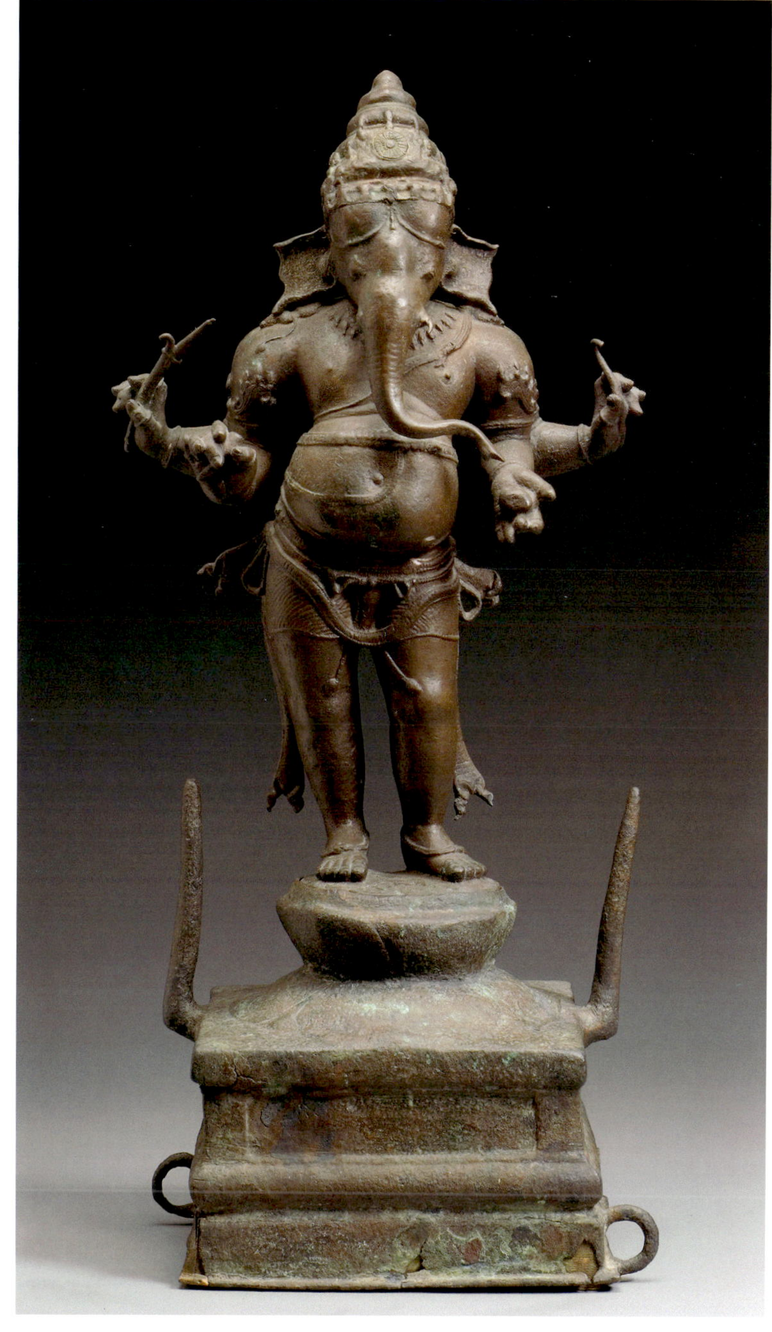

a sweet in his lower left hand that he is eating with his trunk. He holds his own right tusk, referencing a story when it was broken off in a struggle, in his right hand. His upper hands hold a *kuthara* (ax) and a *pasha* (noose), now broken. This figure was created following a different canon of proportions, visible in his rather elongated body, triangular-shaped head, and spindly, low-swung trunk. He wears an elaborate tiered crown and ornate jewelry. The medium used to create this standing Ganesha is bronze, which allows for ease of modeling and fine detailing. It was created in southern India during the Chola dynasty (850–1279), a period renowned for its mastery of bronze.

Unlike the Dancing Ganesha, this Chola sculpture lived inside a temple, likely residing in a subshrine of a large complex. It was created to be venerated both at its shrine and during festivals, when dowel rods would have been inserted through the rings in the base, enabling the sculpture to be moved and carried in processions.[32] This use underscores the function of the sculpture: it is an icon, a vessel intended to contain the invoked presence of a living deity. When it was enshrined, it would have looked on its worshippers directly, as they looked upon it. The power of the divine was transferred through the activity of seeing, known as *darshan*. To serve this function, a sculpture's form and casting had to be as perfect as possible. Such perfection is still evident in this bronze image of Ganesha a thousand years after it was made.

Lintel Fragment with Indra on his Three-Headed Elephant

10th century
Cambodia
Khmer dynasty (802–1431)
Sandstone
22½ × 16¼ inches (57.15 × 41.28 cm)
PURCHASE: William Rockhill Nelson Trust, 49-20

Indra, the king of the Hindu gods, resides in a palace at the summit of the mythical mountain Mahendraparvata. In the year 802, Indra's palatial abode was made manifest on earth at Phnom Kulen, on a plateau in a small mountain range in the jungles of northwestern Cambodia. In this year a local king, Jayavarman II (ca. 770–850), commissioned two ceremonies that initiated him as a *chakravartin,* a universal sovereign, and invested him with the protection of a local royal guardian deity. These actions gave birth to the Khmer Empire (802–1431), one of the most magnificent civilizations of the pre-modern world.

From the inception of their kingdom, the Khmer were prolific builders. This is evident on Indra's mountain, where in 2013 archaeologists reported the discovery of Jayavarman's first city, which included over thirty undocumented temples, connected to other ruins by a complex of roads and hydro engineering works.[33] The construction of elaborate temples continued during the rule of subsequent Khmer kings, and reached its most exquisite and ornate phase in the mid- to late tenth century, at temples such as Banteay Srei, consecrated in 967, north of the Khmer capital at Angkor. Temples from this period exhibit a harmonizing combination of compact forms and flat surfaces covered with dense reliefs. Based on Indian prototypes, individual shrines and structures from this period impress the viewer through their use of vigorous and ornate decoration.

Some of the most intricate carvings on Khmer temples are found on the lintels crowning temple doorways. These lintels are filled with carvings of lush foliage, which is inhabited by Hindu gods and mythical beasts. The god Indra frequently appears in lintel reliefs, usually atop his royal elephant Airavata, who is depicted with three heads in Southeast Asian art. The relief depicting Indra on Airavata in the Nelson-Atkins collection appears to be related to the phase of Khmer art that produced Banteay Srei, or its direct antecedents, both in terms of its iconography and style.[34] Note the deeply carved fleurons that undulate across the composition. The artist has carefully drilled and undercut around rows of lobed leaves, which emerge as curling, overlapping forms projecting outward into our space. A coiling rope of leaves appears to emerge from a chalice held by one of Airavata's trunks, to the far left of the relief. Indra balances upon his elephant mount, knees bent as if dancing. He holds an object, likely a *vajra,* his lightning-bolt weapon, in his raised right hand. Above the god, a row of alternating *yogin*s and floral motifs form the upper border of the composition.

The exuberant tenth-century style continued to influence the treatment of temple lintels and pediments into the eleventh century, and can be seen in monuments ranging from Angkor to southern Thailand. The energetic scene on the Nelson-Atkins relief would have likely formed the center of a late-tenth-century to eleventh-century door lintel, and may have graced a temple north of Angkor, where monuments of tan sandstones were more often found.

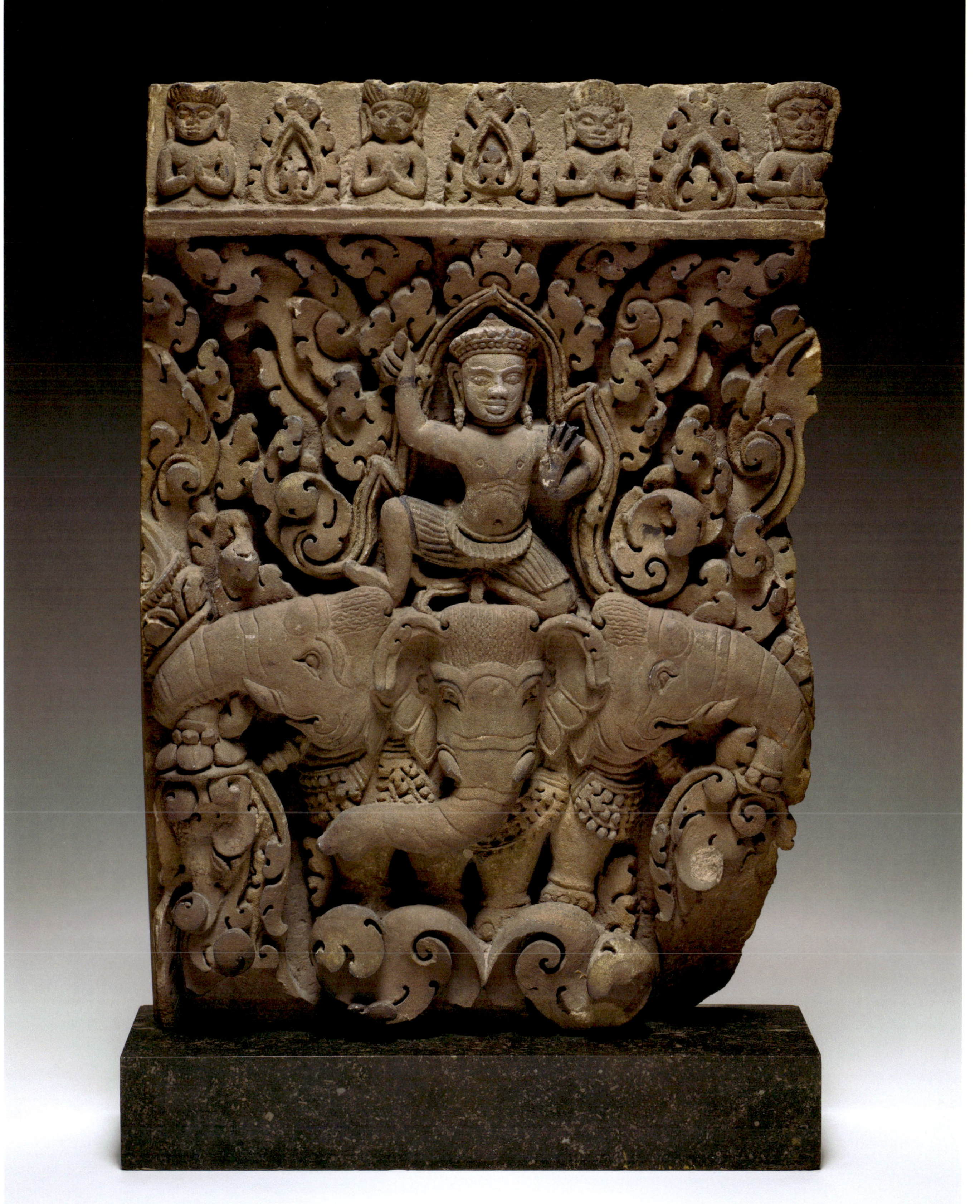

 | *Standing Male Figure*

11th century, Baphuon Style
Cambodia
Khmer dynasty (802–1431)
Sandstone with traces of gilding
28½ inches (72.39 cm)
PURCHASE: William Rockhill Nelson Trust, 46-34

Perhaps no other phase of Cambodian figural sculpture better represents the crystallization of the mature Khmer aesthetic than the Baphuon style, which is wonderfully represented in the Nelson-Atkins collection by this sculpture of a male figure. The Baphuon style takes its name from the Baphuon, the great pyramidal temple built in the mid-eleventh century by King Udayadityavarman II (r. 1050–66). This artistic style, which is used in the sculptures on the Baphuon, dominated Khmer art of the eleventh century. The Baphuon style is also associated with sculptures created during the reigns of two other Khmer kings, including Udayadityavarman's predecessor Suryavarman I (r. 1002–49), and his brother, Harshavarman III (r. 1066–80).

Baphuon-style sculptures are noted for their sense of grace and harmony. This is achieved through several innovations that built upon the sculptural styles of the tenth century. The sculptors of this figure followed a new canon of proportions. Gone is the thick torso and flared hips of early Khmer figures. Instead, the artists rendered this young man with a compact, non-muscular, and extremely narrow body. His hips have been reduced to gentle curves that slope downward into tubular legs. The large size of his legs is a holdover from earlier sculptural styles and is likely a structural necessity to allow the sculpture to support its own weight. Indeed, a freestanding figure like this would have likely stood as an object of focus inside a shrine. The figure's head is large in proportion to his torso and exhibits a flat jaw line, full lips, and wide features. It engages us with open eyes and a warm smile. While the figure's pose is taut, its flesh is smooth and gives the impression of softness, similar to the treatment of flesh in the earlier freestanding sculptures from Banteay Srei. The appearance of softness is further accentuated in this sculpture by the weathering of its surfaces, which has reduced the crispness of sharply carved areas and incised lines, like the double outlining of the eyes.

Also notable in the Baphuon style is the treatment of the figure's lower garment, known as a *sampot*, which consists of a long cloth wrapped around the waist and through the legs, and secured by a belt. The top of this figure's *sampot* rises high at each side of the waist, creating a deep arc that frames the navel. The garment is gathered into wide folds on the left thigh, with thin pleats elsewhere. The ends of the cloth extend out over the figure's belt in front and back, with an extra piece of loose cloth tied onto the girdle on the right side. This depiction of the *sampot* is common in Baphoun sculptures and must have been based upon court fashions of the period. The contrast between the rough surfaces of the folded and incised garment and the smooth surfaces of the figure's body is another innovation found in Baphuon sculpture.

While it is easy to place this figure in time, it is harder to identify who he is. He wears dreadlocks pulled into a knot on his head, a sign of asceticism and a trait of the Hindu God Shiva. Indeed, Shiva is a frequent subject in art from this period, and the Baphuon temple itself is dedicated to Shiva. However, the figure here is missing Shiva's third eye, which would normally be indicated on his forehead. The absence of this feature led previous scholars to speculate that this sculpture may represent a secular figure rather that a divinity, hence it is identified only as a male figure.[35] The sculpture was gilded, and patches of gold leaf are still visible across its surface. Whoever the figure represents, it is clear that he was once considered a person or deity of importance.

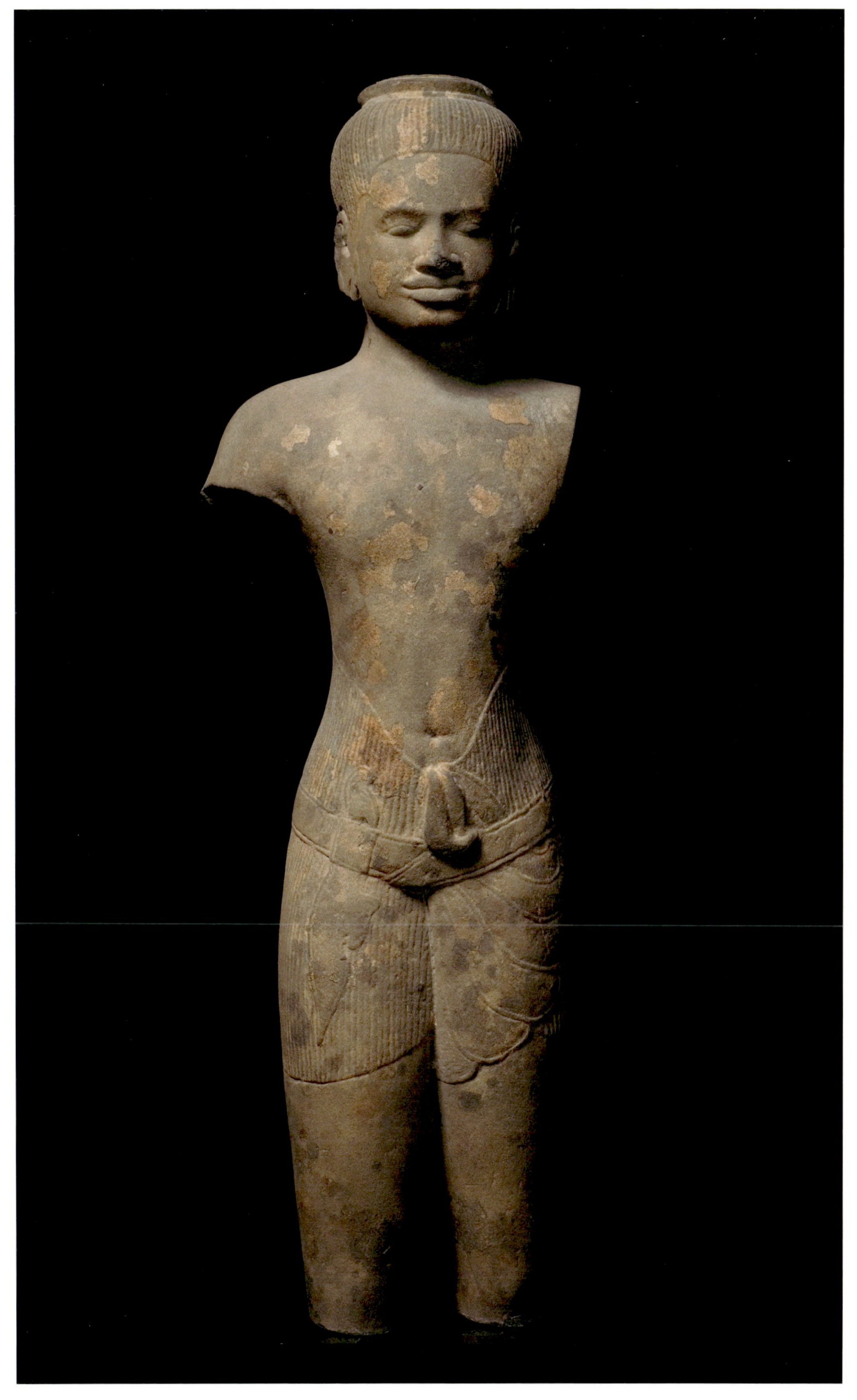

  Shiva and Parvati on the Bull Nandi and *Shiva and Parvati* (Uma-Maheshvara)

956–973
India, Rajasthan, Sikar, Harshagiri
Purana Mahadeva Temple
Chauhan (Cahamana) dynasty (956–1301)
Buff sandstone
18 × 33¾ × 5¾ inches (45.72 × 85.73 × 14.61 cm)
PURCHASE: William Rockhill Nelson Trust, 35-304

9th–early 10th century
India, Uttar Pradesh
Gurjara-Pratihara dynasty of Kanauj (9th–10th century)
Sandstone
36 × 24 × 7 inches (91.44 × 60.96 × 17.78 cm)
Pedestal: 42 × 24½ × 11 inches
Gift in honor of Dr. Satish C. Bansal from Dr. Roopa
Bansal, 2010.61

Shiva and Parvati form one of the most important unions in Hinduism, celebrated in these two roughly contemporary sculptures in the Nelson-Atkins collection. Shiva, known as Mahadeva (great god) was an unmarried ascetic living in the wilderness of the Himalayas at the time he met Parvati, "daughter of the mountains." The Hindu *Purana*s describe their courtship and marriage. Parvati, also known as Uma, was devoted to Shiva from a young age, and it was prophesized that she would marry him. Because of her desire for the god, her father Himavat approached the ash-covered Shiva while he was meditating and asked if his daughter and her maids could attend him. After the intervention of Kama, the god of love, Shiva became attracted to his beautiful servant, but then renounced his desire and returned to his austerities. Parvati realized that she could win the heart of Shiva only by performing extreme penance and cleansing herself as well. She succeeded after years of fasting and meditation, and Shiva asked her to become his bride. After some convincing, Parvati's parents, Himavat and Mena, agreed to the marriage and hosted a grand wedding, where the god Brahma performed the ceremony in the presence of the gods, sages, demigods, mountains, and rivers.

In a tenth-century relief from Rajasthan, the divine couple is shown at the center of a long relief, seated on Shiva's mount, the bull Nandi, surrounded by dancers and musicians. This dynamic sculpture may be a narrative scene depicting the divine couple's wedding procession, which is frequently represented in the format of a long horizontal composition. This finely carved sculpture was once part of a long frieze

that decorated an important Shiva temple, now known as Purana Mahadeva Temple, at Harshagiri in Rajasthan. Situated on top of a hill, this grand monument was created between 956 and 973. The dedicatory inscription states that it was commissioned by a Brahmin ascetic named Allata and completed under his disciple Bhavadyota.[36] The temple also received royal support; the local Chahamana king Simharaja (r. 944–964?) was described as placing a "golden shell" (*andaka*) on the spire of the temple and endowing it with villages.[37] Although the Purana Mahadev Temple was destroyed in later conflicts, its architectural foundation survives at the site, and numerous sculptures from it are preserved at the local museum at Sikar and in several collections around the world. Many of these sculptures feature processional reliefs with musicians and dancers, such as a relief of musicians at the site that shares the same serrated foliate ornament beneath the figures that appears at the bottom of the Nelson-Atkins sculpture. The subject of these reliefs likely references the offering of music and dance at the temple, as suggested by Pratapaditya Pal,[38] and recalls the revelry of the marriage story. Even in its current state, with some of the figures damaged, the high quality of sculpting on the Nelson-Atkins relief is evident, with its deeply carved voluptuous figures in jaunty angular poses, accented with crisply detailed hair and jewelry. These Harshagiri reliefs share many qualities with the exquisite sculptures from the nearly contemporary Harsha Mata Temple at Abaneri, about 200 kilometers to the southeast. The beauty of the Harshagiri Temple when it was completed must have enthralled visitors. Indeed, the dedicatory inscription

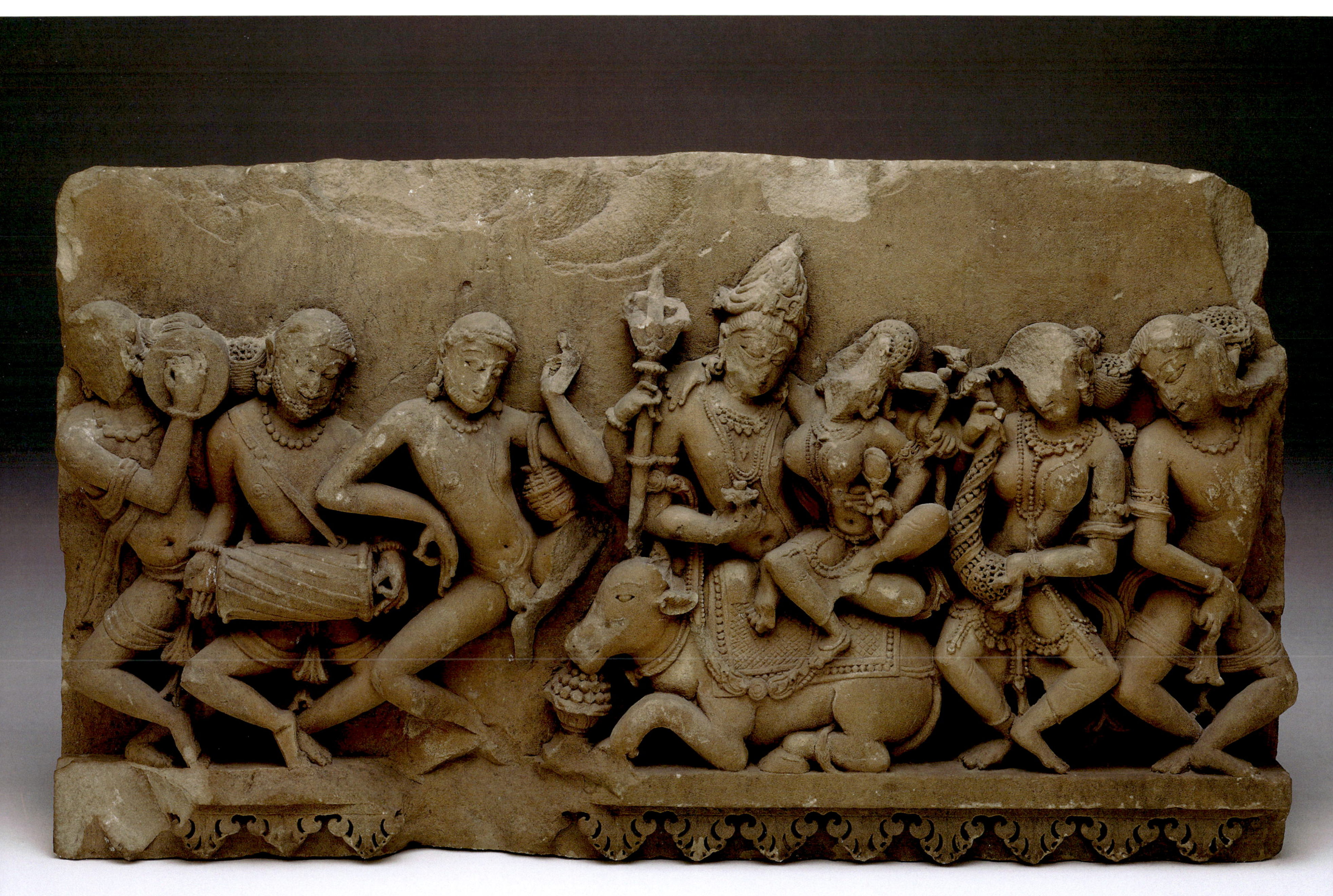

lavishes praise upon the architect, Chandashiva, who "built this delightful house of Shankara [Shiva] with its chapels, the beautiful porch containing all the gods, like a portion of heaven made by the creator himself."[39]

After their marriage, Shiva and Parvati came to embody loving devotion and domesticity. Though Hindu literature describes episodes when Shiva sets off to meditate, leaving Parvati at home alone, he always returns to her. Together, they sport with one another and raise two divine children, Ganesha, the elephant-headed god, and Karttikeya, also known as Skanda, the six-headed warrior god who rides a peacock. The depiction of the divine couple, often titled "Uma-Maheshvara," became an iconic subject in medieval Indian art, as exemplified in another sculpture of Shiva and Parvati in the Nelson-Atkins collection. Seated comfortably together in the center of this large stele, the smiling gods gaze lovingly into each other's eyes. Shiva gently caresses Parvati's shoulder with one of his four hands and clutches a large fruit to his chest with another. She leans into him, resting her hand upon his ankle. This tender sculpture is also a family portrait. Shiva's bull vehicle, Nandi, sits below them as their children, Ganesha and Karttikeya, stand to the right and left, respectively. Shiva and Uma are also attended by four ascetic devotees at the bottom center and sides of the composition, and there is evidence that at least two more figures were originally included at the top left and right sides of the stele, which is now broken. The skeletal figure in the bottom center of the scene is likely the sage Bhringi, who drew Parvati's anger because he refused to worship her as well as Shiva. In the story, Shiva chastises Bhringi, telling him that he and Parvati are two parts of a single godhead, and that to worship one is to worship the other. Here Bhringi seems to have learned his lesson, as he turns his head upward in the direction of Parvati.

This sculpture was created in the Gujara-Pratihara Kingdom, which controlled the Gangetic Plain of northern India from the eighth to the early eleventh century. In the late ninth and early tenth century the Gujara-Pratiharas were also the overlords of the Chahamana kingdom, where the relief from the Harshagiri temple was created. The Uma-Maheshvara sculpture in the Nelson-Atkins collection shares features with other Gujara-Pratihara sculptures, such as the wide-faced figures that are derived from Gupta stylistic models. The large size of the central figures in the stele in relation to the attendants is striking. This use of hierarchic scale emphasizes the importance of Shiva and Parvati, who on occasion in later examples of this subject appear to be swallowed up by a myriad of subsidiary figures. The back of the stele has been cut through, creating negative space that highlights the silhouettes of the figures, drawing even greater attention to them. Also notable is the use of buff-colored sandstone, which is seen in other Gujara-Pratihara sculptures. The color and softness of this stone contributes to the warmth and lifelike qualities of the sculpture. This fine stone enables the sharp carving of Shiva's coiffure while allowing for the modeling of pooling flesh at his waist and the round swelling of Parvati's abdomen. The most striking feature of this sculpture, however, is how effectively it communicates the emotional connection between Shiva and Parvati. Alone, Shiva is the absolute embodiment of untamed masculinity and asceticism. Parvati herself is the embodiment of *shakti*, the feminine power that pervades and energizes the universe. In marriage they become something more: the union of male and female power that constitutes universal divinity and an archetypal couple whose idyllic love transcends time.

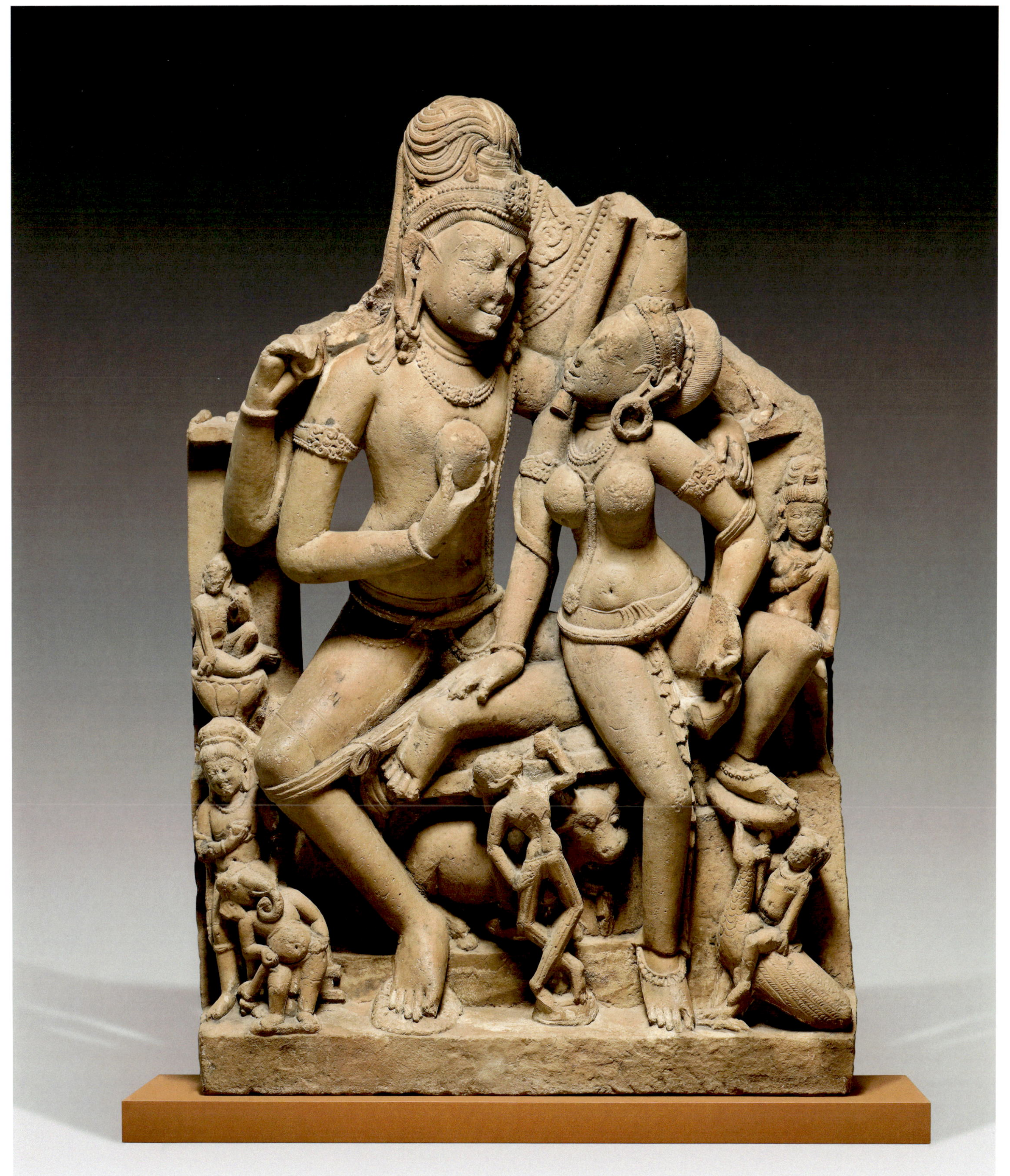

A Celestial Nymph, or Apsara and *Pillar Fragment of a Devata*

ca. 1000
India, Khajuraho
Chandella dynasty (ca. 825–1310)
Tan sandstone
23¾ × 10¼ inches (60.33 × 26.04 cm)
Bequest of Mrs. George H. Bunting, Jr., 81-27/26

Late 13th–early 14th century
Cambodia
Khmer dynasty (802–1431)
Gray sandstone
30¾ × 13 inches (78.11 × 33.02 cm)
PURCHASE: William Rockhill Nelson Trust, 49-21

Both of these sculptures belong to a class of minor female deities broadly known as *apsara*s, or "lovely celestial females." *Apsara*s have ancient origins. In Hindu mythology, they were believed to be one of the auspicious products of the Churning of the Ocean of Milk at the beginning of time. As these deities were believed to inhabit the heavenly realms, they were frequently reproduced on Indian and Southeast Asian temples, which were conceived as palaces on the top of the cosmic mountain where heaven and earth meet. These elegant women are idealized, resembling court attendants, and are beautifully, if only partially, adorned in luxurious textiles, heavy jewelry, and complex elegant coiffures.

This celestial nymph, an *apsara* or *apsaras,* from the Chandella period in Central India is an outstanding example of medieval Indian architectural sculpture. She stands with her back turned to us, balanced on her left leg. Her body twists as she raises her right arm to bind her long hair, as a mischievous monkey pulls the thin garment from her hips. Now we see her alone, but she would have been part of a group of idealized male and female figures engaged in mundane and amorous activities populating a band of registers in the upper superstructure of a northern Indian *nagara*-style temple, like other similar figures depicted on the temples at the Chandella capital of Khajuraho. This particular statue would have been placed at a projecting corner of a temple exterior, well above our heads, a position confirmed by the partial carving of the figure's proper right side, and her downward gaze that would have met our own.

Indian texts identify a specific subgroup of these celestial goddesses known as *surasundari.* These goddesses represent women engaged in specific types of activities, such as gazing in a mirror or plucking a thorn from a foot. The *Shilpaprakasha*, an architectural manual from the eastern state of Odisha, attributed to the twelfth century, describes a *surasundari* named Gunthana who matches the pose and activity of the Nelson-Atkins deity. "Gunthana is a woman concealing herself with a veil, always showing her back. [She is] standing firmly in a virile attitude (*virasanan*). The left leg is stretched straight down in a graceful manner."[40] This description provides the basic template for this Nelson-Atkins figure. However, the inventive Chandella artists added delightful narrative details, such as the monkey actively pulling off her lower garment, revealing her buttocks, as she clings to the cloth with her left hand. The humorous and seductive content of this sculpture was intentional, and it was expected to inspire an emotional response in the viewer, as discussed in the introduction.

This figure displays the hallmarks of Chandella sculpture, which is notable for its highly stylized and sensuous forms. Figures have long, tubular limbs, fleshy, full-figured torsos, and elegant faces with wide almond-shaped eyes and large arching brows. This instantly recognizable style is considered to be a high point of Indian sculptural art. The Nelson-Atkins sculpture demonstrates the great skill of its medieval creator. Notice how the artist carefully worked the forms of the nymph's body in alignment with the grain of the stone. The softness and warmth of the sandstone contributes to the rendering of the body, which appears almost like clay, modeled by a master's hands.

The second celestial being, known as a *devata* in Cambodia, is also an idealized representation of a beautiful woman, this time derived from Khmer concepts of beauty. Unlike the Chandella goddess, this

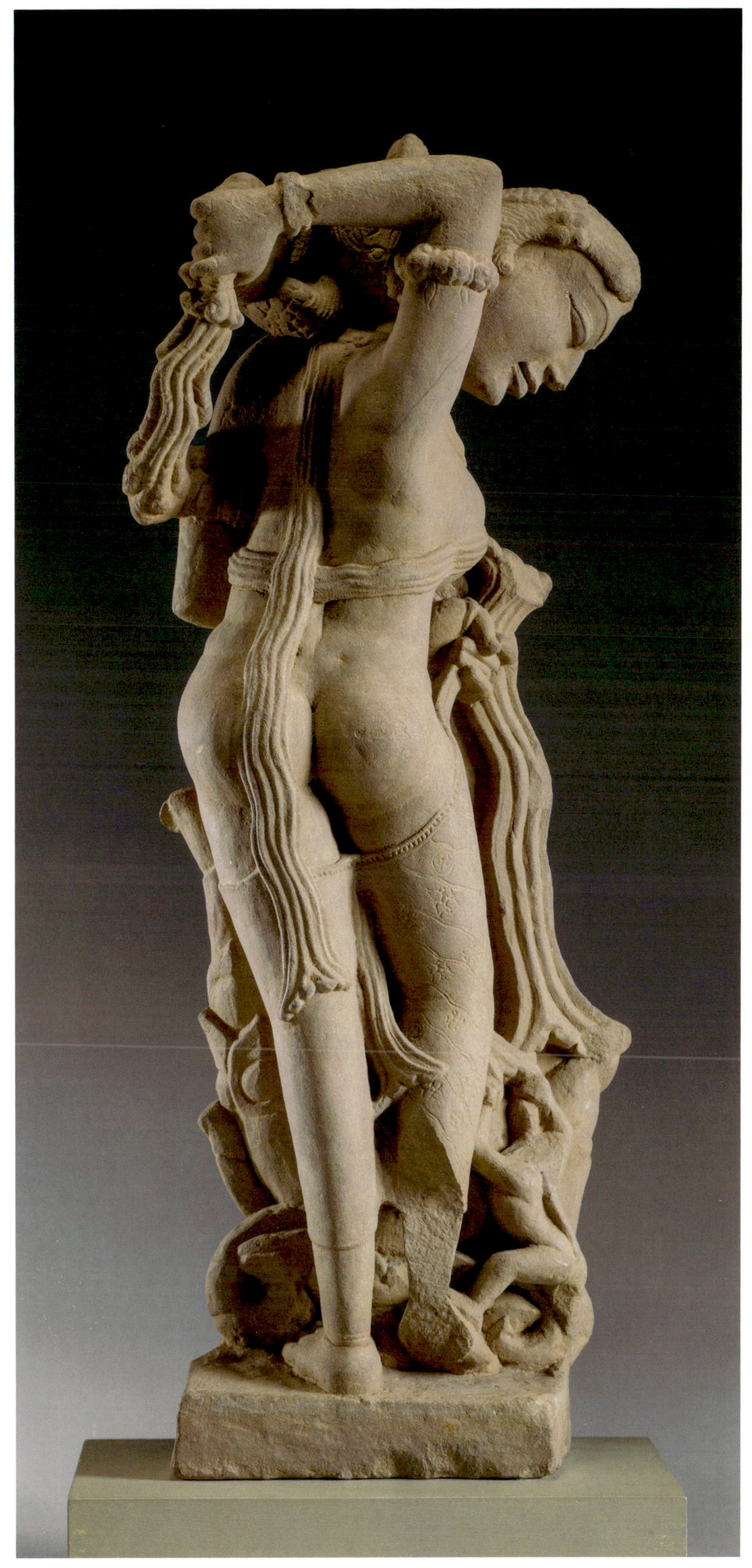

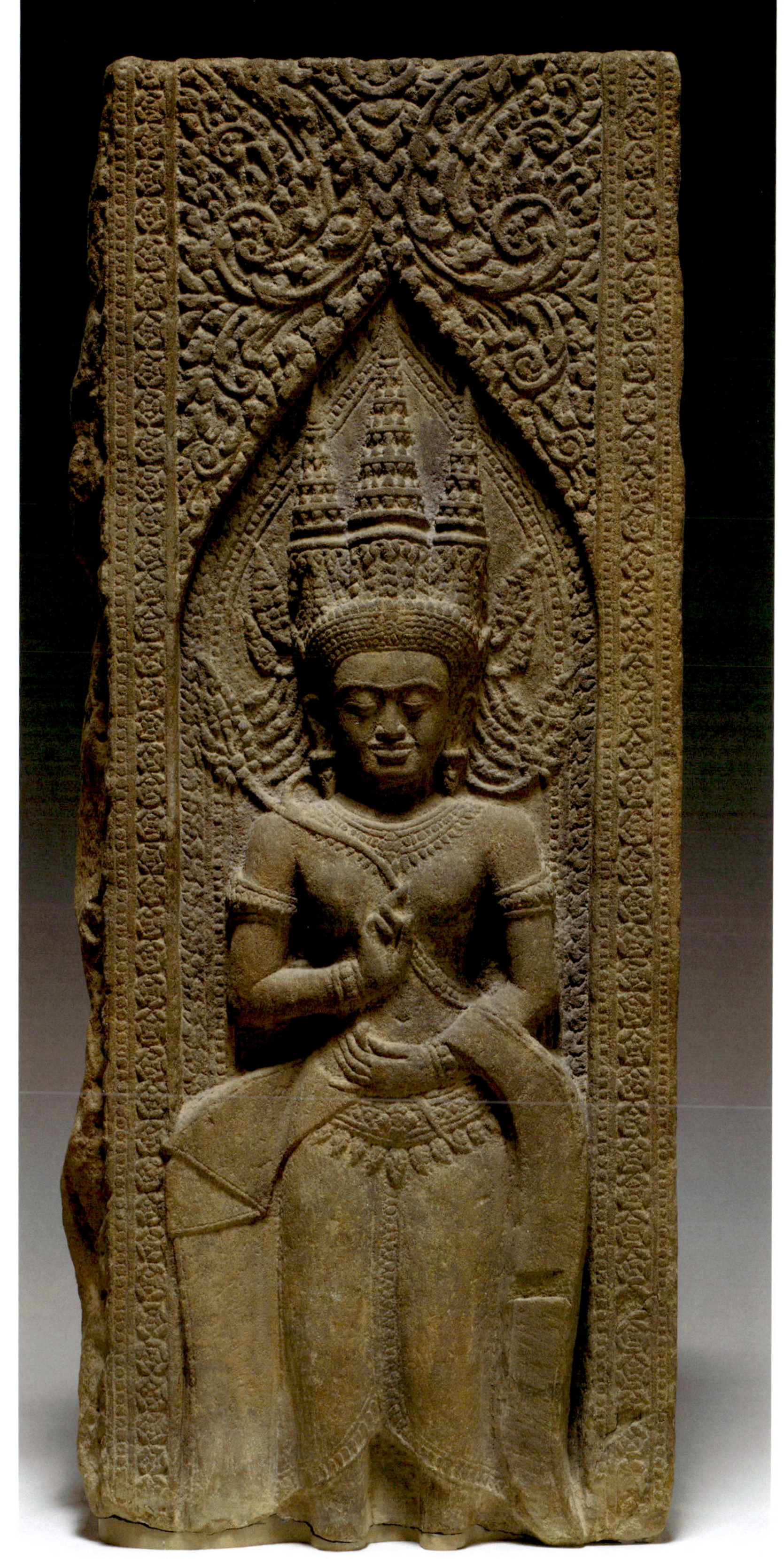

figure faces us directly, greeting us with downcast eyes and a gentle smile. She stands unbending within a tall pointed niche, surrounded by ornate bands of rosettes and plumes of foliage rendered in shallow relief. This *devata* was likely one of many goddesses from a wall or railing of a late Khmer temple from northern Cambodia or the region of Angkor itself.

Though also stylized, the *devata*'s features are different from the central Indian *apsara*. Her smooth body is stockier, less elongated, and exaggerated in shape. Her face features a wide forehead, square jaw, and full lips. Her brows are formed by a wide double arch, which frame two curving eyes, shaped like the silhouettes of birds, an influence from the abstracted forms used in Gupta art. This Khmer goddess holds the stalk of a flower across her body, grasping it delicately in each hand. She is similarly dressed as a courtier, wearing a long skirt with a bejeweled belt, a wide scarf that wraps behind her and falls in flat folds at her sides, heavy jewelry, and a large tiered crown. The shape of the crown is notable as it mimics the multiple curving temple towers, or *prasat*s, found in later Khmer temples. This feature, along with the general stockiness of the figure, helps us date this sculpture to the thirteenth to fourteenth century.[41]

Like Indian temples, upon which they were modeled, Khmer temples were heavily adorned with celestial females. In Khmer art, some scholars have recently divided them into two specific types of figures, applying the broad category of *apsara*s only to goddesses depicted as dancing. The figures of standing deities like the Nelson-Atkins figure, not dancing, have been classified as *devata*, meaning simply "divine beings."[42] Khmer temples symbolized a microcosm of the universe and recreated the abode of the gods. In this celestial court, *apsara*s and *devata* were depicted in great numbers. Archaeologists have identified nearly 1,800 individual relief sculptures of *devata* at the temple of Angkor Wat alone. The ubiquitous appearance of these figures in Khmer temples relates to their roles as graceful and auspicious attendants and embodiments of female power, who sanctify the space and honor the gods enshrined inside by their presence.

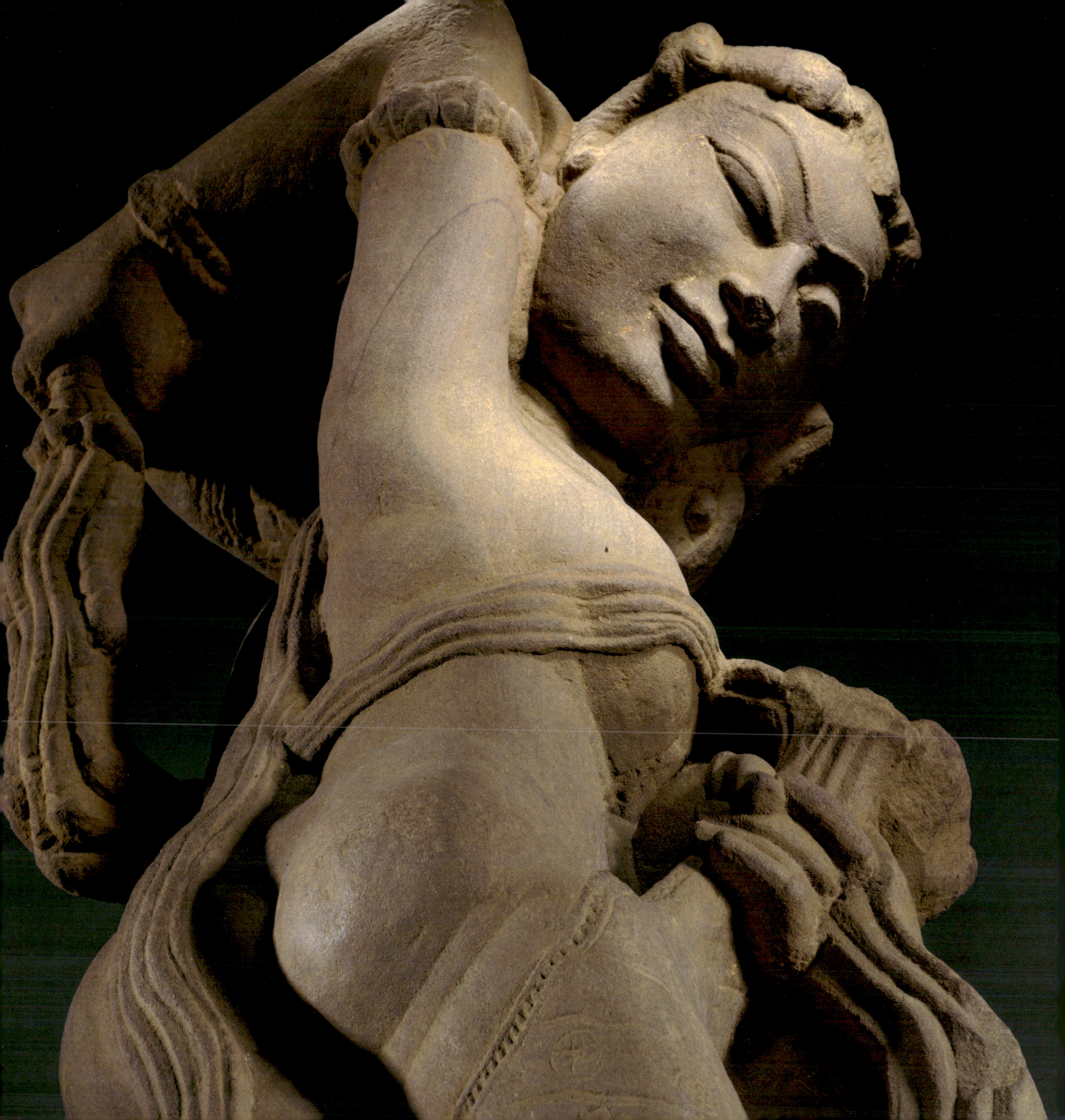

Late 9th–early 10th century
India, Kanchipuram or Kaveripakkam
Chola dynasty (848–1279)
Greenstone
52½ inches (133.35 cm)
PURCHASE: William Rockhill Nelson Trust, 44-27

Awesome, mesmerizing, and intimidating, this seated woman confronts us from her pedestal in the gallery. She sits upright, legs bent in a yogic pose, holding what appears to be a bell with a clapper in her one surviving hand. She is our size, and she interacts with us face-to-face in a direct and personal manner. Except that she is not a person. Look more closely. Four arms extend from her shoulders, two fangs protrude from her lips, and her wide-open eyes grasp the viewer in their gaze.

This large-scale sculpture depicts a *yogini*, a member of a class of powerful female deities that rose to importance in medieval India. The term *yogini* means a female practitioner of yoga. However, sculptures like this represent one of a set of dangerous tantric goddesses that were ritually worshipped as a group. Temples dedicated to *yogini*s appeared in central and eastern India in the tenth through the twelfth century; however this sculpture demonstrates that a *yogini* shrine was constructed as far south as Tamil Nadu.

While *yogini* worship developed in the late first millennium, the desire to access the power of goddesses in India is much older. In the ancient Indian world-view, the universe is gendered. Power, known as *shakti*, permeates creation and gives life. *Shakti* is feminine and is manifest within the earth and in living beings, including humans and divinities. The goal of tantric practitioners and their patrons was to harness the power of *shakti* for a variety of spiritual and earthly purposes, including physical protection, military prowess, and healing powers. Through the ritual worship of *yogini*s, some ascetics hoped to achieve unearthly powers, such as magic and flight.[43] Although many *yogini*s were associated with the Hindu god Shiva, sets of *yogini*s were also propitiated

by Buddhists, and similar tantric goddesses were worshipped by Jain monks. Thus *yogini*s could provide a wide range of medieval audiences with one of their most immediate and powerful sources of *shakti*.

The dangerous nature of the Nelson-Atkins *yogini* is evident in the way she is presented. Certainly, this *yogini* embodies lifegiving and nurturing feminine power through the depiction of her nubile female body. There is tension, however, between her idealized beauty and aspects of her demeanor. Contrast the *yogini*'s somewhat relaxed pose in the slight sway in her torso and her gently bending limbs with the wildness of her gaping eyes framed by tight, arching, and curling brows. Dreadlocks shoot straight out from behind her head in all directions, as if shocked with electricity. Her slightly open mouth reveals pointed fangs. Even her jewelry gives a sense of danger, with ferocious lion heads on her bracelets and crown and a jewel-spewing *makara,* a dragonlike river monster, snaking out from behind her right ear. These juxtapositions conform to the content of *yogini* sculptures found in central and eastern India, which combine threatening and benign imagery.

The Nelson-Atkins *yogini* was discovered in the southern Indian city of Kanchipuram, which was under the control of the Chola dynasty in the tenth century when she was created. She was part of a group of at least nineteen related sculptures. Of these, eleven large-scale *yogini*s are known to have survived and are in museum collections in India, Europe, and the United States.[44] While the original temple and its configuration are unknown, it is likely that the Kanchipuram *yogini*s were arranged in a manner that enveloped worshippers, surrounding the viewer with multiple goddesses, as is the case in the circular *yogini* temples found in central and eastern India. Imagine what it must have been like to be confronted by so much fierce beauty.

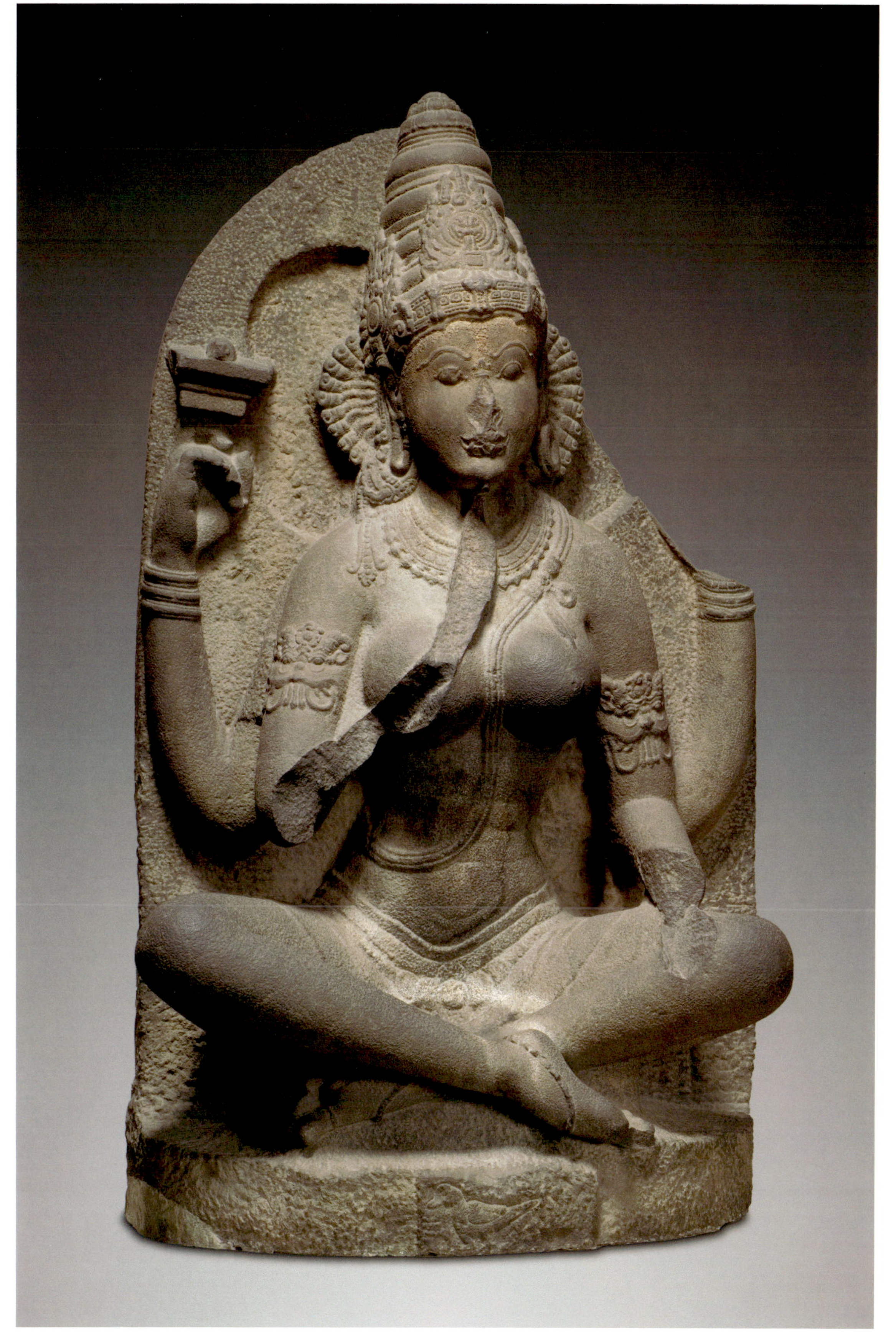

 | *Karaikkal Ammaiyar, a Shaiva Saint*

11th century
India, Tamil Nadu
Chola dynasty (848–1279)
Bronze with deep green patina
Overall: 19⅝ × 8⅞ × 5½ inches (49.85 × 22.54 × 13.97 cm)
PURCHASE: William Rockhill Nelson Trust, 33-533

It is hard to imagine that one so slender and frail can sit so erect, so wide-eyed and alert. Her ribs protrude, breasts sag, and her limbs are reduced to long narrow extensions interrupted by sharply angular bends at her joints. Karaikkal Ammaiyar, the "Mother of Karaikkal," was once a real woman who lived in the sixth century. She was the first of the Nayanmars, the great saints from southern India who dedicated themselves to the Hindu god Shiva. In Shaivite literature she was originally known as Punidavadi, the wife of a wealthy merchant and a woman who was fiercely devoted to Shiva.

Shiva was an active presence throughout Punidavadi's young life. She had divine visions as a child and later experienced a miraculous event, when a mango she had offered to a wandering mendicant was divinely replicated to be offered to her husband, as the mendicant was actually the god Shiva himself. Punidavadi's love for the god was too strong to be limited by social constraints, so she left her husband, became an ascetic, and walked to Mount Kailash in the Himalayas to be in the presence of Shiva. As a reward for her penance, she was granted the vision of being forever in the god's presence when he danced. The woman, now emaciated, returned to her coastal city of Karaikkal, where she was given the revered name Ammaiyar, "mother," and where she was feared as a kind of witch or powerful woman. She lived her life as both a holy woman and an outcaste, composing devotional songs and poems in honor of Shiva. Historians believe that this poetic description of a female demon is an autobiographical reference to the author herself:

A female ghoul with withered breasts, bulging veins,
Hollow eyes, white teeth, shriveled stomach,
Red hair, two fangs,
Bony ankles, and elongated shins,
Stays in this cemetery, howling angrily.
This place where my Lord dances in the fire with a cool body,
His streaming hair flying in the eight directions,
Is Tiruvaalankaatu.[45]

While Karaikkal Ammaiyar does appear in the sculptured stone programs of southern Indian temples, fine bronze sculptures of her are exceedingly rare. We see her in the Nelson-Atkins bronze as a woman transformed: rail thin, focused, and fiercely devoted as she plays the cymbals to the rhythm of Shiva's eternal dance.

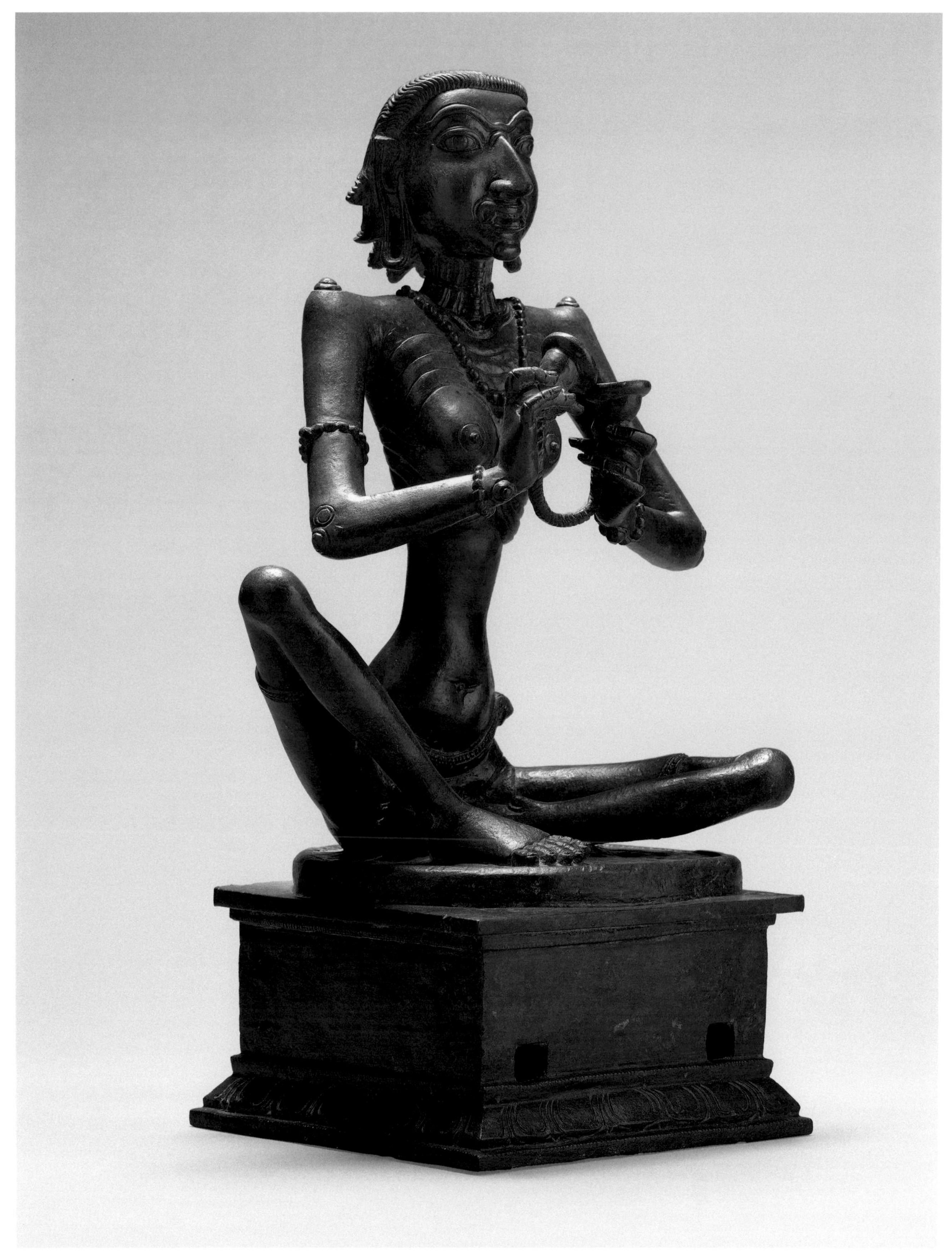

Early 13th century
India, Tamil Nadu
Chola dynasty (848–1279)
Bronze
34¼ × 27½ × 13 inches (87 × 69.85 × 33.02 cm)
PURCHASE: William Rockhill Nelson Trust, 34-7

Has Your beautiful hand become red because of
the fire dancing in Your hand?
Or because of the beauty of Your beautiful
hand, did the fire become red?
You who perform an awesome dance in the
forest where the ghouls dance,
Your hero's anklets shaking, holding fire in Your
hand,
You tell me this!"[46]

There may be no Hindu deity more recognizable in the Western popular imagination than Shiva in his form as *Nataraja*, The Lord of Dance. In this masterly crafted bronze, the god appears before us with raised limbs, perfectly balanced, frozen in motion. Shiva lifts his left leg, ready to transition into his next posture. In the early twentieth century, art historian Ananda Commaraswamy offered a reading of the symbolism and meaning of Shiva Nataraja that is now the popular interpretation of this iconographic type.[47] The god stands upon a small, dwarflike figure that symbolizes ignorance, demonstrating that Shiva is the conqueror of that earthly flaw. Shiva has four arms, which signify his divine status and allow him to present multiple gestures (known as *mudra*s) and attributes. The double drum in Shiva's upper right hand plays the rhythm of creation: the rhythm of his dance. Shiva unfolds his upper left hand to reveal a flickering flame, the elemental energy associated with destruction. Shiva holds his lower right hand in *abhaya mudra*, the "fear not gesture," as a sign of blessing and comfort to his followers. This reassuring message is echoed in Shiva's calm expression, which greets the viewer's gaze with wide, partially opened, almond-shaped eyes, soft features, and full lips pursed in a gentle smile.

Sculptures of Nataraja were also iconic to their original audiences in southern India during the Imperial Chola period (848–1279). The great proliferation of Nataraja imagery under the Chola kings was the result of several factors. The Chola rulers themselves were Shaivites, sectarian followers of the great god Shiva, whom they revered as their patron deity. In the ninth century, the Cholas took control of the eastern Kaveri River delta and its surrounding lands. This was 'Shiva country,' and the crowning Chola acquisition was the ancient coastal city of Cidambaram, a sacred center associated with the god. Religious texts and devotional hymns from southern India describe Cidambaram as the abode of Shiva, where the god lived in the sanctum of the temple and performed various dances in the lush groves and terrifying cremation grounds around the city. Images of Nataraja were produced in great numbers during the Imperial Chola period, including in workshops in the royal capital city of Thanjavur. Indeed, the scholar Padma Kaimal suggests that the iconic form of Shiva as Nataraja and his deep connection to the region may have had special significance as both a religious symbol and political emblem for the Chola kings.[48]

The Nelson-Atkins Nataraja was created to serve as a processional image and would have been installed in a subshrine of a Hindu temple, to be removed and carried on special ritual occasions. It would have been encircled by a separately cast *mandorla* depicting a ring of flame, which is now missing. Like other Chola bronzes, this sculpture was created using the lost wax technique. An original sculpture was modeled in wax, which was then packed around with clay to form a mold. Sculptors poured a molten copper alloy into an opening, which vaporized the wax original and filled the cavities of the mold. The sensuous, projecting limbs and details found on sculptures of Nataraja have caused several scholars to suggest that this sculptural type was likely first conceived of in bronze, which is suited for supporting this form, and was only later copied in stone.[49] Unlike other sculptural traditions,

bronzes from southern Indian had to be solid-cast to be appropriate hosts for the living deity. The artistic skill and technical knowledge needed to cast flawless large-scale sculptures in solid bronze was perfected in the Chola workshops over 1000 years ago. This achievement, which is difficult to replicate even with modern techniques, has earned Chola metal sculptures, like this beautiful representation of Nataraja, recognition as one of the greatest sculptural traditions in the history of world art.

Of Shiva's many dances, his most famous is his *Thandava* dance, shown here. It is performed to bring an end to the *Kali Uga*, the era of corruption that we all currently inhabit in the Hindu cyclic system of mythic time. It will be in the cremation grounds of Cidambaram where Shiva comes to dance. In this way, Shiva will perform one of his most important duties as a great god: as the destructive force at the end of time, who will usher in the birth of a new golden age.

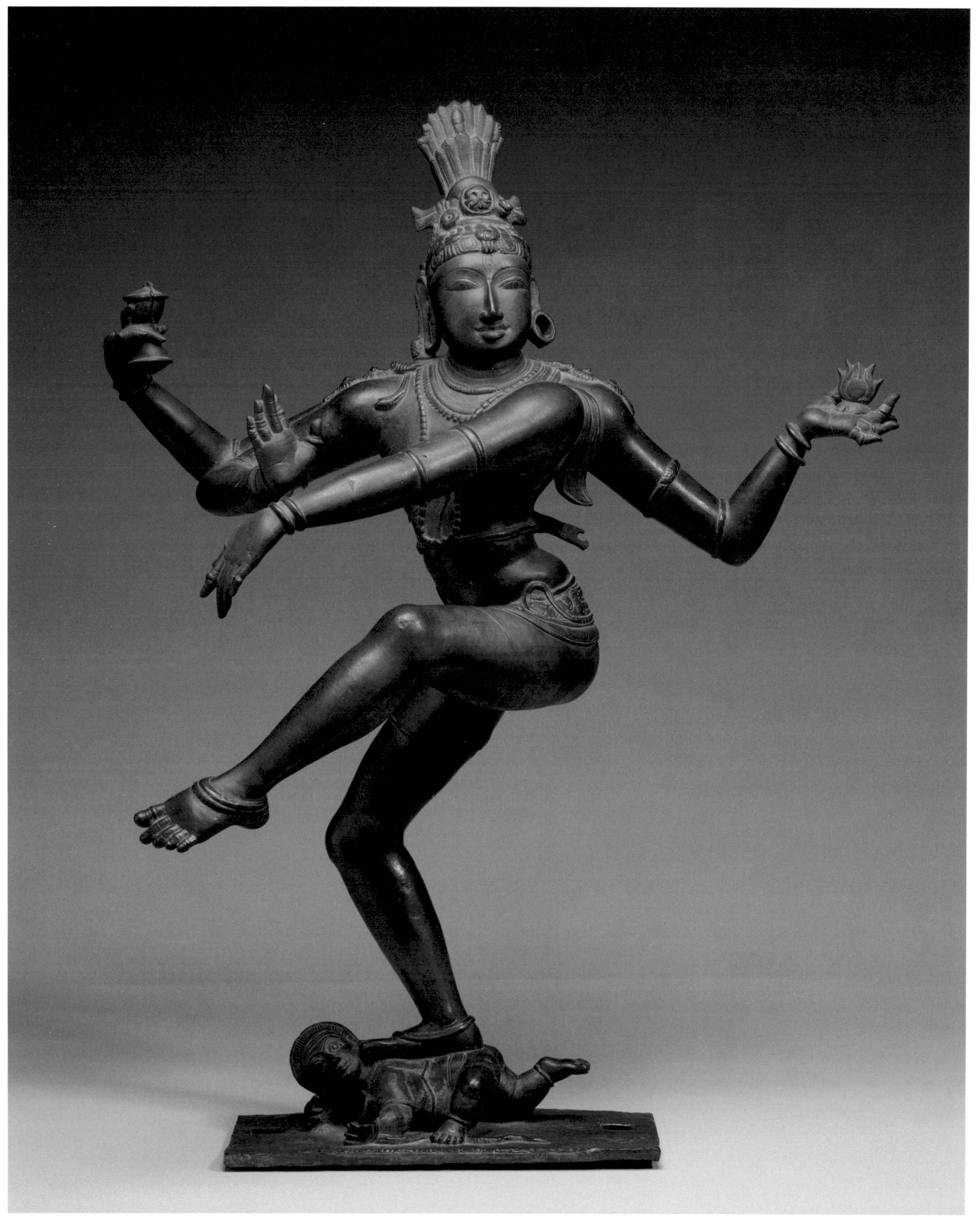

Sambandar, a Shaiva Saint

13th century
India, Tamil Nadu, probably Thanjuvur District
Chola dynasty (848–1279)
Bronze
26 inches (66.04 cm)
PURCHASE: William Rockhill Nelson Trust, 34-5

Even as a young child Sambandar was devoted to Lord Shiva. He expressed his love and piety by reciting hymns and performing dances, ancient Hindu forms of honoring and worshipping the gods. Here Sambandar is shown in his most iconic form, perfectly balanced with his right foot raised and left arm extended in the pose of *gaja hasta*, replicating an elephant's trunk, in the middle of performing a dance. His calm gaze and relaxed appearance conceal the physical strength and precision needed to master this posture.

Sambandar was one of the Nayanmars, the great Shaivite saints of southern India. These Hindu saints served as models of piety and helped to disseminate a new form of personal devotional practice, known as *bhakti*, across southern India. Like Karaikkal Ammaiyar (Cat. 21), Sambandar was a historical figure famous for his intense devotion to Shiva. He lived in the seventh century, and is credited with converting the Pandyan king of Madurai in southern Tamil Nadu from the Jain religion to Shaivism, thus contributing to the rise of Hinduism as the dominant religion in southern India.

Sambandar is depicted as a child because of his brief life span. The stories of Sambandar's life state that he began on his devotional path after a miraculous experience at a Shiva temple at the age of three. At age sixteen, he vanished from the world in a burst of brilliant light created by Shiva. During those thirteen years, Sambandar composed over four thousand hymns in praise of Shiva. This form of Sambandar is similar to depictions of another famous child in the Hindu tradition, the god Krishna. When Krishna is depicted as a youth, he is frequently shown in the same dance posture. The two figures can be distinguished, as Sambandar points upward with one finger on his right hand, an allusion to the miracle at the temple when he was three; images of Krishna usually show him offering the protective *abhaya mudra*, or "fear not gesture," with his right hand.[50]

This outstanding sculpture presents characteristics of the mature Chola sculptural style. The figure is lifelike, proportionate, and fully modeled in the round. Though the treatment of the figure's smooth, muscular limbs reveal the build of a mature dancer, his round face with its gentle smile and fleshy torso retains the youthful appearance of the child saint. There is a pleasant balance between the emphasis on the modeled contours of the saint's body and the detailing of his jewelry. This sculpture is rendered in bronze, a favored medium used to create processional images for temples in southern India. The holes in the base of the sculpture were made to allow carrying devices to be attached, indicating that this Sambandar sculpture was intended for processional use.

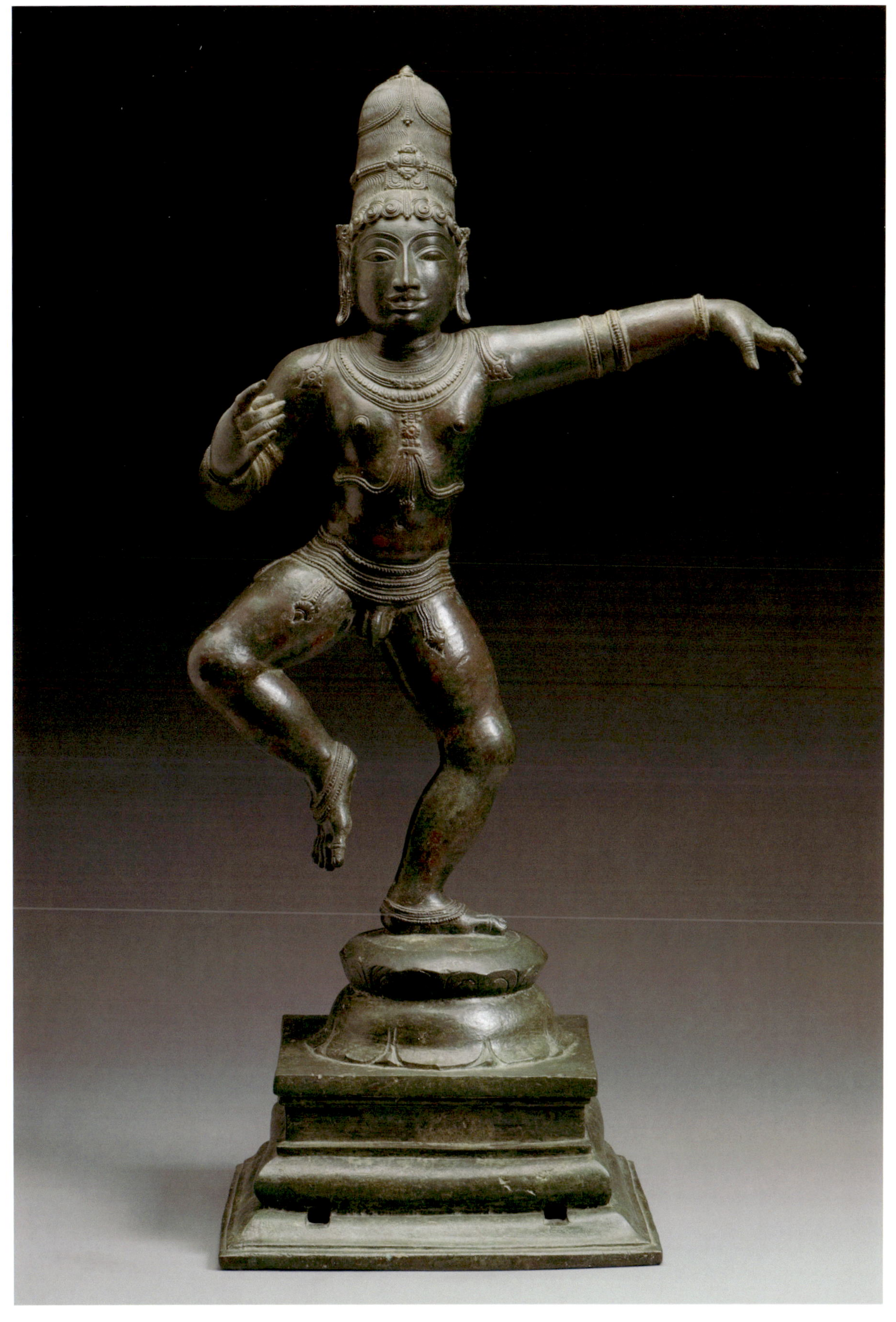

24 | *Mahishasuramardini, Durga as the Slayer of the Buffalo Demon*

16th century
India, Tamil Nadu
Vijayanagar dynasty (1336–1646)
Greenstone
48 inches (121.92 cm)
PURCHASE: William Rockhill Nelson Trust, 34-3

Standing tall and facing forward, with one hand on her hip, a defiant goddess meets our gaze. This is Durga, the great mother and warrior goddess of the Hindu tradition. In southern India, sculptures like this are frequently found in external niches on the north side of Hindu temples. The four-armed goddess wields two weapons, an axe in her upper left hand and a *chakra*, the throwing disc favored by the Hindu god Vishnu. This suggests that this depiction of Durga was created to be part of the sculptural program of a Vaishnavite temple.

Though the sculpture belonged to a temple dedicated to Vishnu, Durga is a supreme deity in her own right. The Sanskrit root of her name, *durg*, means fortress, and she has frequently been worshipped because of her strength and protective powers. In the *Devi Mahatmya*, a fifth- to sixth-century text dedicated to the great goddess, Durga reigns supreme.[51] She is called upon by the great male gods, including Vishnu and Shiva, when they are unable to defeat the destructive demon named Mahisha. In a famous story, Durga takes the weapons of the male gods, which include the *chakra* and axe, and battles the shape-shifting demon across the universe. In his last incarnation, Mahisha takes the form of a buffalo. Durga and her lion mount finally capture the demon and the goddess cuts off his head. Mahisha emerges from the body of the buffalo, bows to the goddess in surrender, and becomes her obedient devotee. This episode is referenced in this sculpture by the inclusion of the buffalo head that lies beneath Durga's feet. The composition that we see here of Durga standing triumphantly above the buffalo's severed head is first seen in a fifth-century sculpture from Besnagar in northern India. It is commonly used in southern Indian sculptures of this subject, as seen in the standing Durga carved in the eighth-century Trimurti Cave at Mamallapuram. Beyond the story of Mahisha, the buffalo head also reminds us of the ancient practices of animal sacrifices made to powerful Indian goddesses. These practices have been extinguished in southern India, replaced by sacrificial imagery and symbolic surrogate offerings.

This figure of Durga is an excellent example of later southern Indian temple sculpture. Carved in greenstone, a local stone similar in appearance to granite, the goddess exhibits other regional traits, including an elongated face, narrow waist, tubular limbs, and tall crown. She differs in style from her Chola-era predecessors in her flattened form, the schematic rendering of the masses and joints of her body, and the emphasis upon linear patterning over sculptural modeling, as seen in the treatment of her garments and jewelry. These traits suggest that this impressive sculpture of Durga was created during the sixteenth century, when the Tamil lands were under the control of the Vijayanagar dynasty (1336–1646).

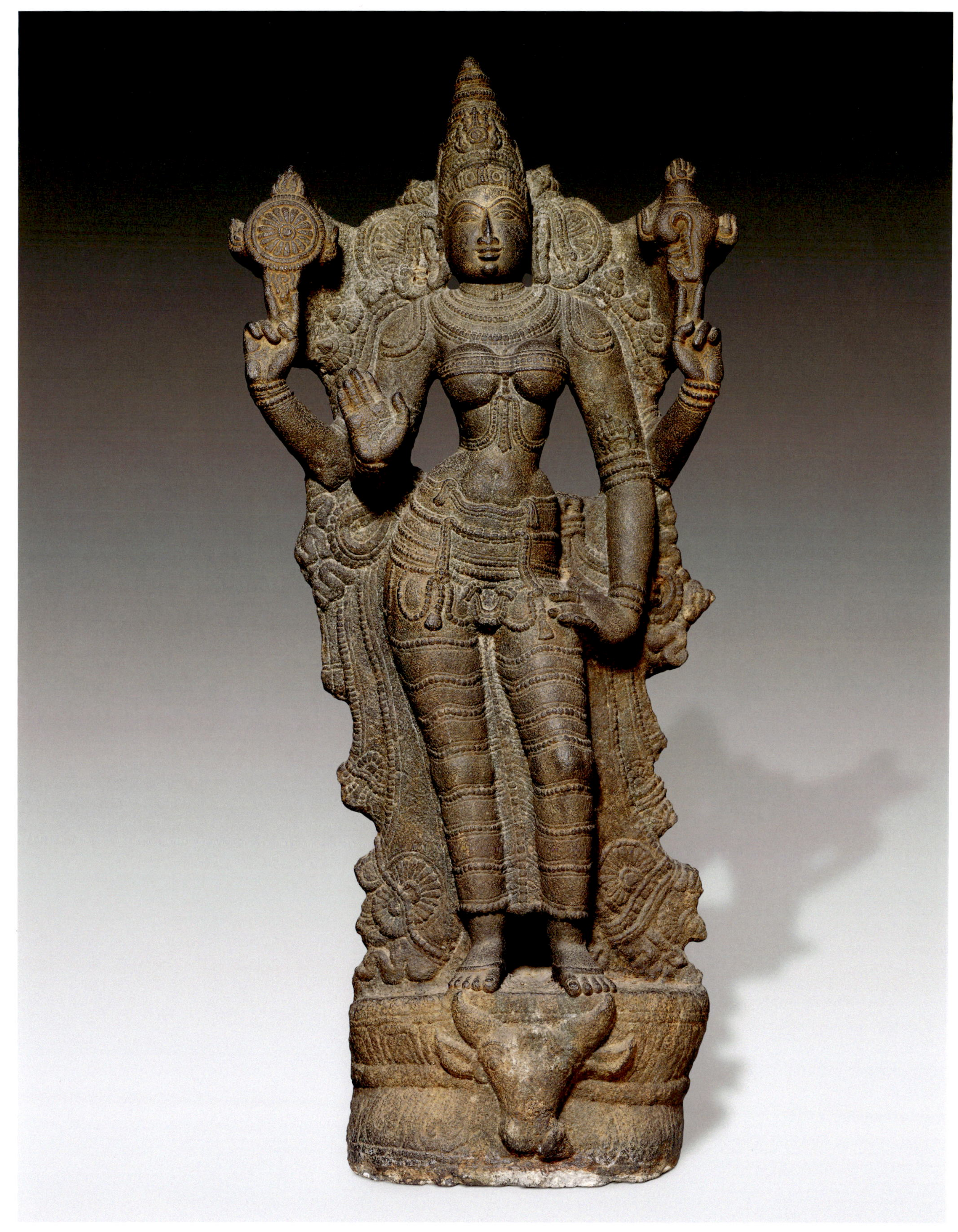

1501
India, Patan
Gujarati Sultanate period (1407–1573)
Ink, opaque watercolor, and gold on paper
Sheet (each): 4³⁄₁₆ × 13³⁄₁₆ inches (10.64 × 33.5 cm)
PURCHASE: the Asian Art Acquisition Fund in memory of
Laurence Sickman, 2011.73

The primary text illustrated in this fine manuscript is the *Kalpasutra*, one of the fundamental texts of the Shvetambara sect of the Jain religion. The *Kalpasutra* documents the lives of Jain teachers, known as *Tirthankaras* (ford makers) or *Jinas* (victorious ones). Written in Prakrit, the text focuses heavily on Mahavira, the last of the *Tirthankaras*, who lived in the sixth century BCE. Key events in Mahavira's life, from his miraculous conception and lustration by the gods at birth, to his youth, asceticism, achievement of the advanced spiritual state known as *kevalajnana*, and his cessation from the world, are illustrated in great detail. Later chapters of the *Kalpasutra* lay out rules of proper conduct for the monastic community, and the text is read aloud at gatherings of monastic and lay Jains during the annual summer Paryusan festival.[52] It is thought that the practice of illustrating the *Kalpasutra* may relate to the performative function of the text, with images relating to the story held up for audiences during narration.

This manuscript is an important example of this tradition because of its completeness, the number and quality of its illustrations, and the two colophons at the end of the text block, which provide historical information about the place and the recipient of the commission. Containing over 150 folios and 97 illustrations, the Nelson-Atkins manuscript is one of the largest and most heavily illustrated texts of the *Kalpasutra* and *Kalakacharyakatha* in an American museum. The illustrations in the current manuscript align with the later phase of the Western Indian Style, a regional painting style that is characterized by rendering forms in heavy outlines and flat colors and lively patterns, with figures displaying a characteristic "projecting eye" when shown in three-quarter views. Illustrations of key events in the narrative are inserted into the text block, with commentaries and descriptive captions running in the margins. Set against rich blue backgrounds created from lapis lazuli and ornamented with gold paint, the illustrations in the Nelson-Atkins *Kalpasutra* and *Kalakacharyakatha* are of very high quality, some of the best of their type from around the year 1500.

This manuscript was a grand gift from an unnamed lay patron to a Jain monk named Devakallola. The colophons state that it was produced in Patan, India, in the western state of Gujarat. Patan was the capital of the early medieval Hindu Solanki dynasty, and then served as the first capital of the Islamic Gujarati Sultanate. Produced in a cultural center that witnessed the ebb and flow of regional political powers and their distinctive artistic styles, the manuscript seems to capture these multicultural influences in many of the illustrations. This is especially true in the illustrations of the *Kalakacharyakatha*, the smaller text inserted at the end of the *Kalpasutra* story.[53] Here, Islamic patterns and figures commingle with traditional Indian forms and motifs.[54] The illustrations of this text are restricted to the first chapter. In this story, the Jain monk Kalaka journeys across the Indus River in order to raise a foreign army to return to India and wage war against the unjust Hindu king of Ujjain. The story of Kalaka was popular and was frequently included with texts of the *Kalpasutra*. As the historic monk Kalaka was credited as establishing the date for the annual Paryusan festival, this text is also frequently read during the observance of the festival.[55]

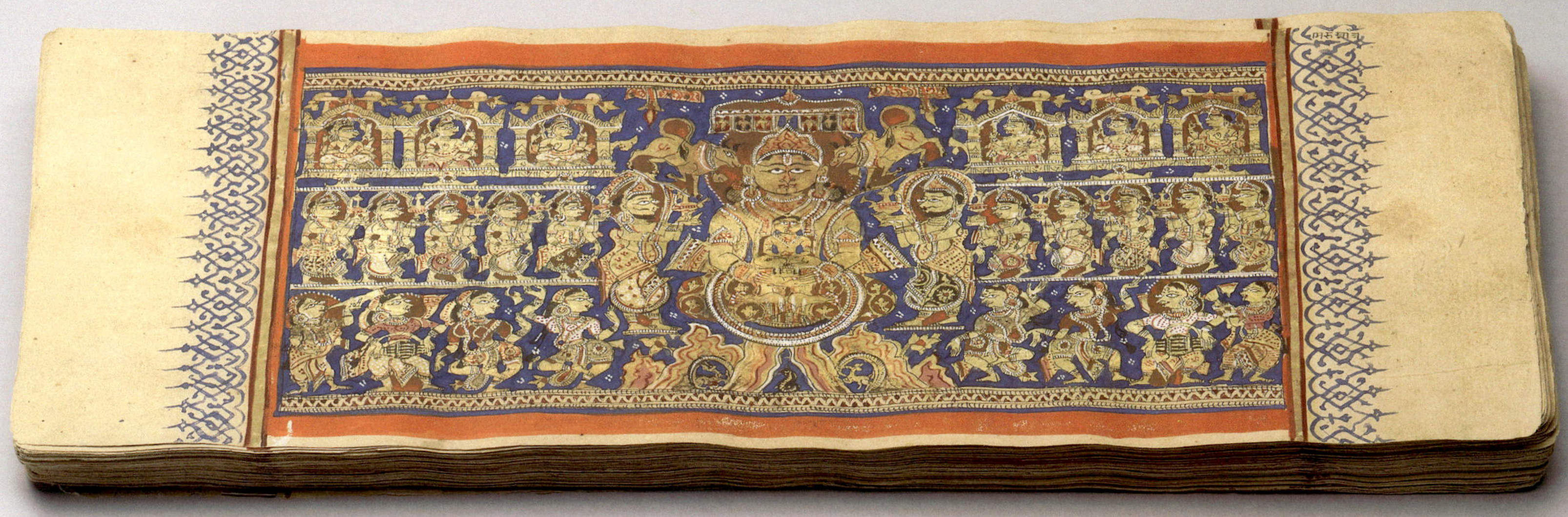

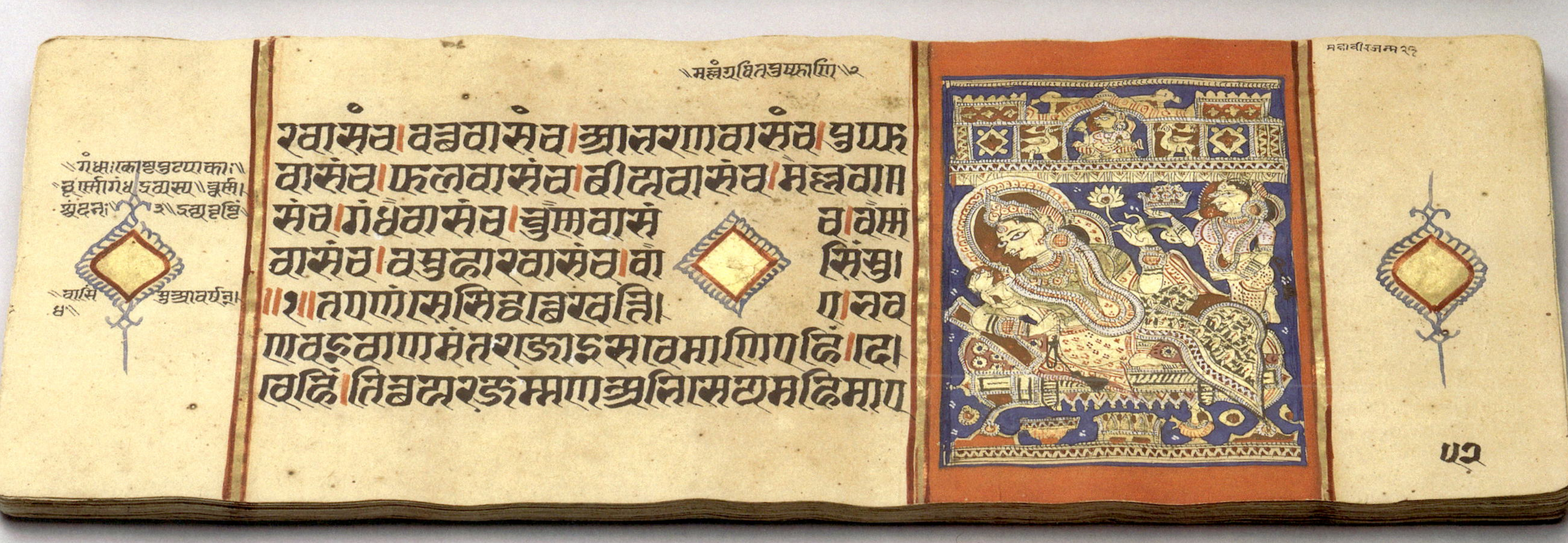

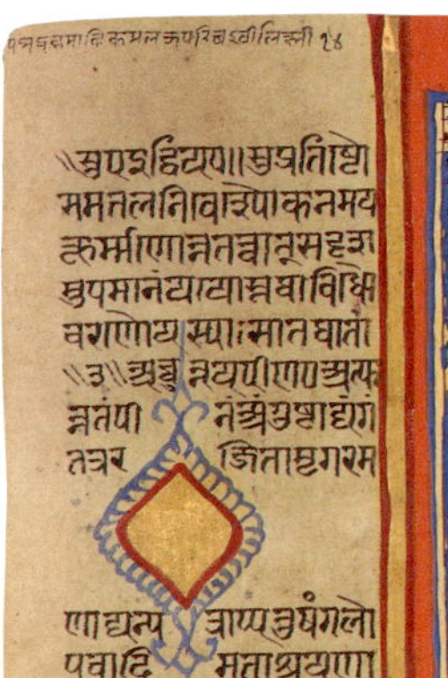

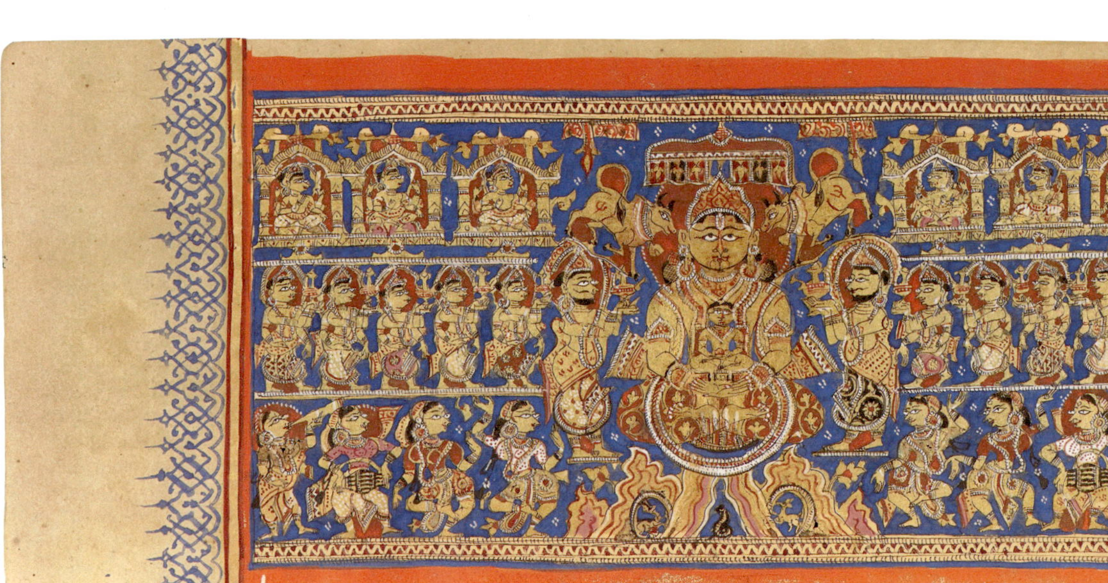

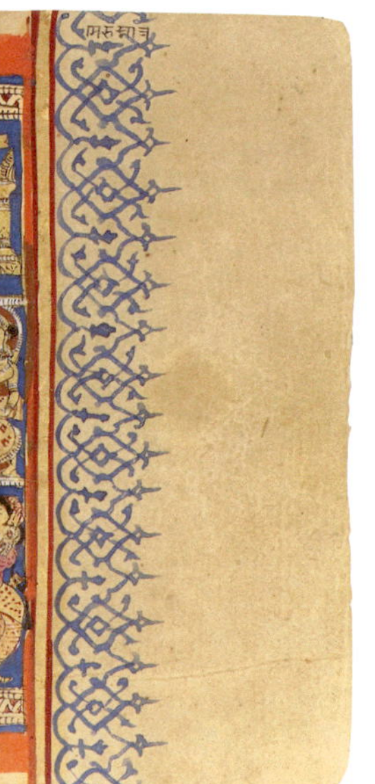

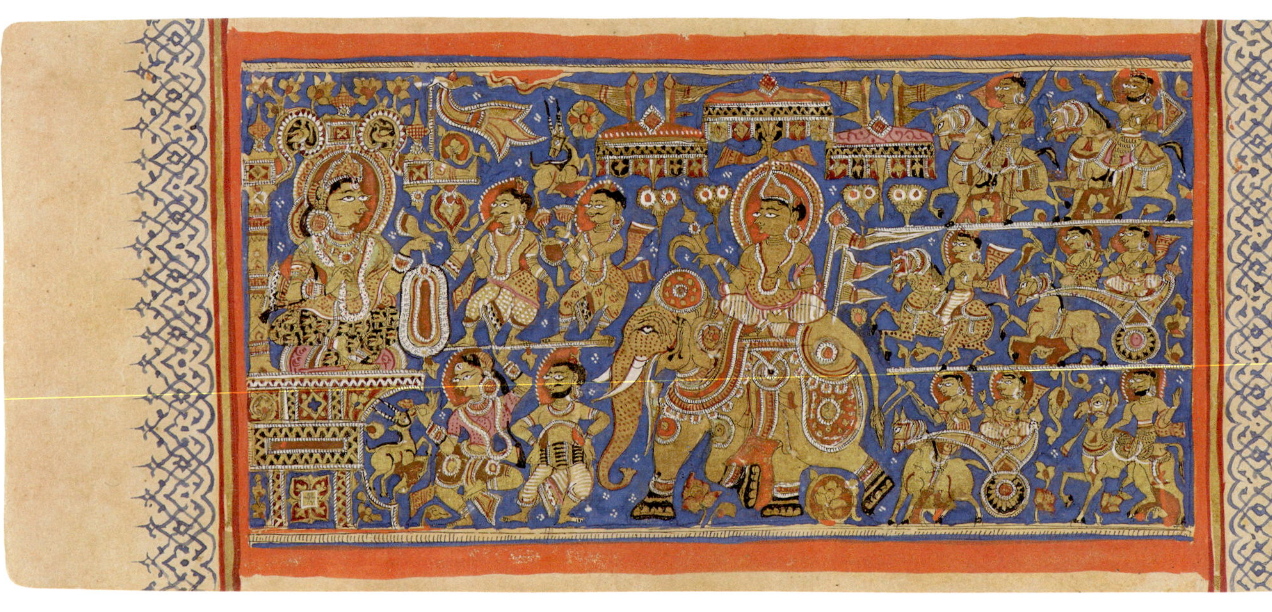

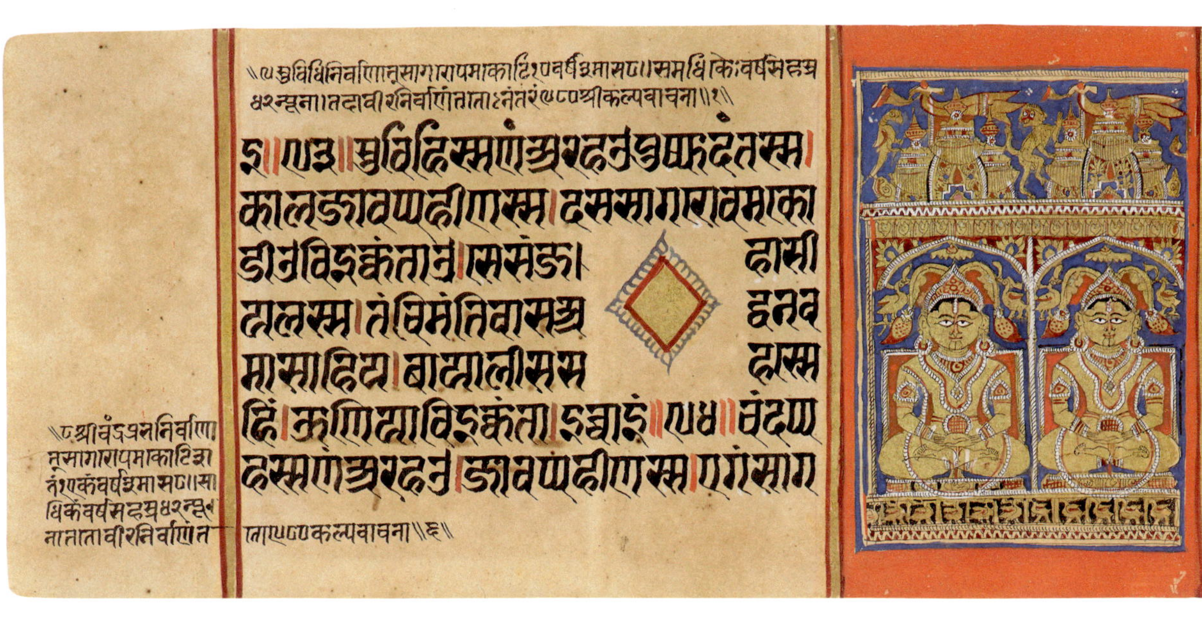

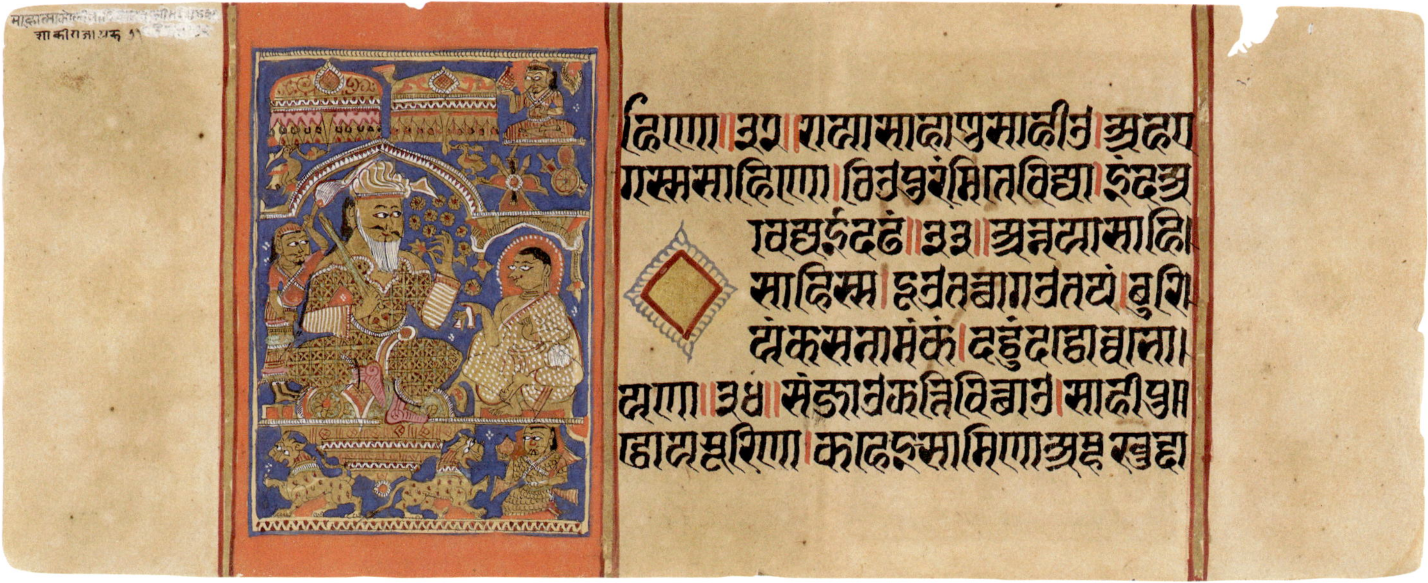

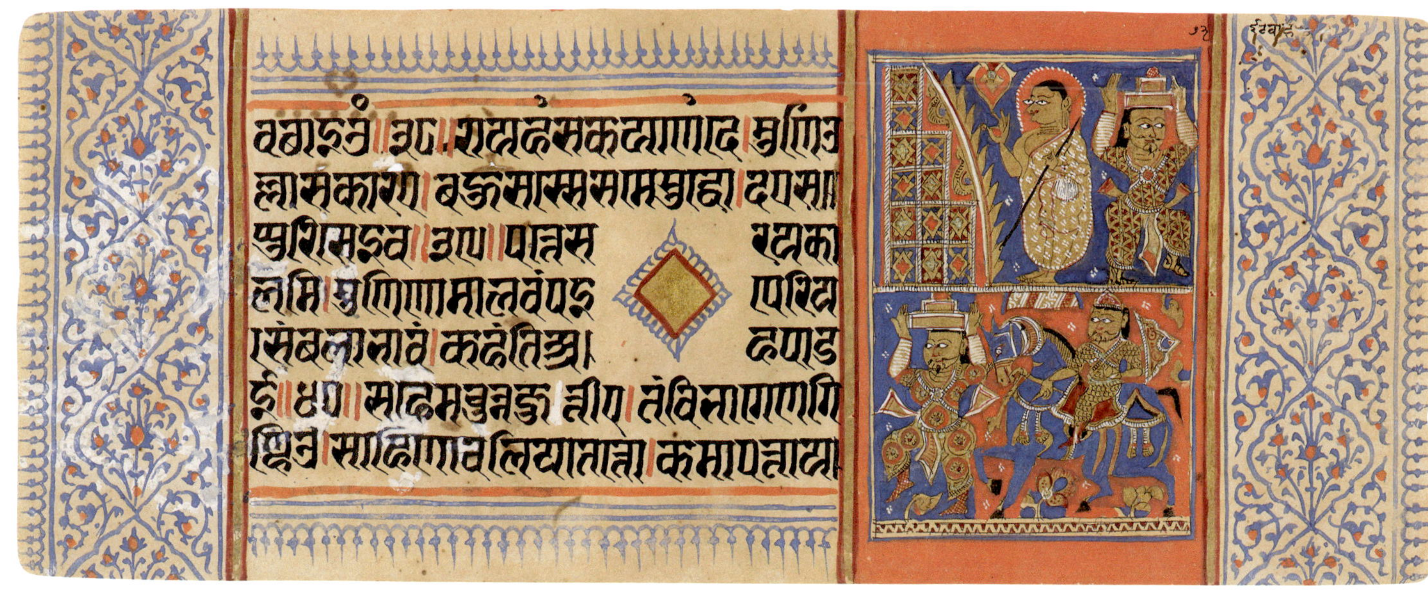

16th to early 17th century
India, Gujarat, possibly Patan
Possibly Gujarati Sultanate period (1407–1573)
Wood, polychrome paint, gold leaf, mirrored glass
Overall: 70 × 57⅝ × 7 inches (177.8 × 146.3675 × 17.78 cm)
PURCHASE: William Rockhill Nelson Trust, 32-136

Jainism is an ancient religion of India. Jainism focuses upon the perfection of the individual through ethical behavior and thinking, and renunciation. The ultimate goal of Jainism is liberation from rebirth; those individuals who have achieved liberation, and serve as exemplars, are known as *Jina* (victor) or *Tirthankara* (ford maker—one who crosses the waters and indicates a way for others).

Jain practice requires daily veneration of an image of a *Jina*.[56] This veneration can take place at a community temple or at a home shrine. It was common practice in western India for wealthy Jains to commission an elaborate *ghar derasar* (home temple) for use in their private homes. Such a shrine was frequently constructed of wood and decorated with relief carvings and polychrome.

Domestic Jain shrines incorporate elements of temple architecture into their design. The elaborately carved lintels depict a *Jina* in the center. The figure here can be identified as Adinath, the first *Jina*, whose bull *vahana* (vehicle) is shown at his feet. Directly beneath him is the goddess of good fortune, Lakshmi, being lustrated by a pair of elephants. This form of the goddess, known as *Gaja Lakshmi*, is frequently depicted on the lintels of Indian temples, where she symbolically blesses and cleanses those who enter into the sacred realm of the shrine. Other fascinating details can be found on the upper lintel, to either side of the seated golden *Jina*. These include a group of figures at the top right that show three white-clad Jain monks performing a ritual for two royally dressed patrons. The seated monk wears a *muhapatti*, a cloth over his mouth that prevents both the inhaling and accidental killing of small insects and organisms and the exhaling of saliva onto sacred texts and objects. To the left of the *Jina* are two yellow and gold footprints, known as *paduka,* which represent the passing of a Jina or enlightened ascetic into nirvana. Beside them, a charming wide-eyed tiger peers outward from behind a curvaceously rendered tree.

The shrine's door panels are packed with symbolic imagery. From top to bottom, the coffered panels depict the fourteen premonitory dreams of the mother of a future *Jina*, which are usually associated with Queen Trisala, Mahavira's mother, carved in deep relief. The dreams include visions of an elephant, a bull, and a lion. The goddess Lakshmi appears, with two garlands, the moon, the sun, a flag on a golden post, a gold water pot, a lotus lake, the stormy ocean, a celestial vehicle, gems, and a smokeless flame. These visions are followed by the *asta mangala*, the eight auspicious symbols sacred to Jainism, which are compressed to fit onto six panels. These symbols comprise the *svastika* (an ancient sacred symbol of South Asia), the *srivasta* (a sacred mark over the heart of Vishnu), the *kailasha* (water pot), the *bhadrasana* (throne), the *nandavarta* (a sacred diagram), the *vardmanaka* (a powder flask), the *meen yugala* (pair of fish), and the *darpan* (mirror.)

The small porch references a *mandapa*, the pillared hall that is constructed in front of a shrine in an Indian temple. The pillars would have supported a lotus ceiling, which represents the floor of the heavens above.

In 2012 and 2013, conservators at the Nelson-Atkins consolidated and cleaned this shrine. A thick layer of brown varnish and grime was removed to reveal vibrant and richly detailed painted and gilded surfaces. The top layer of paint likely dates to the nineteenth century due to the presence of a pigment known as "Emerald Green," but scientific analysis of paint samples revealed the presence of an earlier layer of paint.[57] This original layer had a predominantly red and blue color scheme and included areas of ultramarine blue pigment, made from ground lapis lazuli, which was a very expensive material used on lavish commissions. Carbon 14 testing of wood samples from different sections of the shrine indicates that the shrine was most likely created in the sixteenth century.

The Nelson-Atkins Jain Shrine has had multiple lives. It was originally a highly ornate shrine that served as a fitting residence for a *Jina* image inside a medieval Gujarati home. It must have remained in use until the nineteenth century, when it was considered worthy of renovation. Artists at this time painted it in a bold manner and used modern pigments and materials to refurbish it, uniting an ancient faith with contemporary artistic practices.

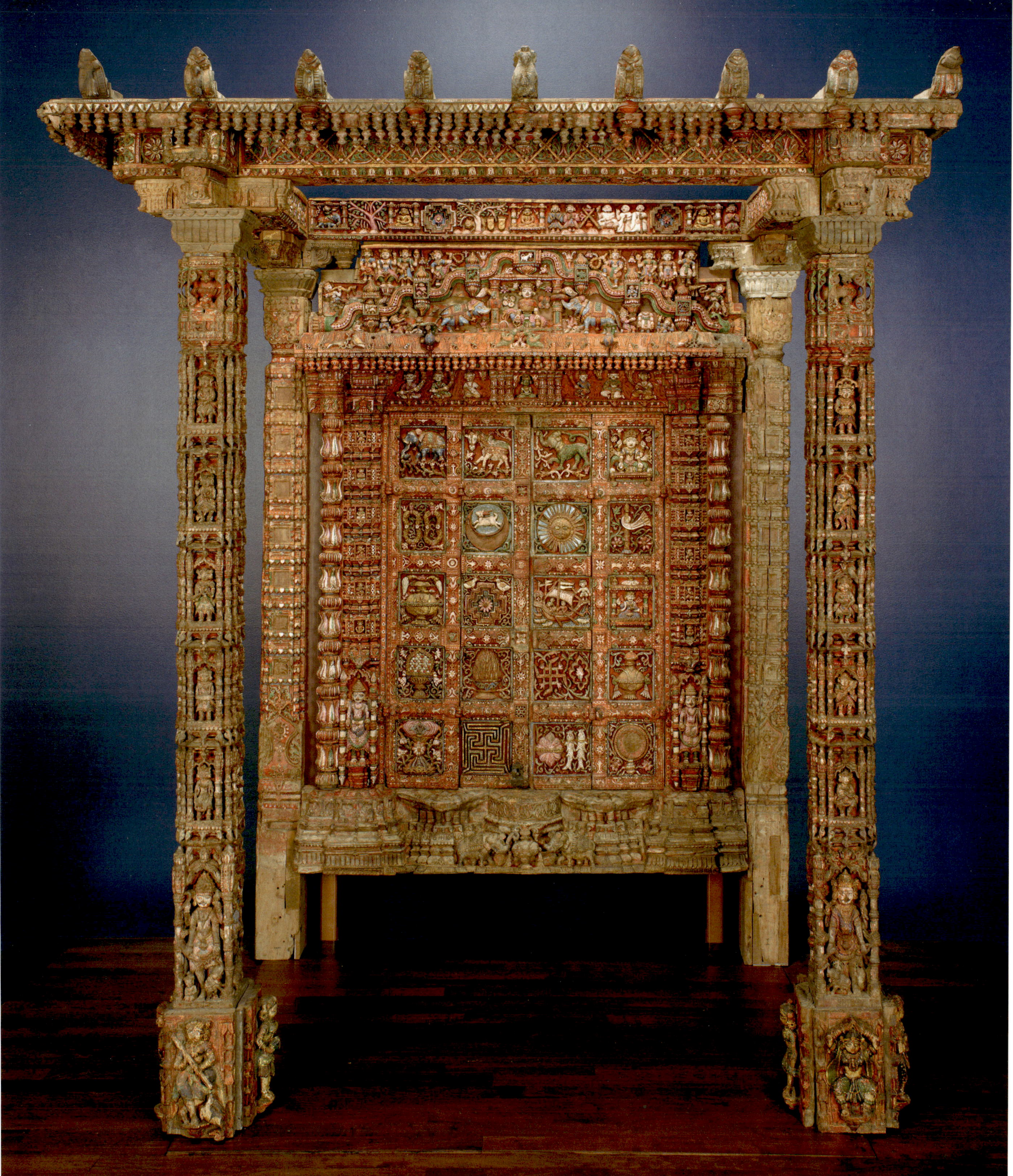

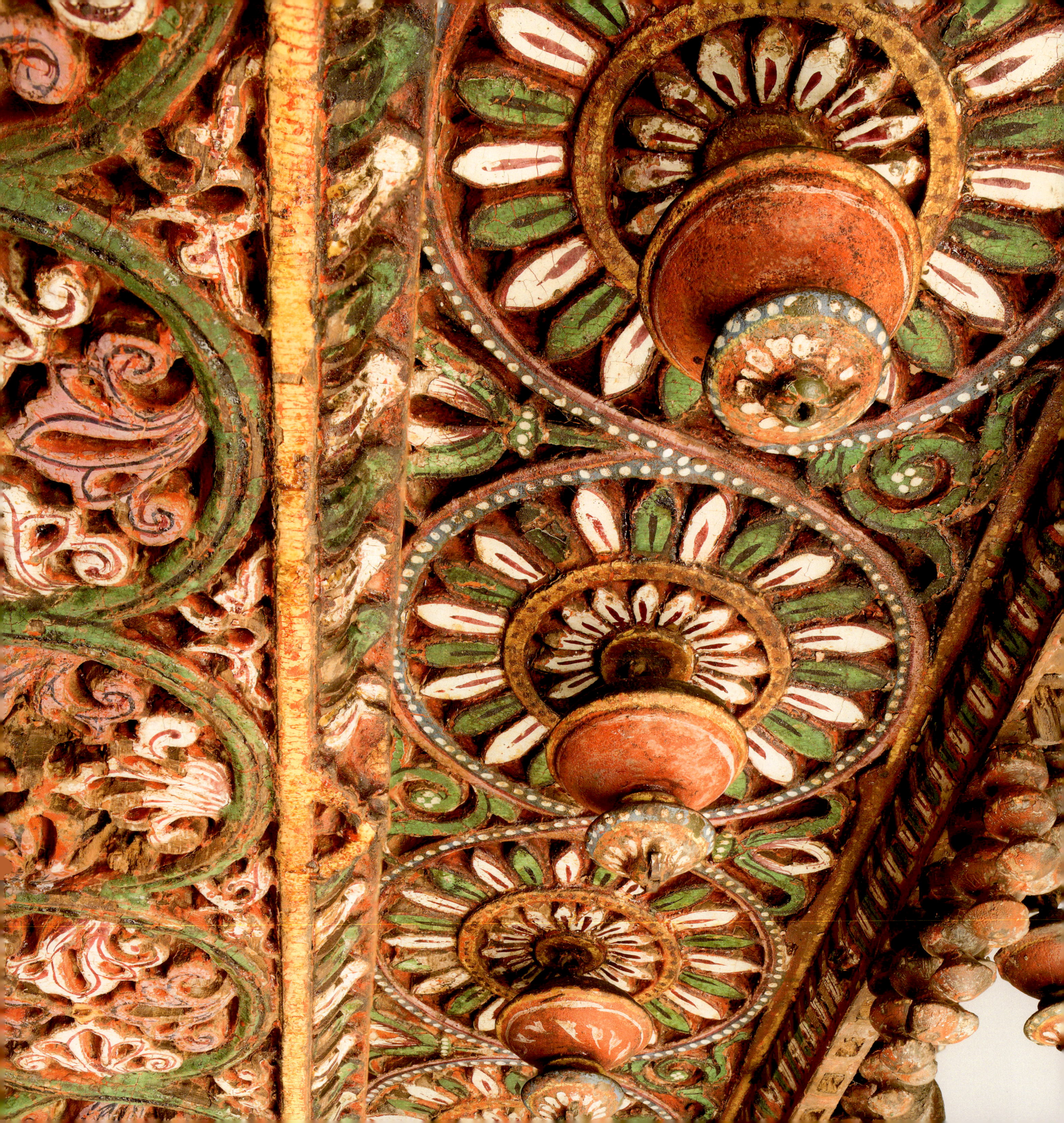

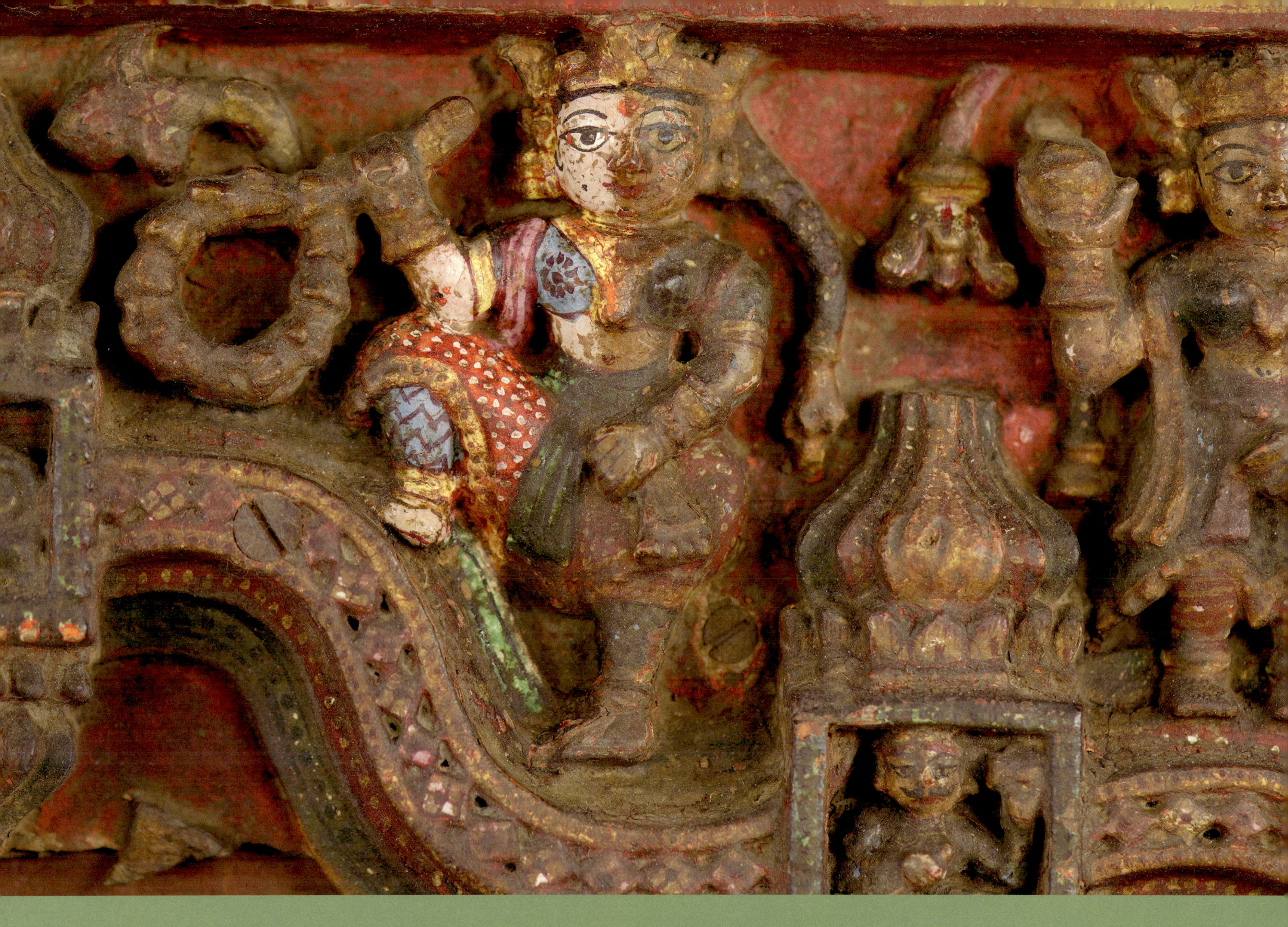

 Kamadhenu, the Wish-Granting Cow

15th–17th century
India, Tamil Nadu or Karnataka
Stone and pigment, with metal attachments
14½ × 23 × 8 inches (36.83 × 58.42 × 20.32 cm)
PURCHASE: William Rockhill Nelson Trust through the
George H. and Elizabeth O. Davis Fund, 2009.15

This lavishly detailed stone sculpture depicts Kamadhenu, the wish-granting cow of ancient and medieval India. Kamadhenu is the 'Mother of All Cows,' an ancient agrarian deity venerated across South Asia. The cow is a sacred animal in Indic religions. It is associated with purity and is recognized for providing both sustenance and ritual materials in the form of milk.

Vedic and Puranic texts identify Kamadhenu as one of the fourteen precious items that were churned from the Cosmic Ocean of Milk by Vishnu. Other stories state that she was the wife of Daksha, the Vedic creator god and the wife of one of the *rshis,* the great ancestral sages. She is also associated with Vishnu's *avatar,* the cowherd god Krishna. In Shaivite traditions, Kamadhenu is believed to have taken residence in one of Shiva's temples in southern India, from where she grants wishes. Although the veneration of Kamadhenu is pan-Indic, the wish-granting cow appears to be especially popular in southern India and is linked by legend to several temple sites.

This caparisoned cow wears a combination of elaborate halters, harnesses, garlands, and a cloth cover (*jhul*) decorated with a flower pattern and carved in deep relief. All elements of the cow and its decoration are carved in the same dense gray stone, with iron clasps used to attach three low-hanging bells loosely to the rest of the sculpture.

An unusual feature of this sculpture of Kamadhenu is that it is hollow, with an excavated tunnel running from the head to the rear of the sculpture and channels connected to the tunnel running to each of the four udders. This interior carving was completed after the original creation of the sculpture, as evidenced by the removable sections cut into the finished stone along the cow's left side. It appears that the Nelson-Atkins Kamadhenu was intended literally to offer milk, suggesting an unusual ritual use of the sculpture.

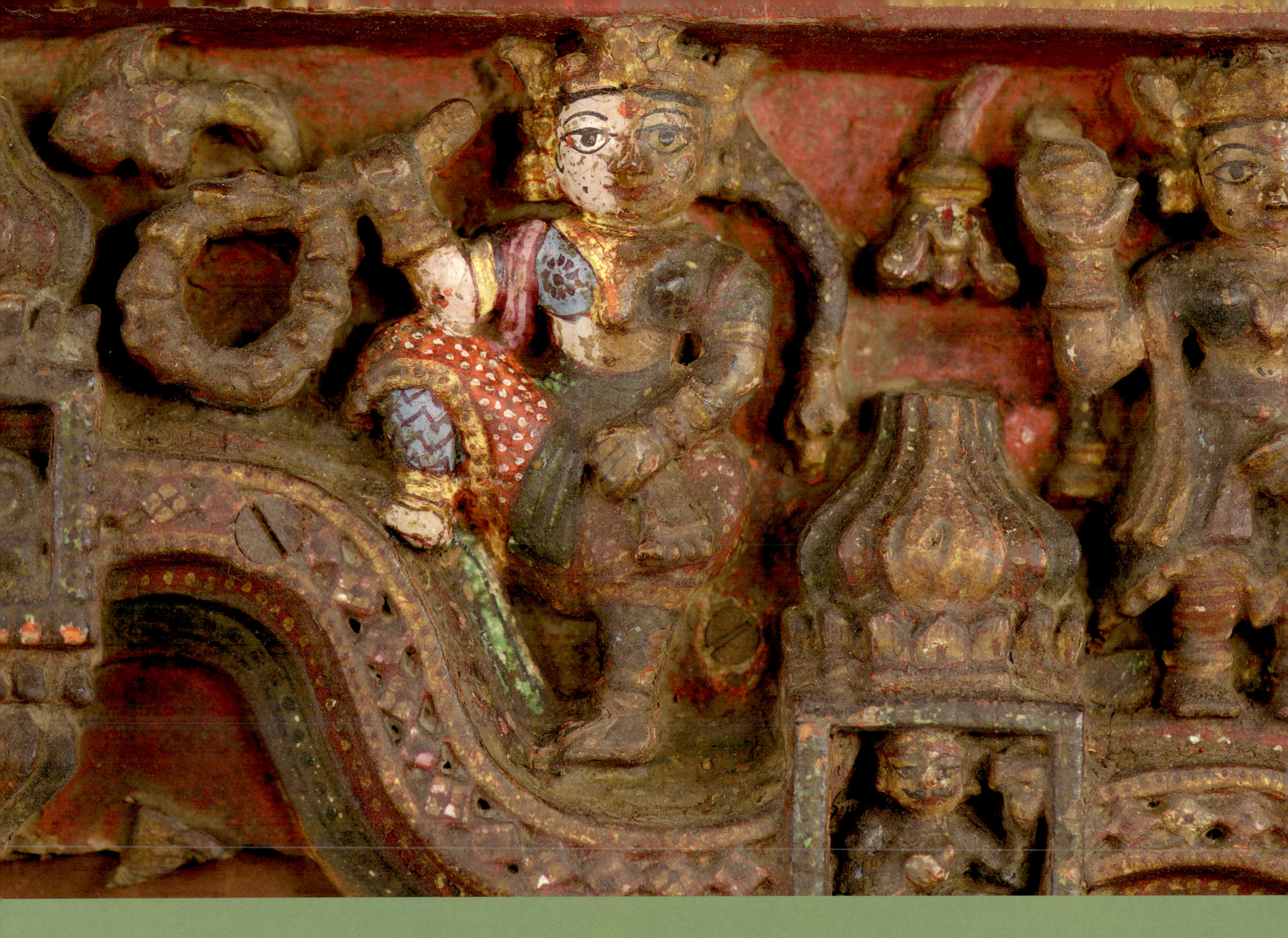

Kamadhenu, the Wish-Granting Cow

15th–17th century
India, Tamil Nadu or Karnataka
Stone and pigment, with metal attachments
14½ × 23 × 8 inches (36.83 × 58.42 × 20.32 cm)
PURCHASE: William Rockhill Nelson Trust through the
George H. and Elizabeth O. Davis Fund, 2009.15

This lavishly detailed stone sculpture depicts Kamadhenu, the wish-granting cow of ancient and medieval India. Kamadhenu is the 'Mother of All Cows,' an ancient agrarian deity venerated across South Asia. The cow is a sacred animal in Indic religions. It is associated with purity and is recognized for providing both sustenance and ritual materials in the form of milk.

Vedic and Puranic texts identify Kamadhenu as one of the fourteen precious items that were churned from the Cosmic Ocean of Milk by Vishnu. Other stories state that she was the wife of Daksha, the Vedic creator god and the wife of one of the *rshis,* the great ancestral sages. She is also associated with Vishnu's *avatar*, the cowherd god Krishna. In Shaivite traditions, Kamadhenu is believed to have taken residence in one of Shiva's temples in southern India, from where she grants wishes. Although the veneration of Kamadhenu is pan-Indic, the wish-granting cow appears to be especially popular in southern India and is linked by legend to several temple sites.

This caparisoned cow wears a combination of elaborate halters, harnesses, garlands, and a cloth cover (*jhul*) decorated with a flower pattern and carved in deep relief. All elements of the cow and its decoration are carved in the same dense gray stone, with iron clasps used to attach three low-hanging bells loosely to the rest of the sculpture.

An unusual feature of this sculpture of Kamadhenu is that it is hollow, with an excavated tunnel running from the head to the rear of the sculpture and channels connected to the tunnel running to each of the four udders. This interior carving was completed after the original creation of the sculpture, as evidenced by the removable sections cut into the finished stone along the cow's left side. It appears that the Nelson-Atkins Kamadhenu was intended literally to offer milk, suggesting an unusual ritual use of the sculpture.

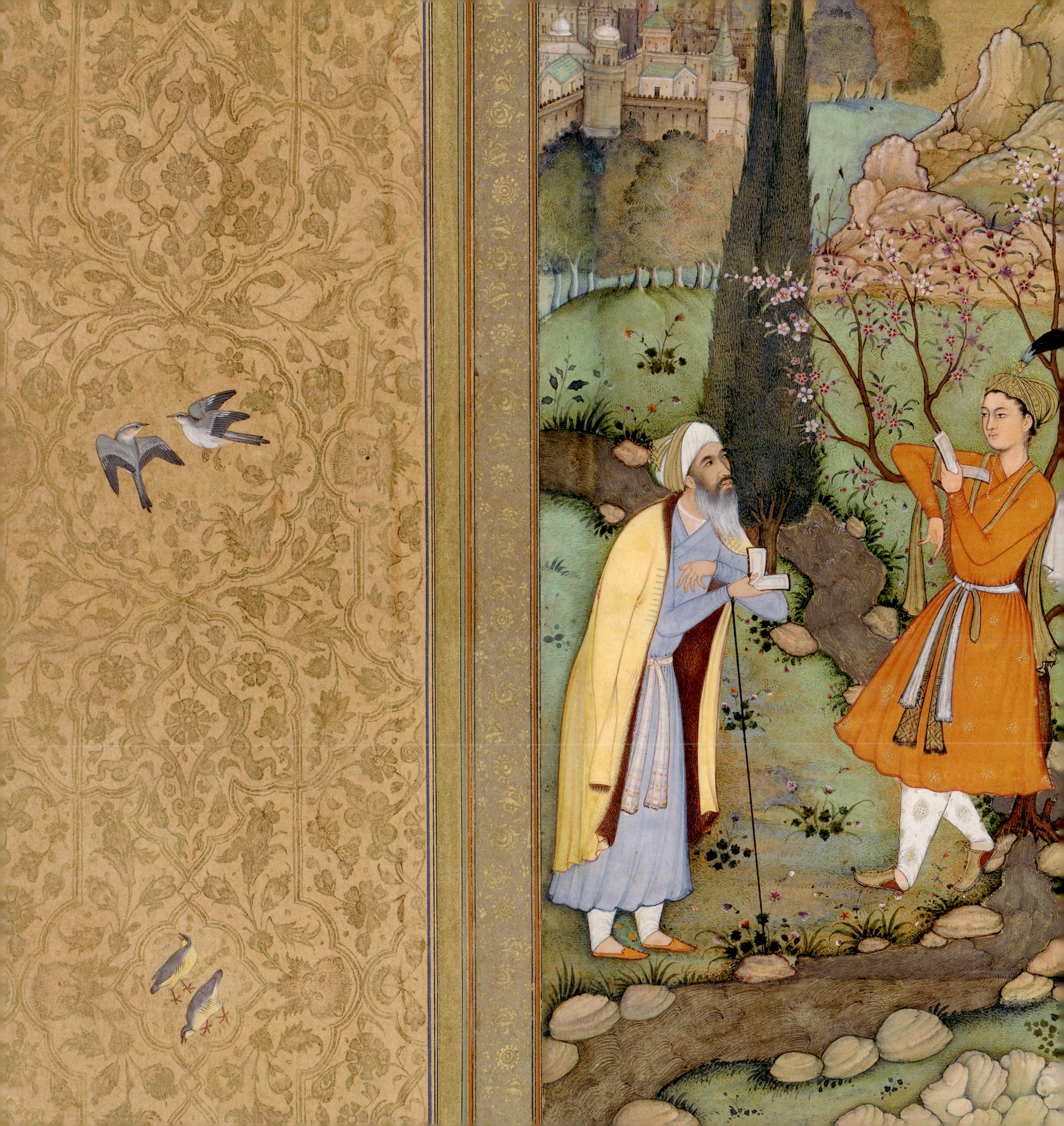

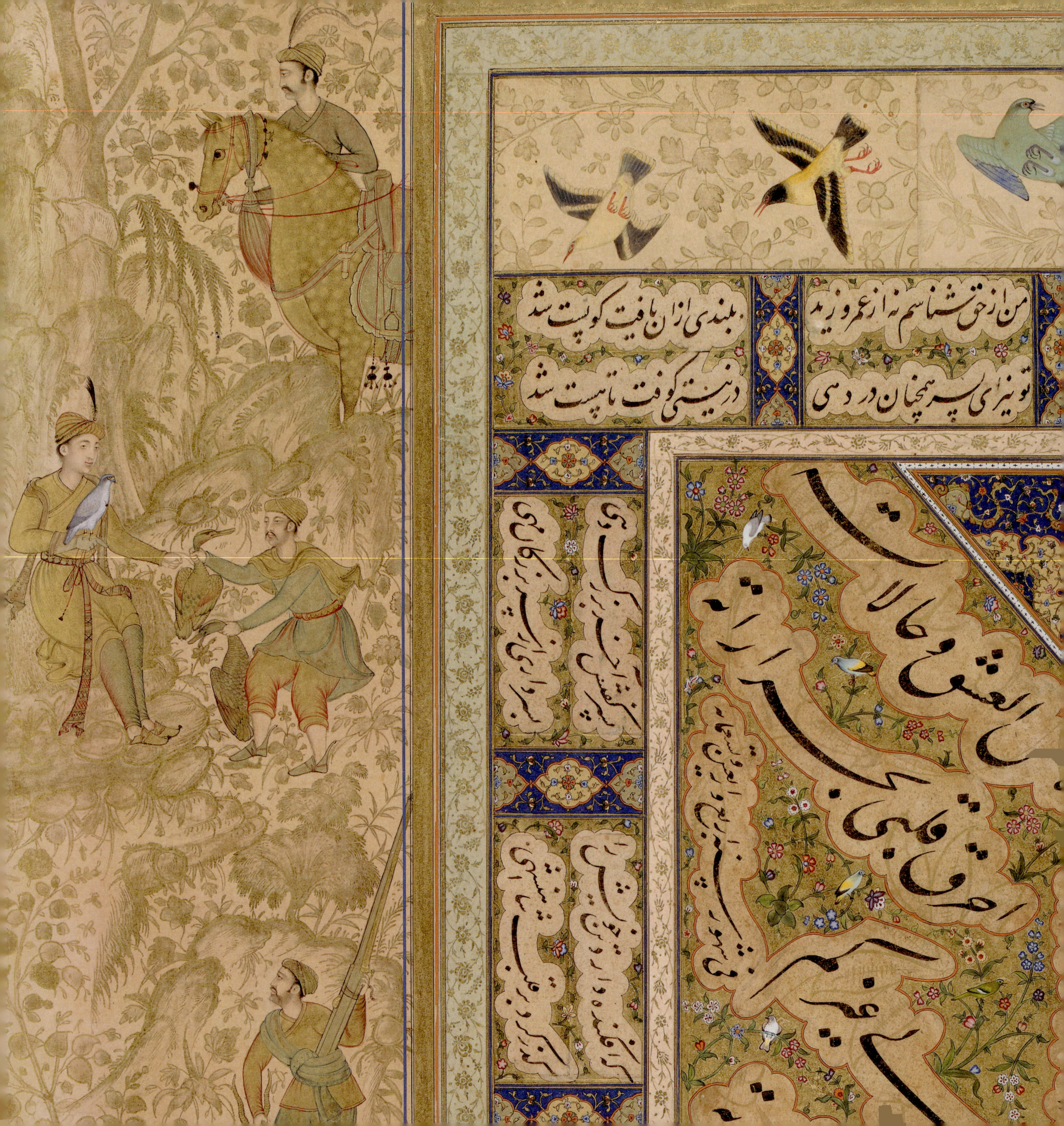

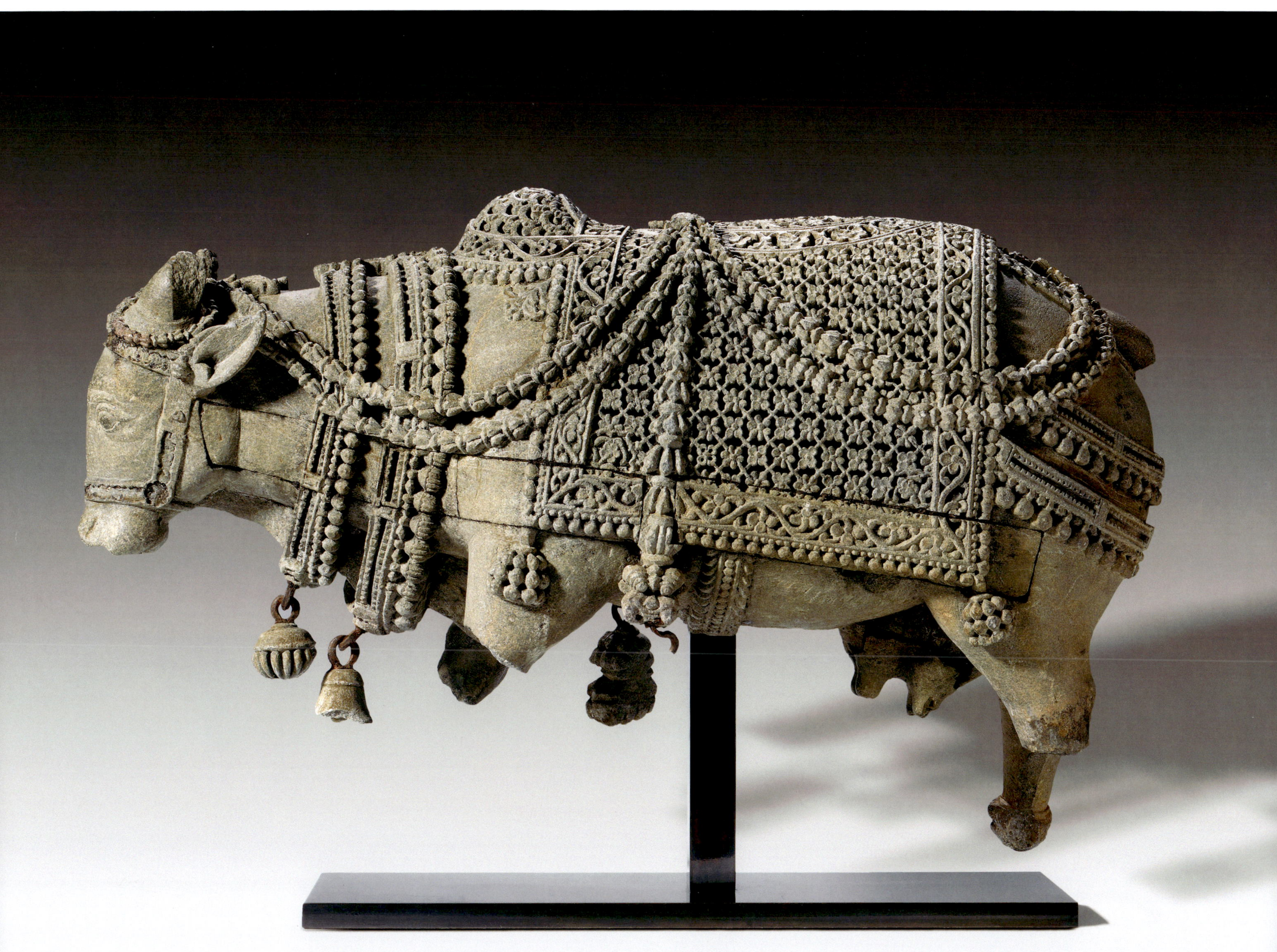

Folio from the Muraqqa Gulshan: The Poet and the Prince (recto), *Calligraphy* (verso) and *Folio from the Muraqqa Gulshan: A Buffalo Fighting a Lioness* (verso), *Calligraphy* (recto)

1595–1597
India, Agra or Allahabad
Mughal dynasty (1526–1857)
PAINTER: Salim Quli, Indian, active ca. 1590–1605
Also attributed to Lal, Indian, active ca. 1590–1605
CALLIGRAPHER: "Fakir Ali" [Mir Ali al-Katib al-Sultani],
Persian (ca. 1476–1556)
Ink, opaque watercolor, and gold paint on paper
Sheet: 16⅝ × 10½ inches (42.23 × 26.67 cm)
PURCHASE: William Rockhill Nelson Trust, 48-12/1 A, B

Late 16th century
India, Agra or Allahabad
Mughal dynasty (1526–1857)
PAINTER: Attributed to Farrukh Chela, Indian, active
ca. 1585–1604
CALLIGRAPHER: Mir Ali al-Katib al-Sultani, Persian
(ca. 1476–1556)
Ink, opaque watercolor, and gold paint on paper
Sheet: 16⅝ × 10½ inches (42.23 × 26.67 cm)
PURCHASE: William Rockhill Nelson Trust, 48-12/2 A, B

I derive such enjoyment from painting and have such expertise in judging it that, even without the artist's name being mentioned, no work of past or present masters can be shown to me that I do not instantly recognize who did it. Emperor Jahangir, from the *Jahangirnama*[58]

This proud excerpt from Jahangir's (r. 1605–27) personal memoirs reveal the fourth Mughal emperor's great interest and expertise in painting. Jahangir applied his connoisseurship to the creation of his own atelier, and both historical documents and inscribed paintings suggest that he patronized a small, select group of master artists. These two folios come from the famous *Gulshan Album*, a bound collection of paintings, drawings, prints, and calligraphies set in richly detailed illuminated borders that was commissioned by Prince Salim in the late sixteenth century, before he assumed the throne and the imperial title of *Jahangir*, "world-seizer." The outstanding quality of the paintings, calligraphy, and ornamentation of this now-dispersed volume earned the *Gulshan* the reputation as one of the most beautiful books ever produced.[59]

The Nelson-Atkins *Gulshan* folios demonstrate how an imperial Mughal *muraqqa*, or album, was organized. Each page is double-sided, with one side showcasing a central pictorial work, usually a painting or tinted drawing; on the opposite side, the composition frames a central calligraphy. The folios in the album would have been carefully arranged to create two-page spreads that alternated between calligraphic

and figural subjects. The roughly 150 surviving folios of the *Gulshan Album* incorporate various works of art into new compositions. They include masterfully crafted verses written by famous Persian calligraphers, old and newly commissioned paintings and drawings created in India and Persia, and paintings, drawings, and engravings created in Europe. These works are carefully mounted and framed with multiple borders featuring illumination and calligraphy.

In *The Poet and the Prince,* a young nobleman and his attendant meet with a bearded poet or sage in the shade of cypress and flowering trees, on the banks of a babbling stream. The style of the poet's turban and long-sleeved robe identify him as Persian, and his gesture with an open book suggests that he is imparting wisdom to the young prince. This Indian painting depicts a common subject found in Persian literature and art: the prince or ruler who seeks knowledge from a *sufi* mystic in the wilderness. The refined style of the work demonstrates some of the great innovations found in Indian painting in the late sixteenth century. At this time, Mughal artists began to incorporate naturalism and observation in the treatment of figures and space, as evident in the light modeling of these men and the setting of a lush, slightly receding landscape. In the background, Persian-style rock formations based on Chinese landscape paintings and a European-inspired cityscape are silhouetted against a vivid late-afternoon sky, highlighted with wispy streaks of gold paint.

We see a different artistic approach in *A Buffalo Fighting a Lioness*, as vibrant, opaque colors and

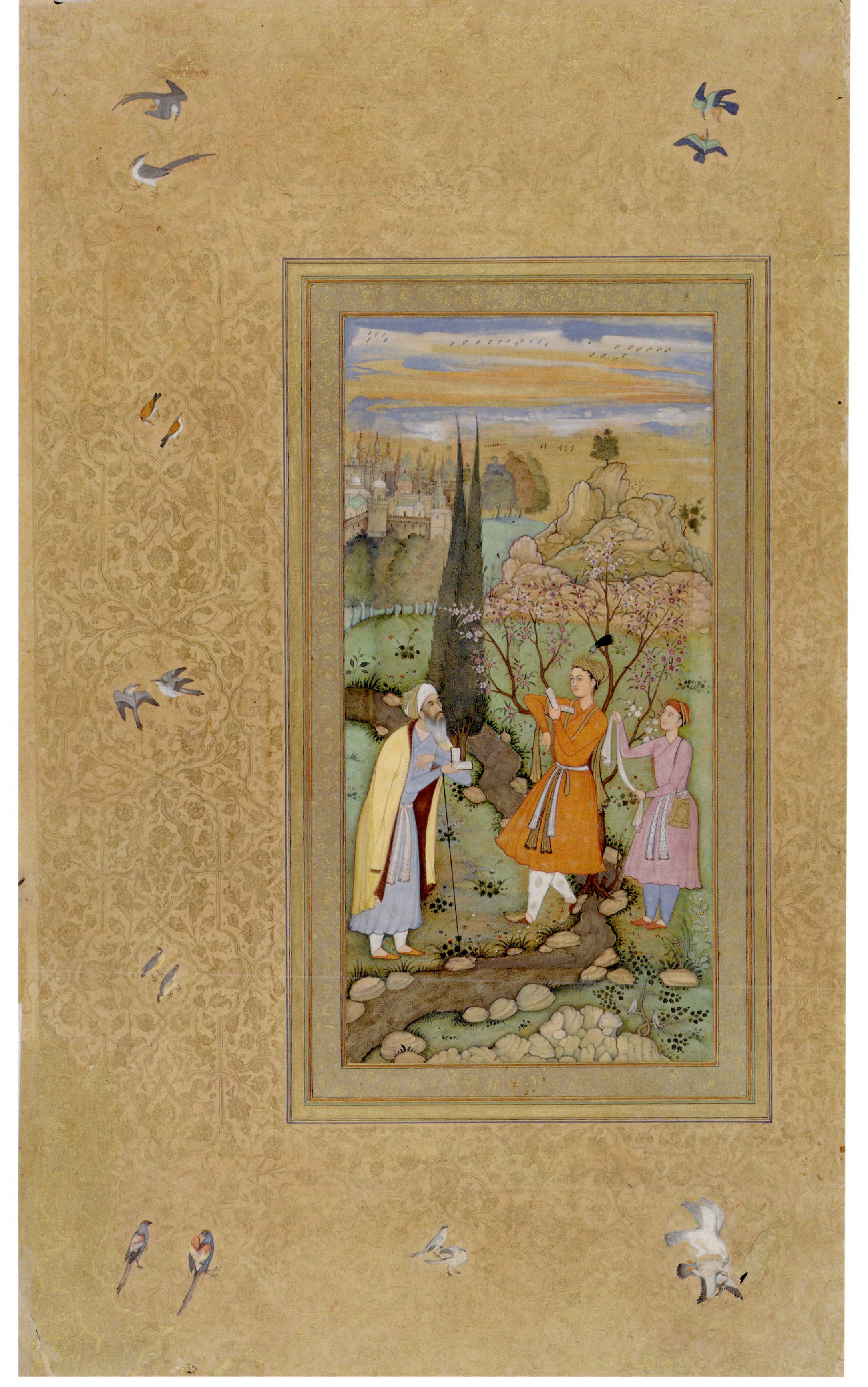

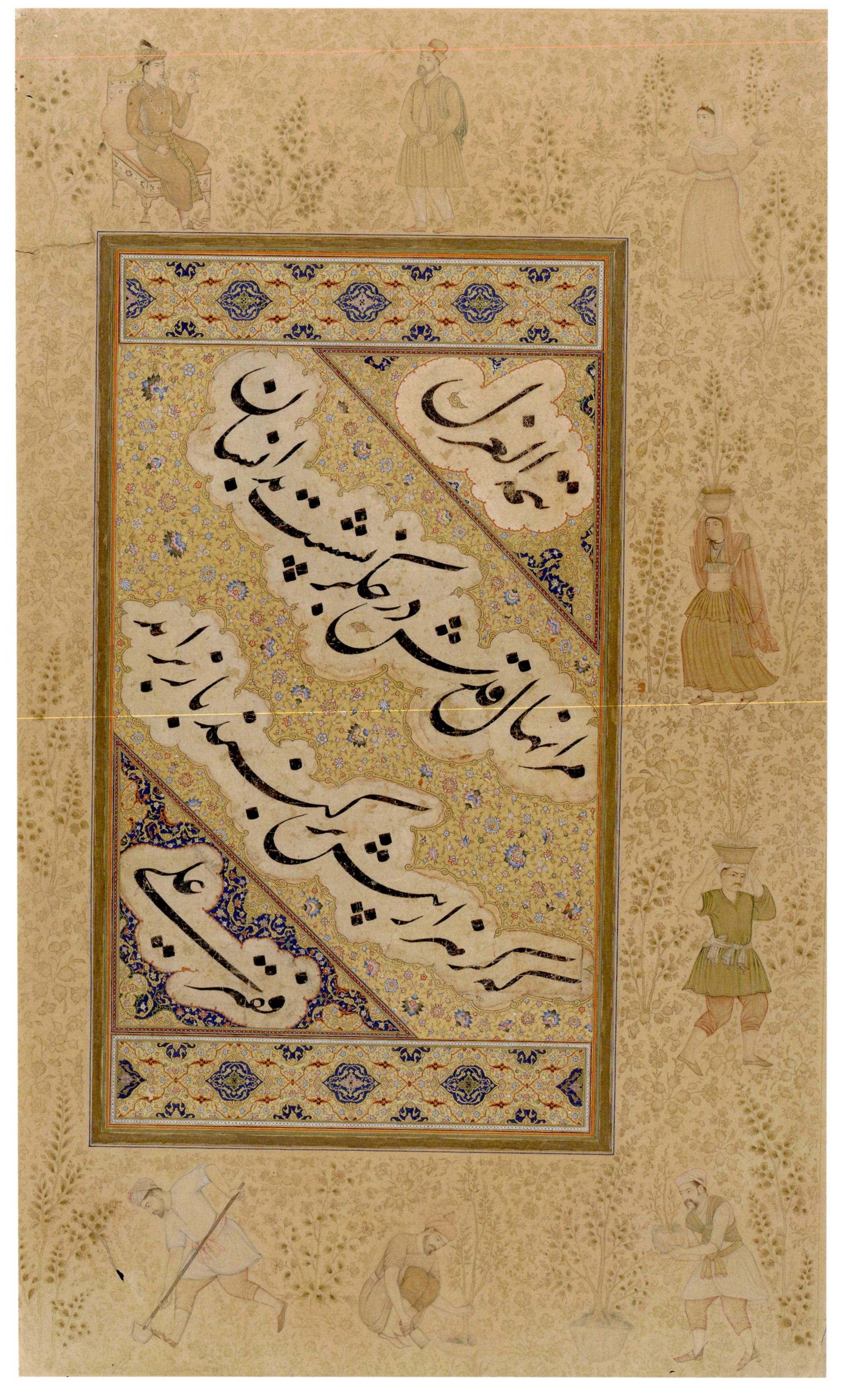

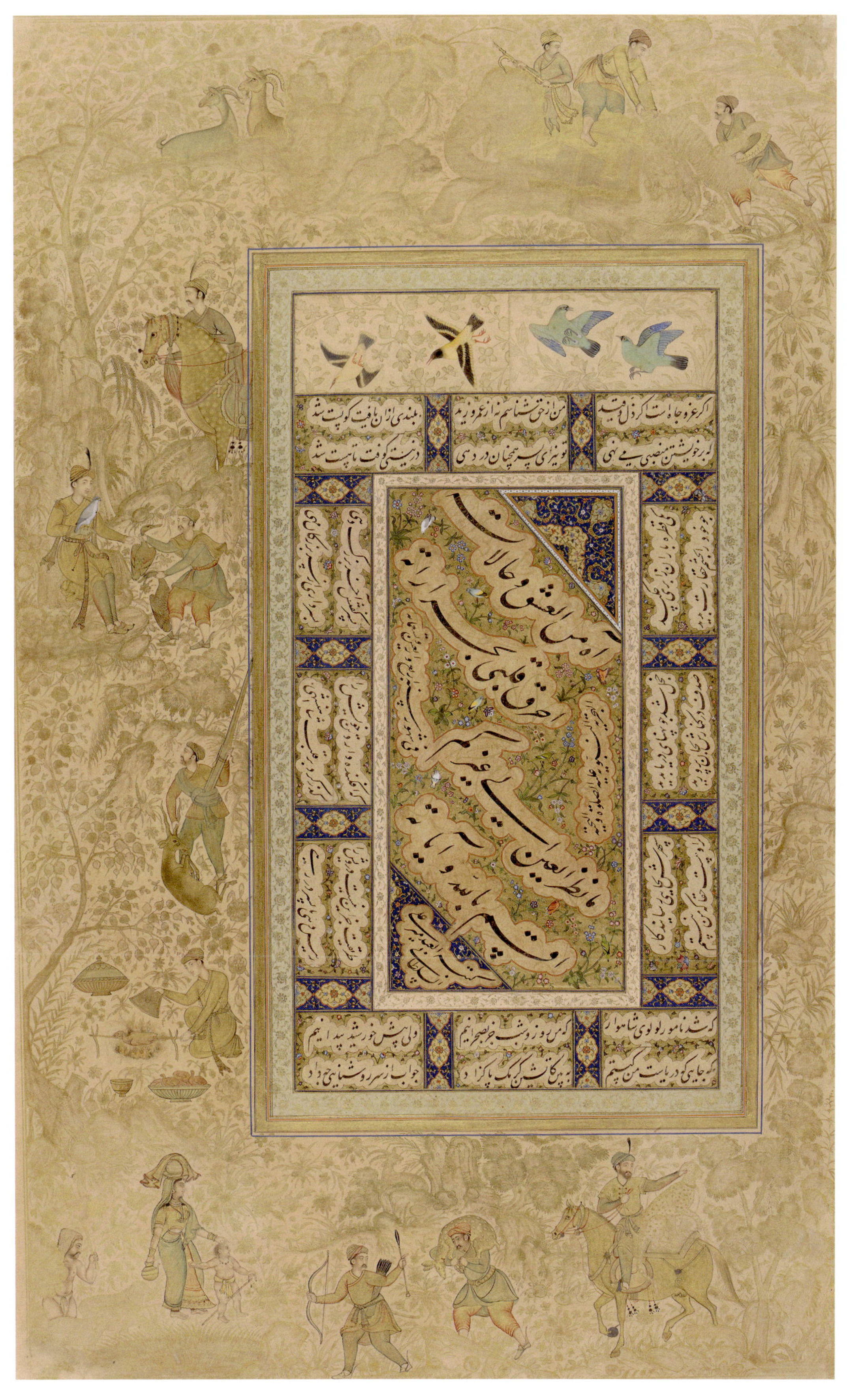

precise forms give way to transparent washes and loosely drawn outlines. This represents a popular art form that falls between a drawing and a painting, known as *nim qalam* (Persian for "half pen"). *Nim qalam* works were highly finished ink drawings that were enriched by the use of transparent washes and stippling, often in shades of brown and green, highlighted with touches of white or gold paint. Here, a rugged landscape, framed by craggy rocks, a mountain stream, and a large banyan tree, provides the setting for a violent scene of animal combat. This work depicts the climactic moment of a lion hunt, as a hunter on a trained buffalo gores an attacking lioness. The diagonal composition adds to the dynamism of the scene, as the buffalo lunges forward and hoists the big cat above its head, her claws extended. This bloody sport was described as a form of of hunting by Abul Fazl, the biographer of Emperor Akbar, Jahangir's father. Fazl states that the hunter rides on the back of a buffalo that is trained to quickly pick up the predatory animal and toss it with its horns. According to Fazl, "It is impossible to describe the excitement of this manner of hunting. . . . One does not know what to admire more, the courage of the rider, or his skill in standing firm on the slippery back of the buffalo."[60]

Some of the most striking imagery in the *Gulshan Album* is found in the densely painted outer borders of the folios. The borders of compositions that showcase paintings and drawings tend to depict animal imagery, landscapes, or floral designs in gold paint, often punctuated by brightly colored birds created with opaque watercolor. In contrast, the calligraphic pages are frequently framed in borders that feature multiple depictions of the human figure, set against lightly rendered scenery or vegetation. These figures, painted in either translucent or opaque watercolor, represent a variety of subjects, and include depictions of daily activities and Christian imagery derived from European art. In several instances in the *Gulshan Album*, the treatment of the outer borders relate directly to the content featured in the center of the folio. For example, in the folio containing the tinted drawing of *A Buffalo Fighting a Lioness,* the theme of an animal combat set in a remote landscape is echoed by the lush scenery and predatory activities featured in the pale blue borders that frame the drawing.

The calligraphic compositions in the Nelson-Atkins folios are as distinguished as the paintings they adjoin. Calligraphy is traditionally regarded as the highest art form in the Islamic world, valued far more than painting or drawing. Mir Ali al-Katib al-Sultani of Herat (ca. 1476–1556), creator of the calligraphies on both folios, was the undisputed master of his age. Large calligraphic compositions like these were produced in royal workshops to be purchased and enjoyed as singular objects in their own right. They contain passages of Persian poetry, often quotations from larger works, written in the elegant, slanted *nasta'liq* script.

The passage backing the painting of *The Poet and the Prince* reads:

> The sapling of his stature took such root in my
> heart
> That if you were to uproot it one thousand
> times, it would still grow.
> [signed] Faqir (the poor) Ali"

The poetry on the reverse of *A Buffalo Fighting a Lioness* reads:

> Alas, from love and circumstances
> My heart is burning with fever
> My eye hasn't looked at anything but you
> I swear by God and his signs.
> [signed] The servant Mir Ali Sultani wrote this
> In the months of the year 944 [1537–38]
> Of the *hijra* of the Prophet, upon him be
> prayers"[61]

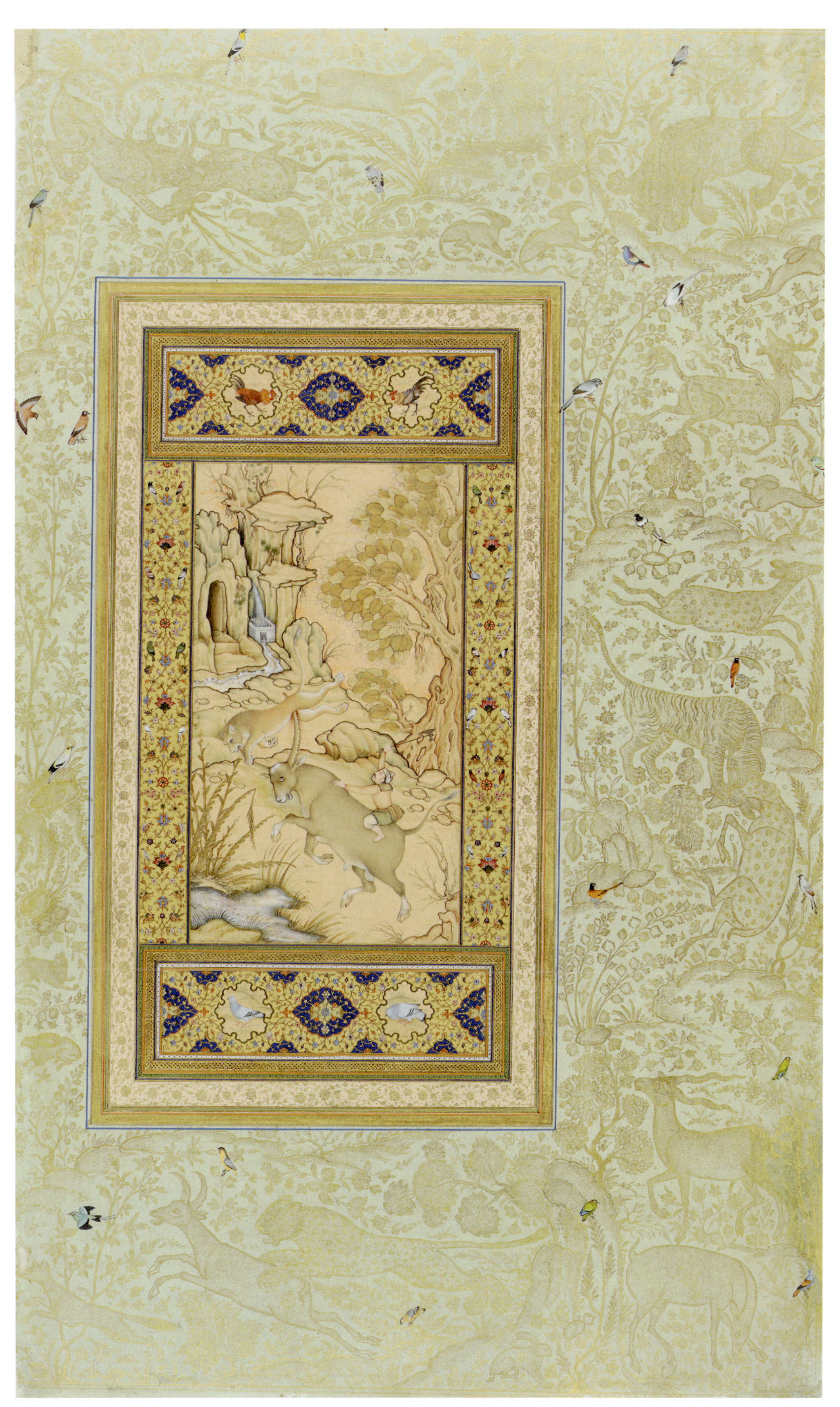

She was waiting for him on a private palace balcony overlooking a grove of mango trees heavy with fruit and a gently flowing river. A luxurious bed was prepared with round bolsters and gold-brocaded textiles. A green carpet with designs of blossoms and curling vines lay beneath. She was bejeweled and dressed in a translucent green bodice, gold- and pink-patterned silks, and a transparent *odhni,* or headscarf, framing her face—she was beautiful.

He was late.

The story depicted here is an illustration of the *Ramakali Ragini,* which is one of the subjects found in the *Ragamala,* or Garland of Musical Modes. The *Ragamala* began as a collection of musical modes or melodies, thirty-six or forty-two in number, that were performed at specific seasons and times of the year and were intended to evoke a particular mood or emotional response. Throughout the medieval period, the *Ragamala* evolved into a multiplatform artistic theme that included poetry and paintings exploring subjects inspired by the music. As the poems and paintings developed within a wider environment of courtly arts, they adopted courtly themes, and much of the content of *Ragamala* poetry and painting is focused on romantic relationships and the emotions they evoke. The multiplatform *Ragamala* was intimately connected with the Indian concept of *Rasa,* an ancient aesthetic theory devoted to the emotional and psychological responses provoked through artistic experiences.

In the story of the *Ramakali Ragini,* the male lover has arrived late because of a tryst with another woman. His beloved receives him angrily as he touches her feet, pleading for forgiveness. However, the woman in the Nelson-Atkins painting is not depicted as a sorrowful victim in this relationship. Note how she appears to push down her kneeling lover's head as both his hands reach toward her foot, the most polluted part of the human body in Indian culture. With a coy glance over her shoulder, she has forced her errant lover to humble himself. To her left, a dark-skinned woman,

perhaps her handmaid and confidante, witnesses the scene from behind a railing.

Further observation of detail and compositional strategy reveals the superior artistry of this painting. Though the forms are rendered with contour lines, notice the soft modeling of the figures, buildings, and rocks, giving them a sense of mass. The landscape is richly detailed; each individual petal-shaped leaf is drawn in a veritable sea of lush foliage, ranging from acidic sap green to terre verte. Beyond the silver river, an ascetic's retreat lies nestled between the rocky banks and a white fortress. Its inhabitants include ten *yogi*s, a *yogini,* and a pair of dogs. In the center of the group, a young acolyte kneels before an older, bearded ascetic with prayerbeads, perhaps his *guru,* or the abbot of the community.

The artist of the *Ramakali Ragini* has used the repetition of forms and planes to great effect. He has drawn multiple shapes along the same diagonal plane, giving a sense of spatial recession and unifying the composition. This is evident in the forward tip of the heads of the two women in the foreground, echoed by the placement of the bolster cushion, the bedrail, the fall of the hem of the man's robes, the spandrel bridge, and the postures of the *yogini* and kneeling *yogi* in the background.

While this folio would have once been part of a complete set of the *Ragamala,* likely including thirty-six illustrations, only five folios from this set are currently known. Four were acquired by the Nelson-Atkins in 1931, and a fifth resided in a private American collection until 2011.[62] The set was created in the early eighteenth century in one of the courts of the Deccan, the wide central plateau that occupies much of southern India. This region supported many dynasties, Hindu and Muslim, and the style of these paintings suggest that they were created either in the sultanates of Hyderabad or, as recently proposed, in the Bidar.[63] The remaining Nelson-Atkins folios depict *Dhanasri Ragini;* a woman making a drawing or gazing upon an image of her absent

lover, *Paraj Ragini;* a woman waiting for her lover as female musicians perform a song of reunion; and *Asavari Ragini,* a woman in the wilderness communing with snakes.

From his study of the five known paintings from this series, art historian Mark Zebrowski has proposed that the hands of three different artists were involved in their production.[64] While all four of the Nelson-Atkins paintings share certain qualities, such as their scale, color palette, settings, and textile patterning, the illustrations of *Dhanasri, Paraj,* and *Asavari Ragini* are similar in style. They depict barely modeled figures set in sparsely detailed landscapes. Their colors are bold, their forms are flat, and the overall use of line is hard-edged, creating a sense of rocklike stillness. These three paintings may even be the work of one artist, but it is a different artist than the one who created *Ramkali Ragini,* who seemed to take delight in rendering every stipple and brushstroke in this lively and intricate scene.

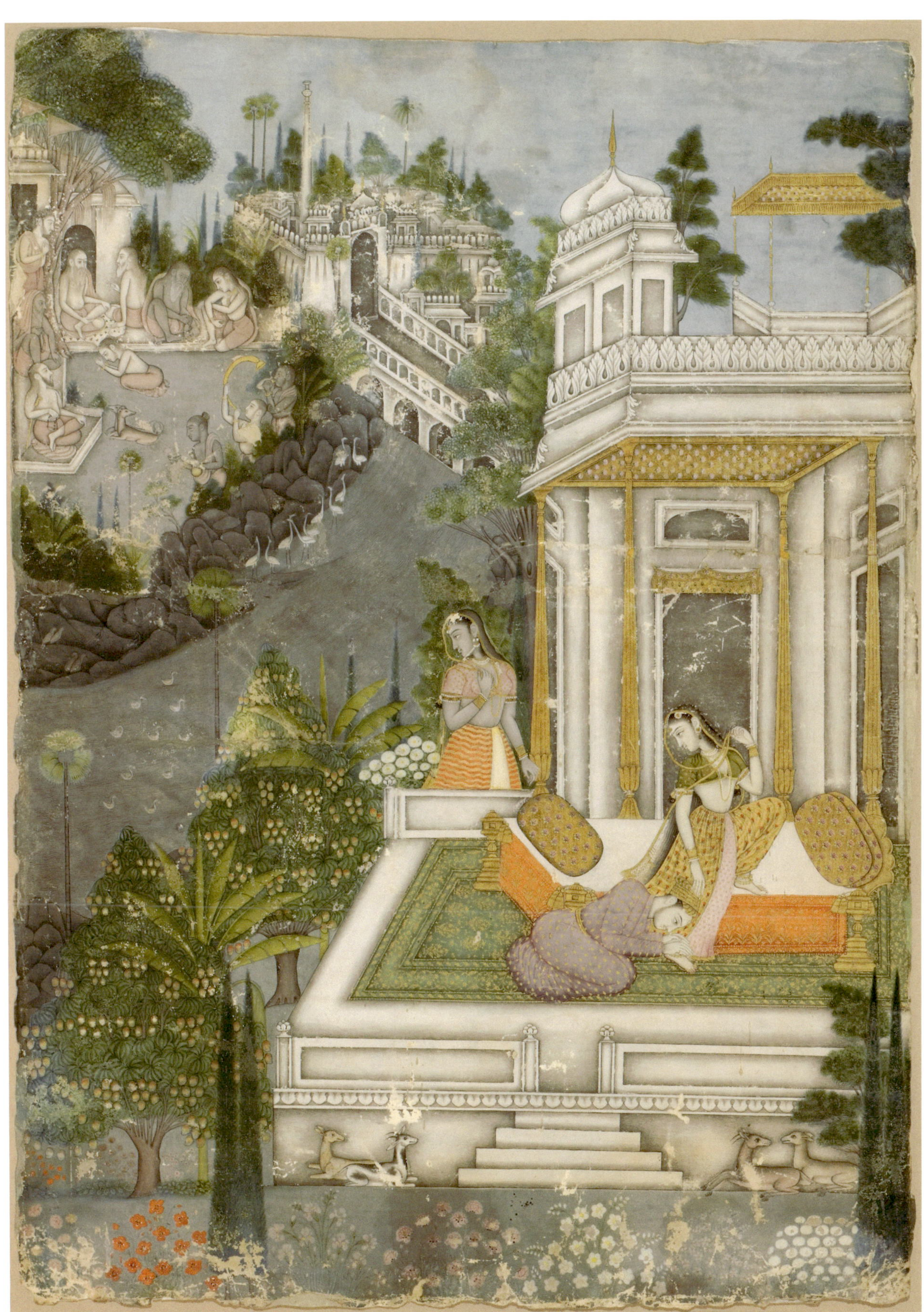

Ramakali Ragini

First quarter of the 18th century
India, Hyderabad or Bidar
Asaf Jahi period (1713–1948)
Opaque watercolor and gold on paper
13 × 9⅜ inches (33.02 × 23.8 cm)
PURCHASE: William Rockhill Nelson
Trust, 31-131/9

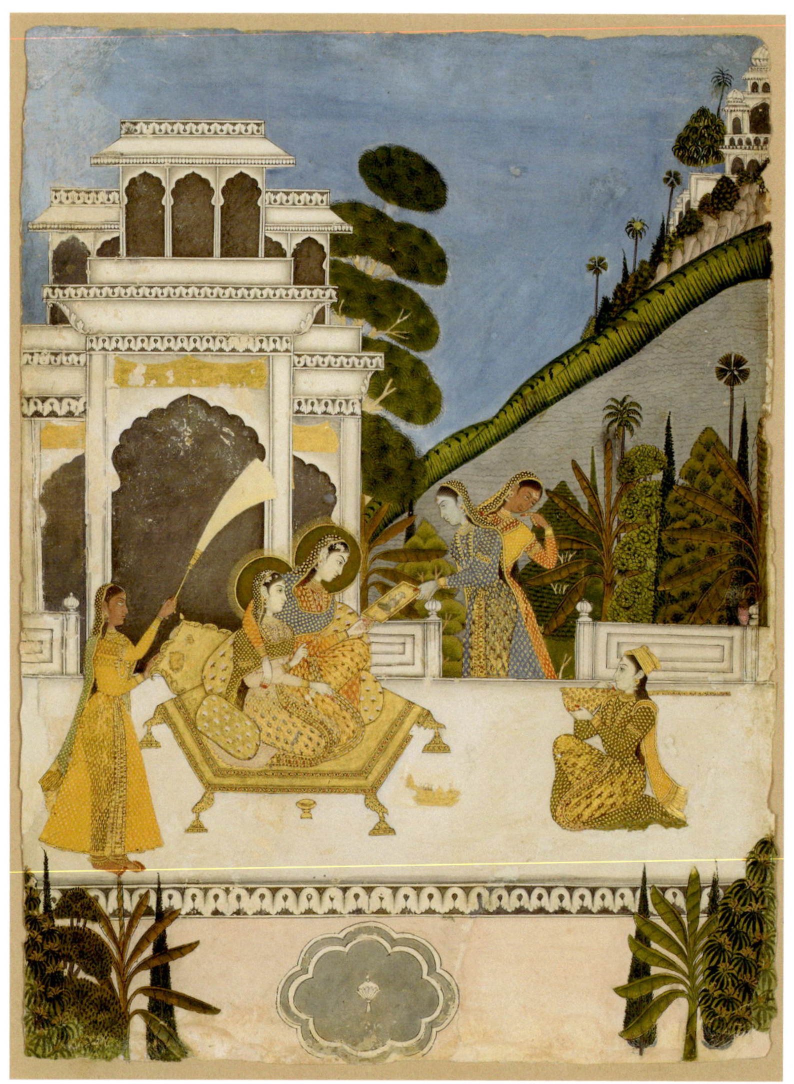

Dhanasri Ragini

First quarter of the 18th century
India, Hyderabad or Bidar
Asaf Jahi period (1713–1948)
Opaque watercolor and gold on paper
12⅜ × 9⅛ inches (31.43 × 23.19 cm)
PURCHASE: William Rockhill Nelson Trust, 31-131/7

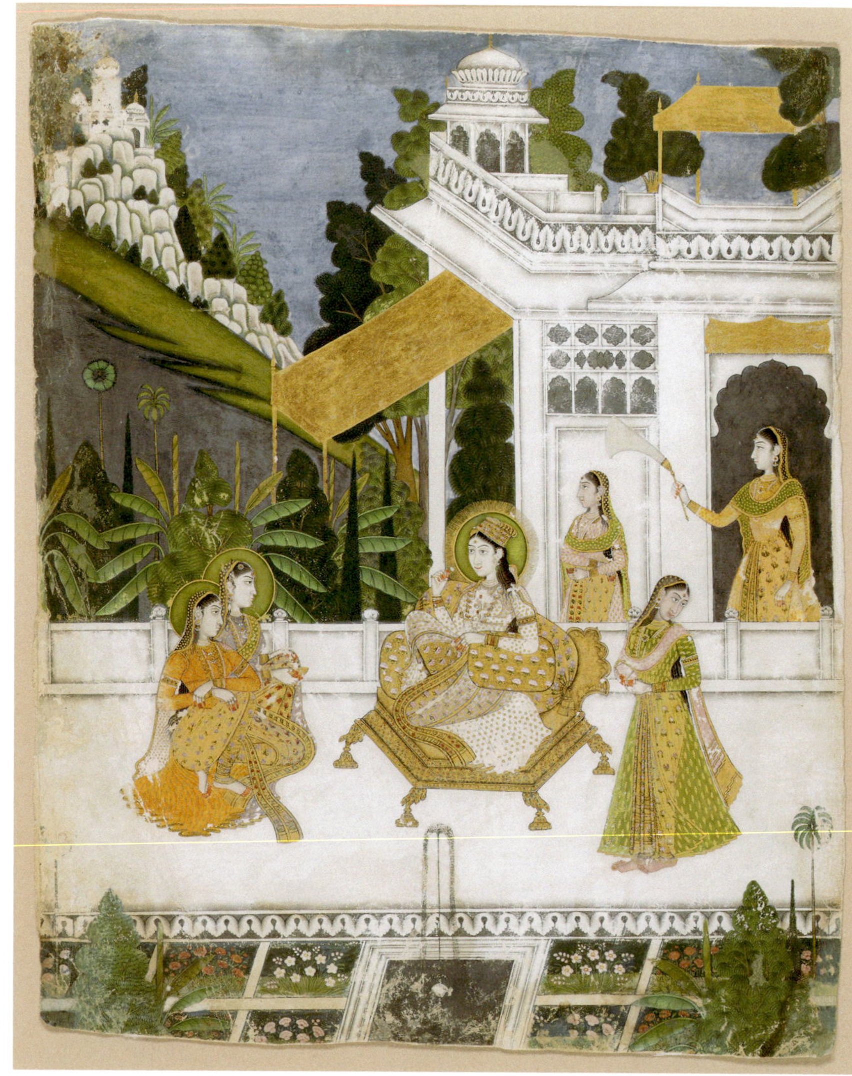

Paraj Ragini

First quarter of the 18th century
India, Hyderabad or Bidar
Asaf Jahi period (1713–1948)
Opaque watercolor and gold on paper
11¾ × 9½ inches (29.85 × 24.13 cm)
PURCHASE: William Rockhill Nelson Trust, 31-131/10

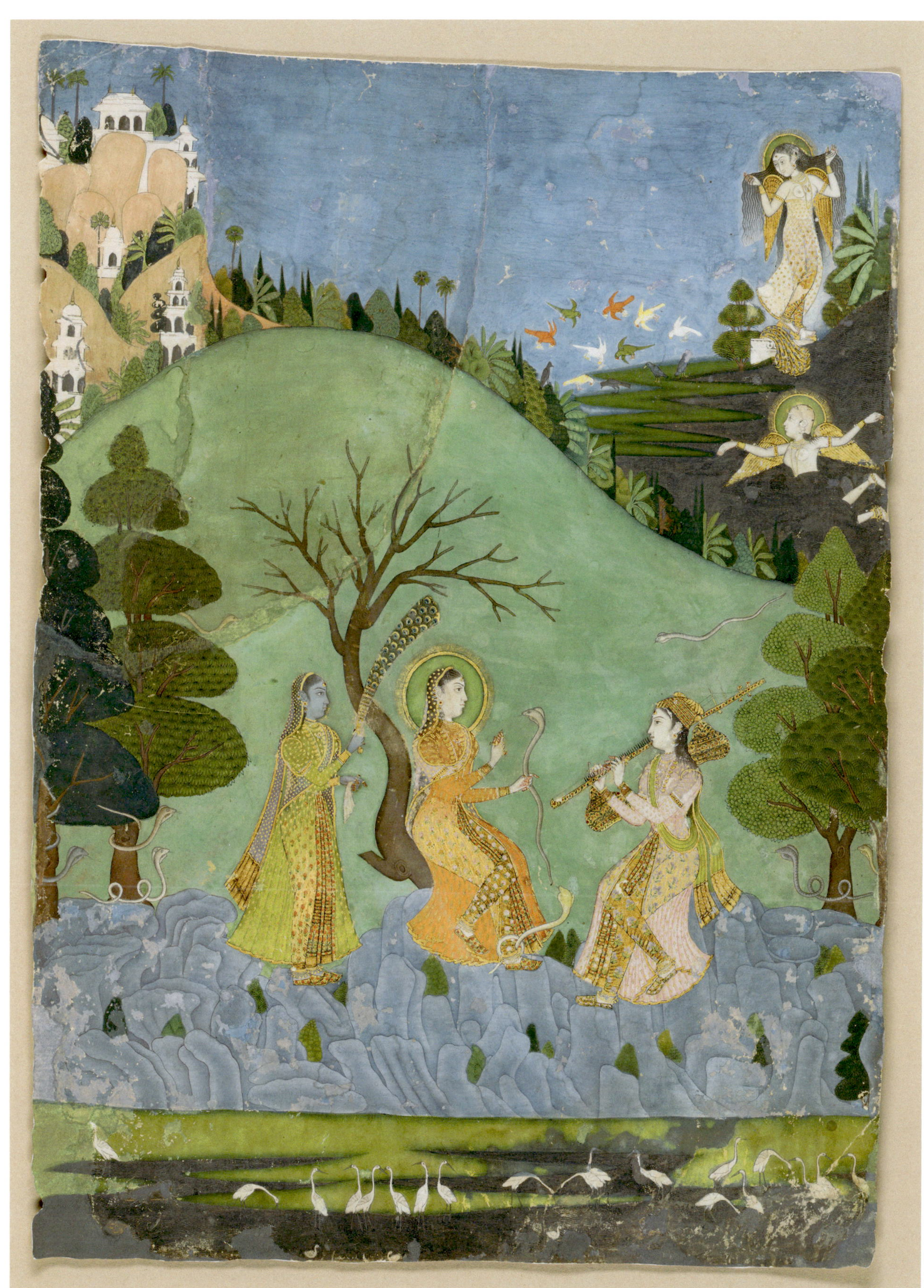

Asavari Ragini

First quarter of the 18th century
India, Hyderabad or Bidar
Asaf Jahi period (1713–1948)
Opaque watercolor and gold on paper
12⅞ × 9⅜ inches (32.70 × 23.81 cm)
purchase: William Rockhill Nelson
Trust, 31-131/11

 Coffered Ceiling and Doors from a Hindu Temple

and Sculptures and Columns from a Temple Cart

18th century
India, Tamil Nadu
Nayaka period (1565–1739)
Teak and Mahwa wood
Overall: 300³⁄₁₆ × 192⅛ inches (763 × 488 cm)
PURCHASE: William Rockhill Nelson Trust, 33-297

Entering a grand temple complex in southern India is a transformative experience. One moves through a series of walled enclosures, multiple courtyards, and pillared halls and rooms, engaging with myriad deities before encountering the main shrine at the heart of the temple. The wooden Temple Room now at the Nelson-Atkins evokes that experience, even though its components come from different structures.

The wooden coffered ceiling and doorways appear to have belonged to the same temple room and are stylistically similar to eighteenth-century carvings from Tamil Nadu. The ceiling features over 126 square coffers that display individualized carved flowers, essentially creating a grand lotus ceiling. The ceiling is girded by a frieze of 128 individual reliefs featuring different Hindu deities. The sculptures of the frieze are similar in shape and scale to the registers of figures that are sometimes depicted in elaborate temple carts from southern India. While the origin of the frieze sculpture is unclear, these similarities led former Nelson-Atkins curator Dorothy Fickle to question whether these sculptures were original to the room or whether they were acquired from temple carts.[65]

The richly carved doors have multiple registers of vegetal motifs depicted in their jambs, while the lintels each present three registers of floral and animal imagery. Unique iconographic features include the female figures—likely representing *yakshis*—grasping tree branches, on the outer jambs; the overflowing vase in the center of the lintel of the east doorway; and the goose flanked by elephants at the center of the lintel of the south doorway.

The ornately carved inset pillars that give the appearance of supporting columns are certainly not original to the temple room, but are manufactured in the form of the projecting struts found on southern Indian temple carts. Like the frieze sculptures, the struts reveal that cart components were sold with the rest of the room components. Indeed, the bold projecting sculptures depicting rearing horses and *vyala* with riders are reminiscent of the elaborately carved pillars found in temple halls in southern India. However, these struts terminate with a bulbous projection shaped like a closed lotus bud above the figural carving, making it clear they were not intended to bear weight. These disparate components were recombined to create an immersive period-room that has been in place in the museum since its opening in 1933. Now known as the "Indian Temple Room," this evocative assemblage of beautiful woodcarving is one of the galleries most beloved by visitors to the museum.

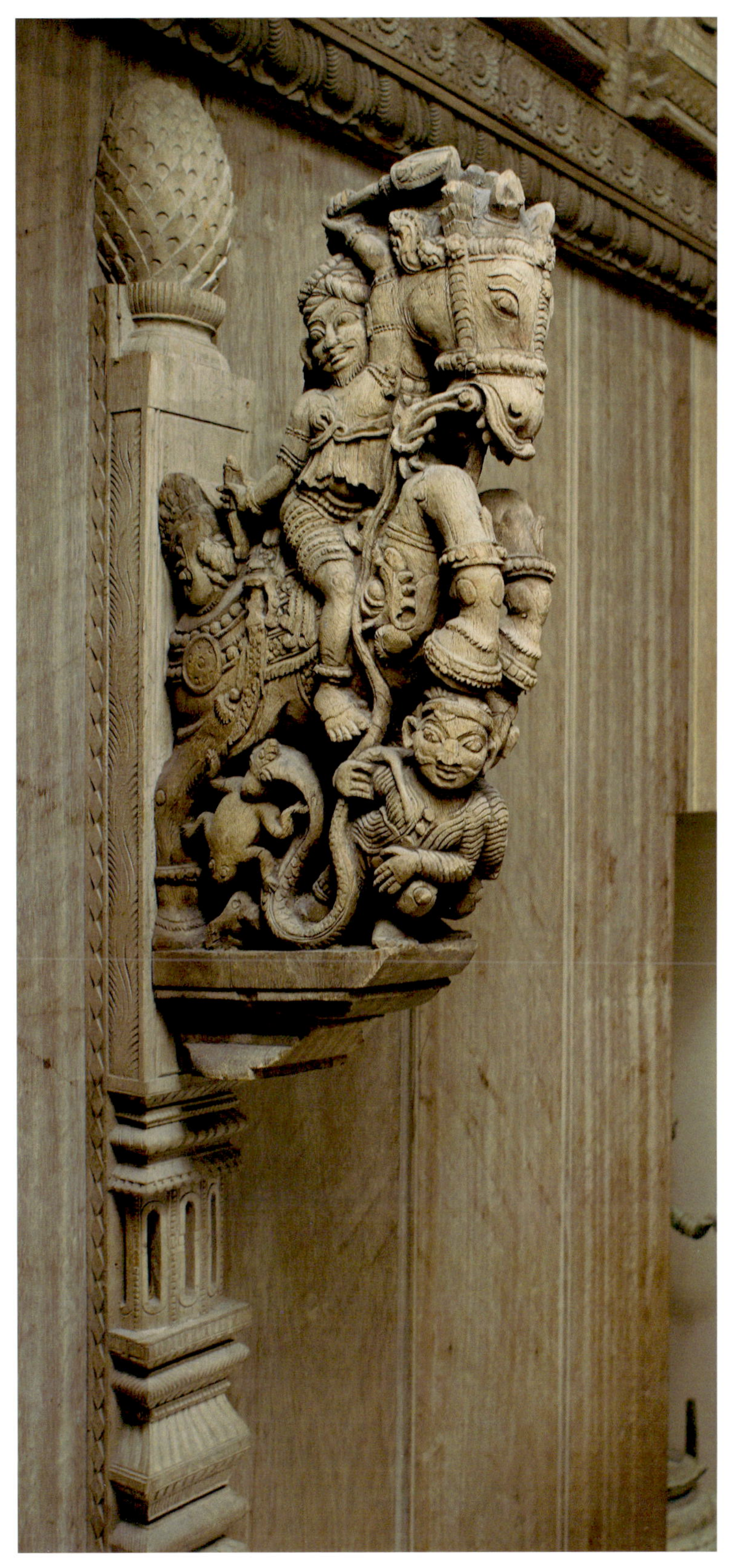

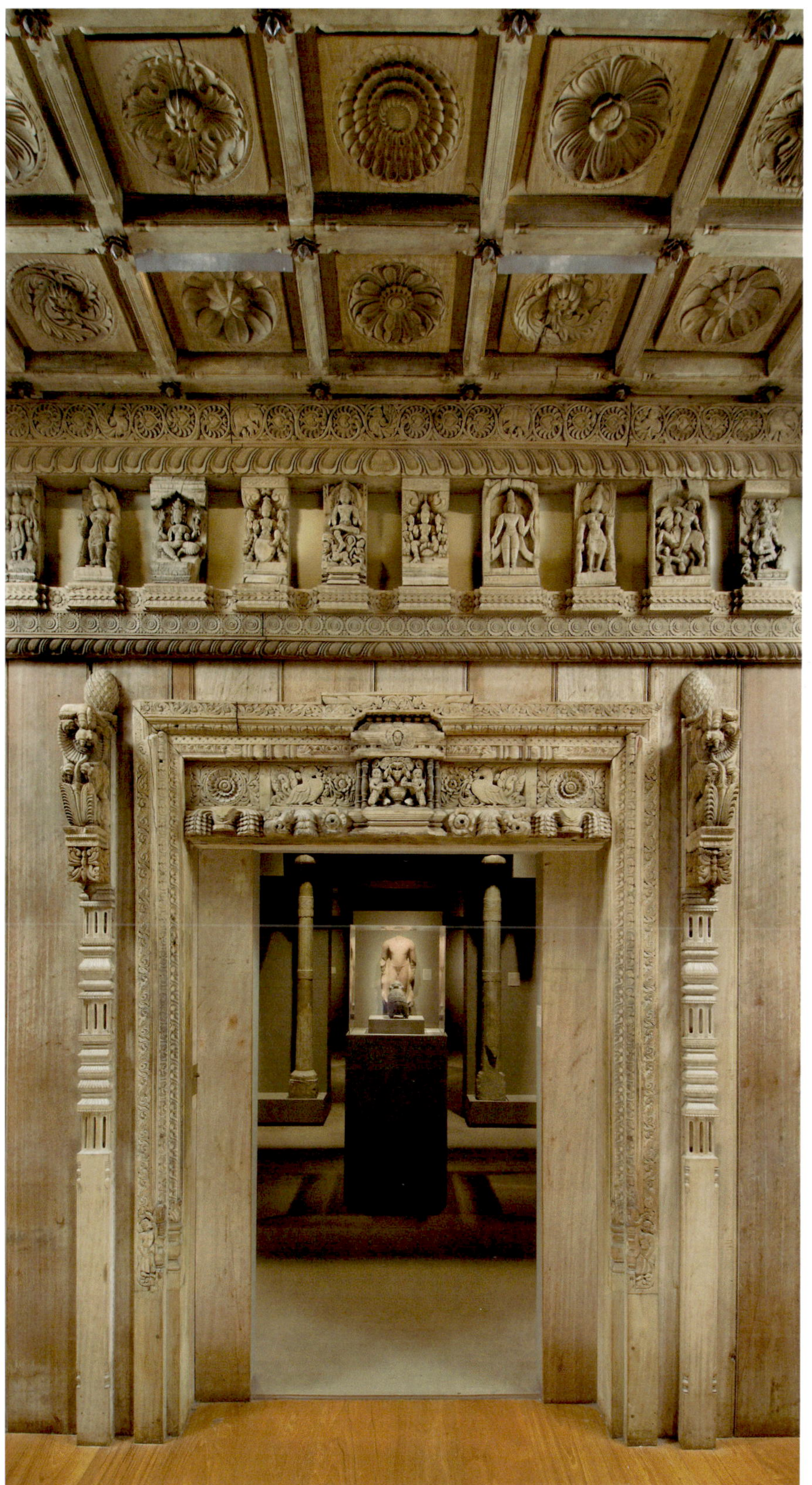

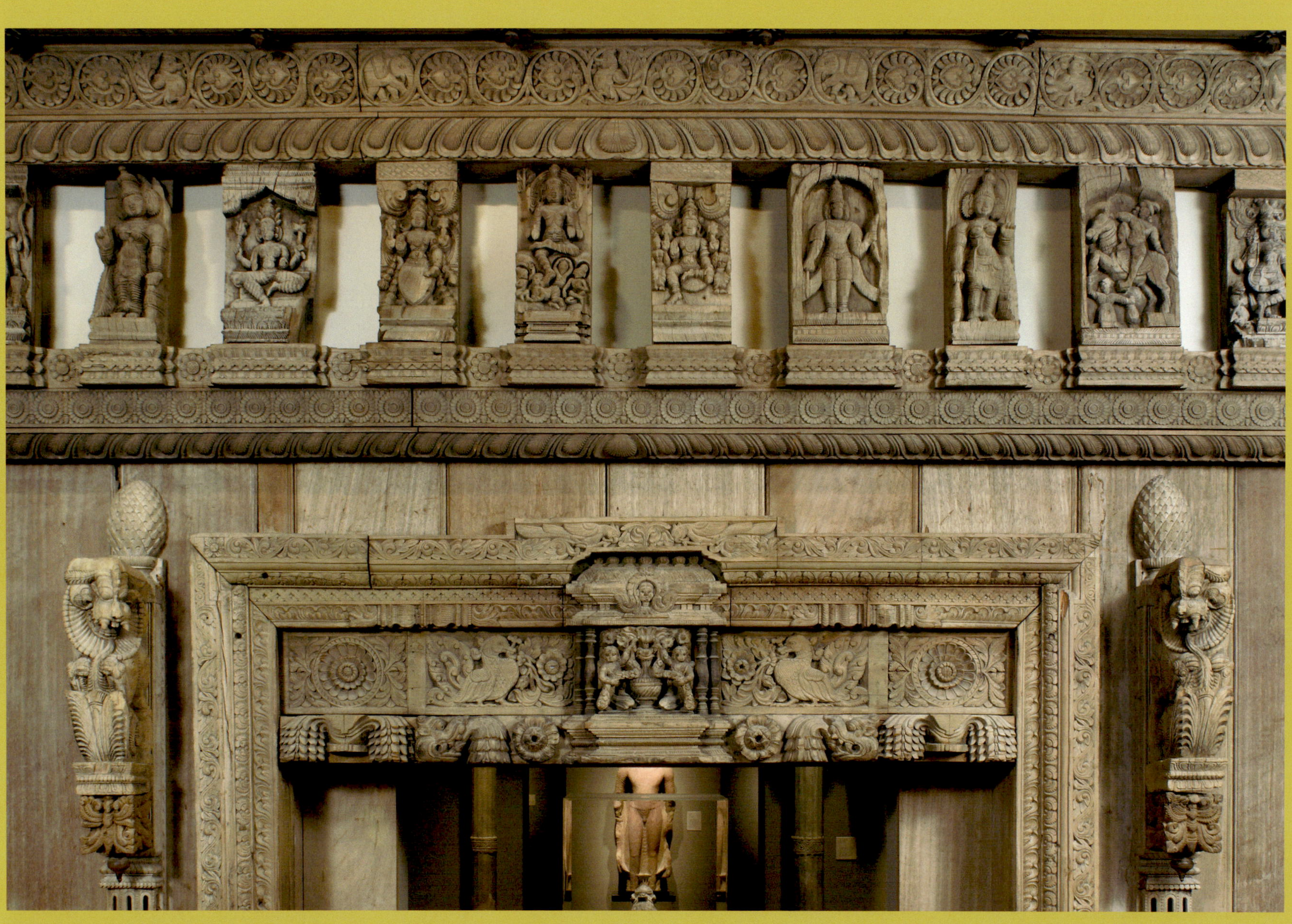

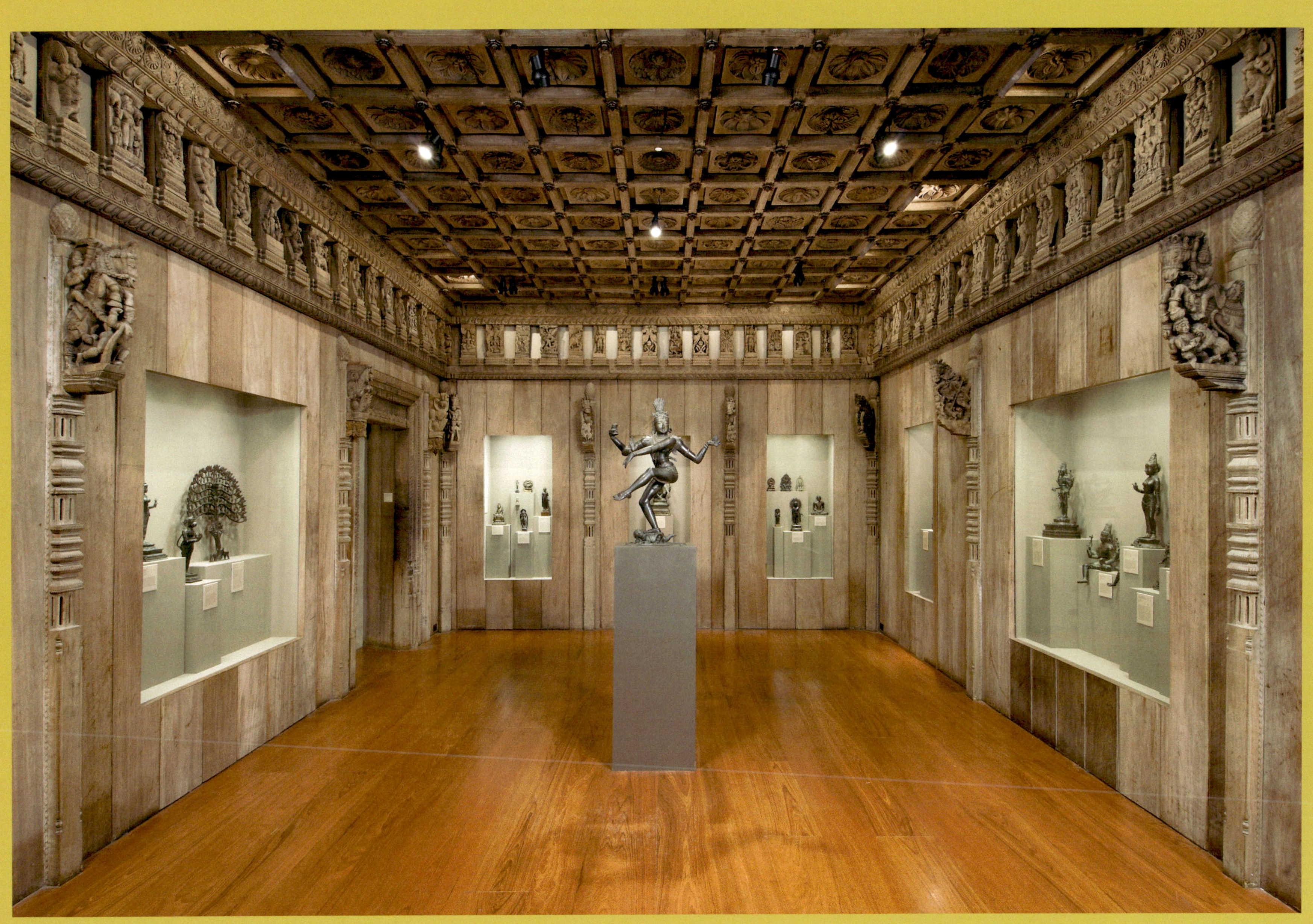

35 | *Krishna's Victory over Aghasura*

Early 18th century
India, Mewar (Udaipur or Nathadwara)
Sisodia dynasty (1326–1949)
Opaque watercolor on paper
Image: 9¾ × 15⅝ inches (24.77 × 39.69 cm)
PURCHASE: William Rockhill Nelson Trust, 60-34

The Hindu god Krishna battled many demons while he lived among the cowherding villagers of Gokula. One of his most memorable encounters was with the great demon Aghasura, which is depicted in wonderful detail in this inventive and fantastical painting. The story of Aghasura is recounted in several sources, most famously in the *Bhagavata Purana*, a Sanskrit chronicle of Krishna stories, which was circulated widely throughout India and is frequently illustrated in Indian paintings. In this telling, Kamsa, the king of the *asura* (demons), asks Agha to kill Krishna, who has previously slain other demons, including Agha's siblings, who had failed at this task. Aghasura takes the form of a gigantic serpent several miles long, and lies in wait in the countryside, mouth agape, pretending to be a cave. Krishna's companions and their herds approach Aghasura and unknowingly enter his mouth. Krishna realizes the danger his friends are in and enters Aghasura's mouth to save them. Once inside the serpent, Krishna's body rapidly grows in size, suffocating the monster. As the serpent takes his final breath, the demon tries frantically to escape the dying body and bursts out through the top of the creature's head. Krishna catches Agha and slays him, while the herdsmen and their cattle escape through the opening in the serpent's head.

A block of text on the verso of the Nelson-Atkins painting is translated below. Written in Marwari, a local dialect, it provides a very close translation of the original passage from the *Bhagavata Purana*. The painting was likely created as part of an album that illustrated scenes of Krishna, which made the canonical stories accessible in the vernacular language.

Shri Krishna sat down in the [demon's] mouth and increased his size. Aghasura's long breaths ceased. Whence he became restless and his life-force escaped with the wind. Gopal emerged from the top of [Aghasura's] head along with the young boys and the calves. Appearing before his friends, he revived them through the heat of his wonderful apparition. By the effulgence of Aghasura, he [Putana's brother] was purified and merged in the Lord."[66]

Aghasura's demise is vividly illustrated in the Nelson-Atkins painting. The drama is set against an indigo sky, flecked with hundreds of tiny stars. Figures appear to float in space, rather than being bound to a ground plain. This stagelike scene removes the story from the physical setting of the pastoral landscapes of Mathura and places it in a cosmic arena, emphasizing the mythic nature of the events. The story is told as a continuous narrative, beginning with Krishna and a companion entering the scene from the right of the composition. The blue-skinned god reappears, this time crouching precariously inside Aghasura's mouth. Krishna's victory inside the serpent is evident from its ruptured head, from which three villagers and a calf emerge. Following the arch of the demon's body, the eye is led to the bottom left of the composition, where a group of seven cowherders and three animals have tumbled to the ground and make their way across the bottom of the scene.

The style of the painting demonstrates the boldness and creativity of the Mewar School of painting in the eighteenth century. Its style is characterized by the use of flat forms and is filled with vivid hues. The color palette of dark blue, deep red, saffron, and acidic green is found in numerous Mewar paintings, and is put to especially fine effect here. The figures are drawn with dark contour lines and are presented in profile, as is common in Indian painting from the

Rajput schools. These figures display a body type and proportionality common to Mewar paintings of the period, which feature wide-hipped figures with squat legs, round heads, straight noses that continue the profile of the forehead, and small chins. Aghasura also adheres to a Mewar template. His fat, curving body with wide-open jaws and curled-up snout is similar in shape to a painting of the same scene dated to the late eighteenth century in the collection of the National Gallery of Victoria.[67] The similarities between the rendering of Aghasura and the figures are so strong in these two paintings that it is likely that they came from the same workshop, even the same hand. The Vaishnavite subject matter of the Nelson-Atkins painting is also common to the Greater Mewar School. Numerous albums featuring stories associated with Krishna were created both in Udaipur and in the nearby pilgrimage center of Nathadwara, where the cult of Krishna was venerated through the image of Shri Nathji. Nathadwara developed its own painting school, which was supported by the vast number of pilgrims who came to Nathadwara to worship at the shrine of Shri Nathji. This school developed as a branch of the Mewar School and bears many of the same stylistic features; it is also notable for its innovative imagery.

Wherever in Mewar the artist of the Nelson-Atkins painting was working, he was a master of his craft and was not afraid to experiment. This is evident in a number of details that enliven the painting, such as the carpet of stars created by flicking white, yellow, pink, and gray paint across the page, to the carefully painted drips of dark red blood pouring from the slain demon's skull, ear, eye, and nostril. Also notable are the animated poses of the figure and calf in the left corner of the painting, depicted in mid-air and falling to the ground, where another figure kneels and raises his hand, as if in thanks. Even the cows contribute to the effect of the narrative, as a loosely outlined

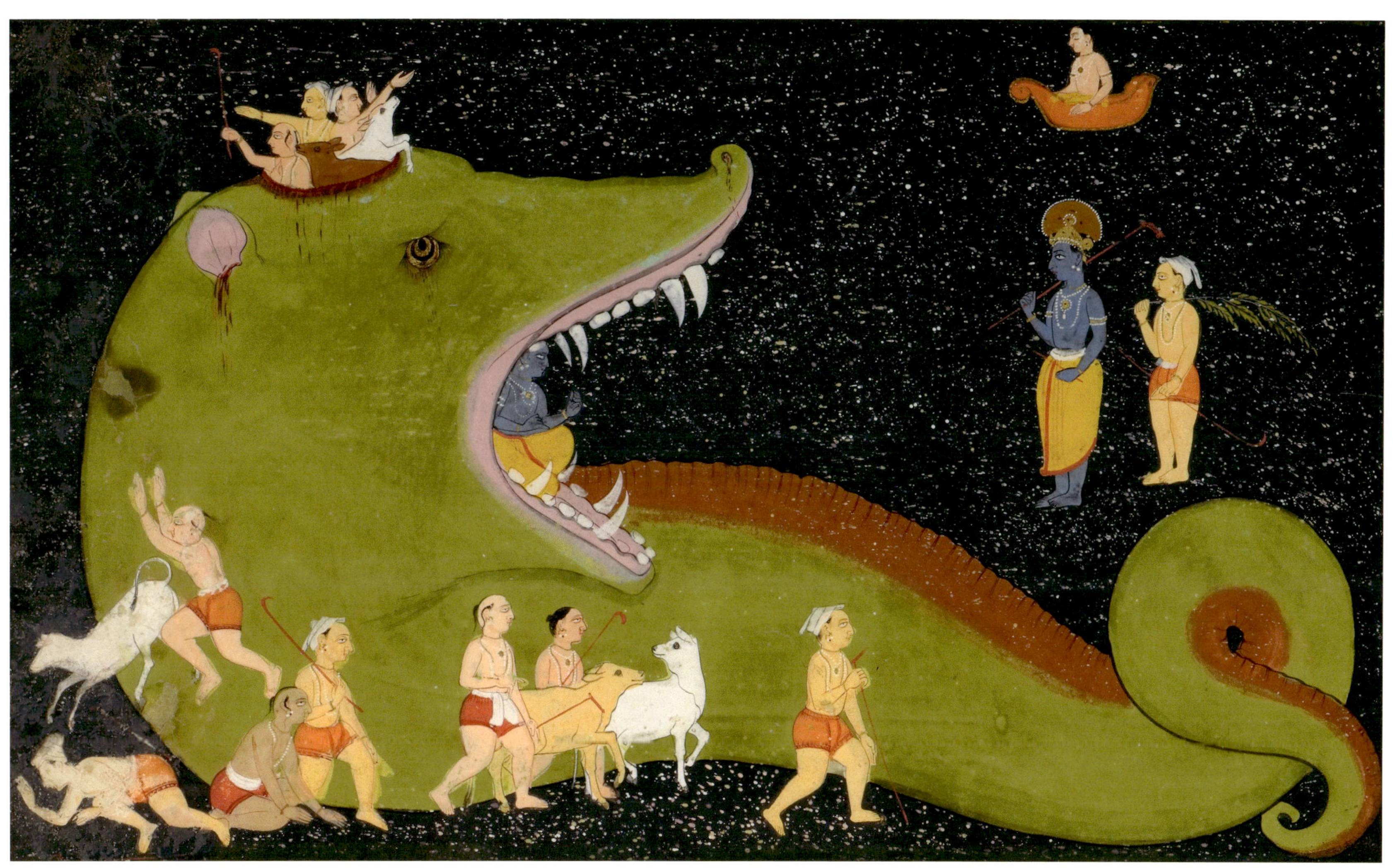

white bovine at the bottom of the scene turns back to look at his tawny companion, as if to say 'wasn't that incredible?' The most striking feature of the painting, however, is Aghasura himself. Though this painting is dedicated to Krishna, it is the serpentine demon that dominates the painting, his body stretching across the composition from the curve of his head in the upper left to his looping tail in the lower right. Aghasura is immense, terrifying, and inhuman. His gaping fanged mouth and cold golden eye evoke one of humankind's most primordial fears, the fear of being eaten. In the hands of a brilliant artist, this painting of Krishna's heroic battle against the reptilian Aghasura needs no translation.

ca. 1770–1800
India, Kashmir
Durrani dynasty (1747–1823)
Wool, double interlocked tapestry twill
61½ × 42 inches (156.21 × 106.68 cm)
PURCHASE: William Rockhill Nelson Trust, 35-299

This elegant and finely woven textile features an early-nineteenth-century elaboration on a decorative subject developed during the seventeenth century in Mughal India. The textile prominently depicts a lobed arch reminiscent of a *mihrab*, or prayer niche, and is composed in the format of a prayer carpet used for the Muslim practice of *salat*. However, this weaving is highly ornate and extremely delicate and was most likely intended to serve as a wall hanging rather than used on the ground for prayers.

A striking feature of the Nelson-Atkins textile is the way the arch, borders, and central field of the design are completely filled with dense and colorful clusters of floral imagery. This style of decoration, known as *millefleur*, is a Mughal design that developed during the seventeenth century; scholars, such as Dan Walker,[68] believe it was inspired by the imagery of European botanical prints. The abundant floral imagery is both decorative and symbolic. It evokes the idea of a lush paradisical garden, similar to other garden carpets. The earliest surviving and best known examples of the Indian *millefleur* design are found in Mughal carpets dating from the late seventeenth to early eighteenth century. These carpets were produced in the northern regions of the empire, in Kashmir or Lahore, and were created with local *pashmina* wool.

Kashmir was a major hub for textile production throughout Mughal history. It is known that Emperor Akbar (r. 1556–1605) favored a double-ply shawl he had had created in Kashmir, which quickly became an important item of fashion at the Mughal court. Indeed, the popularity of the shawls was so great during the rule of the Great Mughals that over 40,000 looms were reported to be working in Kashmir at the time.[69] Early Kashmiri shawls juxtaposed large open fields of flat color with borders or central medallions, as seen in *chandar*, or "moon" shawls, which featured small, tightly woven floral motifs that evolved into the curvaceous *boteh* seen in later examples. By the late eighteenth century, Kashmiri weavers were producing multicolored patterned cloth that was frequently filled with repeated floral motifs, often on a striped or checked ground.

It was in the fertile artistic environment of Kashmir that a kind of cross-pollination took place. The design favored in earlier court carpets was appropriated and refined in the Kashmiri workshops that created tapestry-weave *pashmina* textiles. This relationship is evident in a comparison of the Nelson-Atkins textile with a knotted-pile carpet from Kashmir in the *millefleur* design in the collection of The Metropolitan Museum of Art.[70] Dated to the second half of the eighteenth century, the Metropolitan's carpet provides a close template for the composition, forms, and color palette of the Nelson-Atkin's weaving. The Nelson-Atkins textile has an identical narrow lobed arch, a red central field densely filled with flowers springing from vases, and equally proportioned floral borders. Despite these similarities, subtle changes in design are visible in the weaving of the Nelson-Atkins example, such as the depiction of three vases rather than one, at the top, middle, and bottom of the central field, variations in the sizes and types of flower blossoms, which are quite small and uniform in the carpet, and the dominance of red throughout the weaving. Another *millefleur* weaving depicting a field with flowers emanating from two vases was published with a date of around 1770 attributed by Frank Ames in his volume *The Kashmir Shawl and its Indo-French Influence*.[71] A close comparison with this weaving reveals that the forms and motifs in the Nelson-Atkins textile are even bolder and more exuberant, suggesting that it is slightly later in date.

The Nelson-Atkins textile also presents a *tour de force* of technical accomplishment. This weaving was created using a local variation of the twill tapestry technique. Kashmiri weavers developed an unusual method of weaving the shawl cloth, known locally as *kani*, by setting warp threads in a diagonal orientation on the loom. The patterns were created from colored warp threads, each of which was wrapped around a bobbin in the shape of an eyeless wooden needle, called a *toji*. The threads were inserted in and out of the weave with the *toji*, which allowed for the creation of very detailed designs. A weaver would have used hundreds or more of *toji* to create a patterned textile. A European traveling in Kashmir in the 1820s reported that over three thousand *toji* were used in the creation of one highly detailed shawl.[72] Given the dexterity and attention to minute detail needed to weave these textiles, it is not surprising that each one could take around eighteen months to complete. The work that went into creating the Nelson-Atkins hanging is evident when one looks at the reverse side (detail on pages 102–103). Here we encounter a sea of brightly colored weft threads, including some that are loose and some that overlap and are reinserted into the weave. Each one represents a place where a *toji* was moved in and out of the textile by hand.

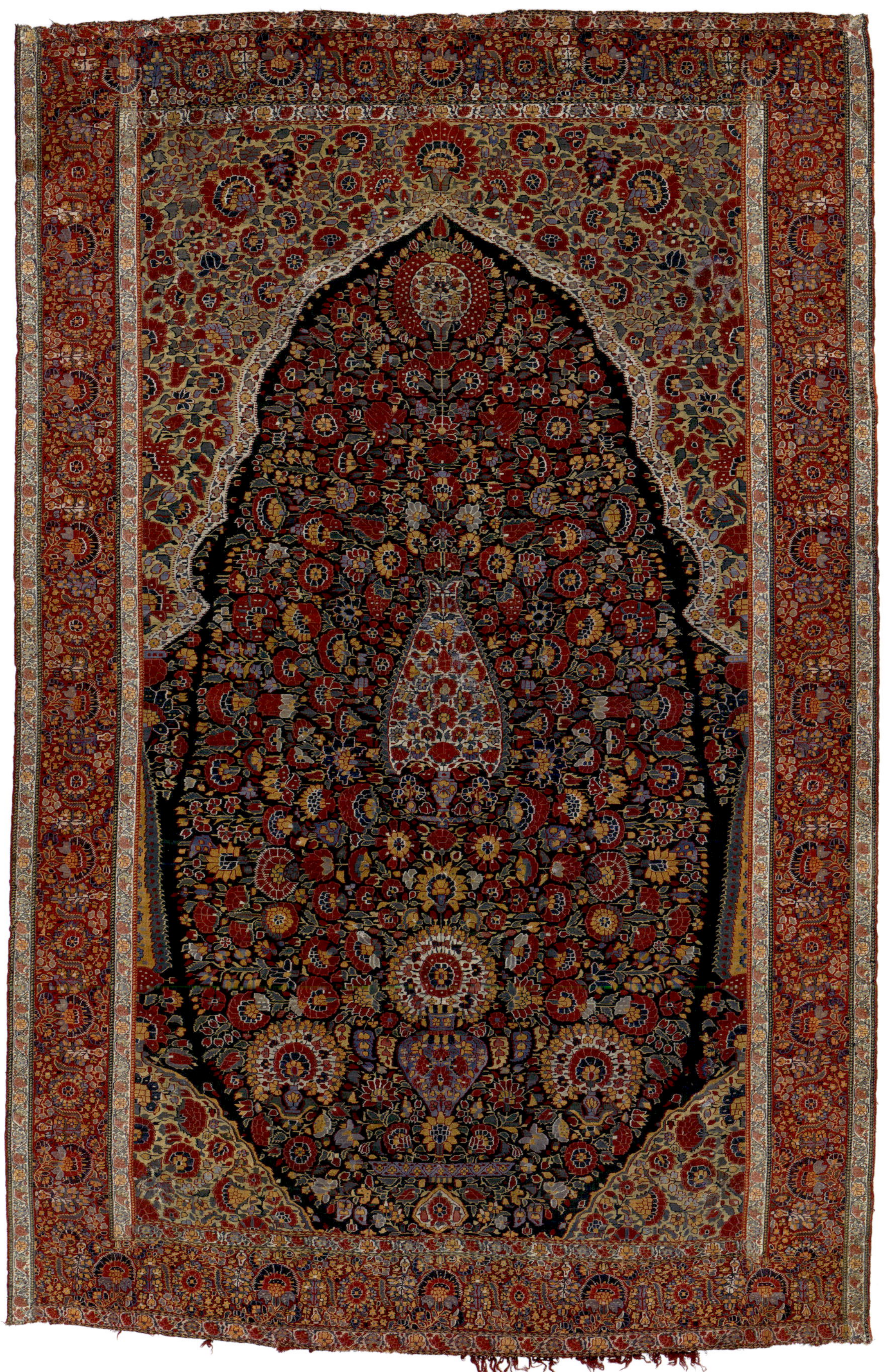

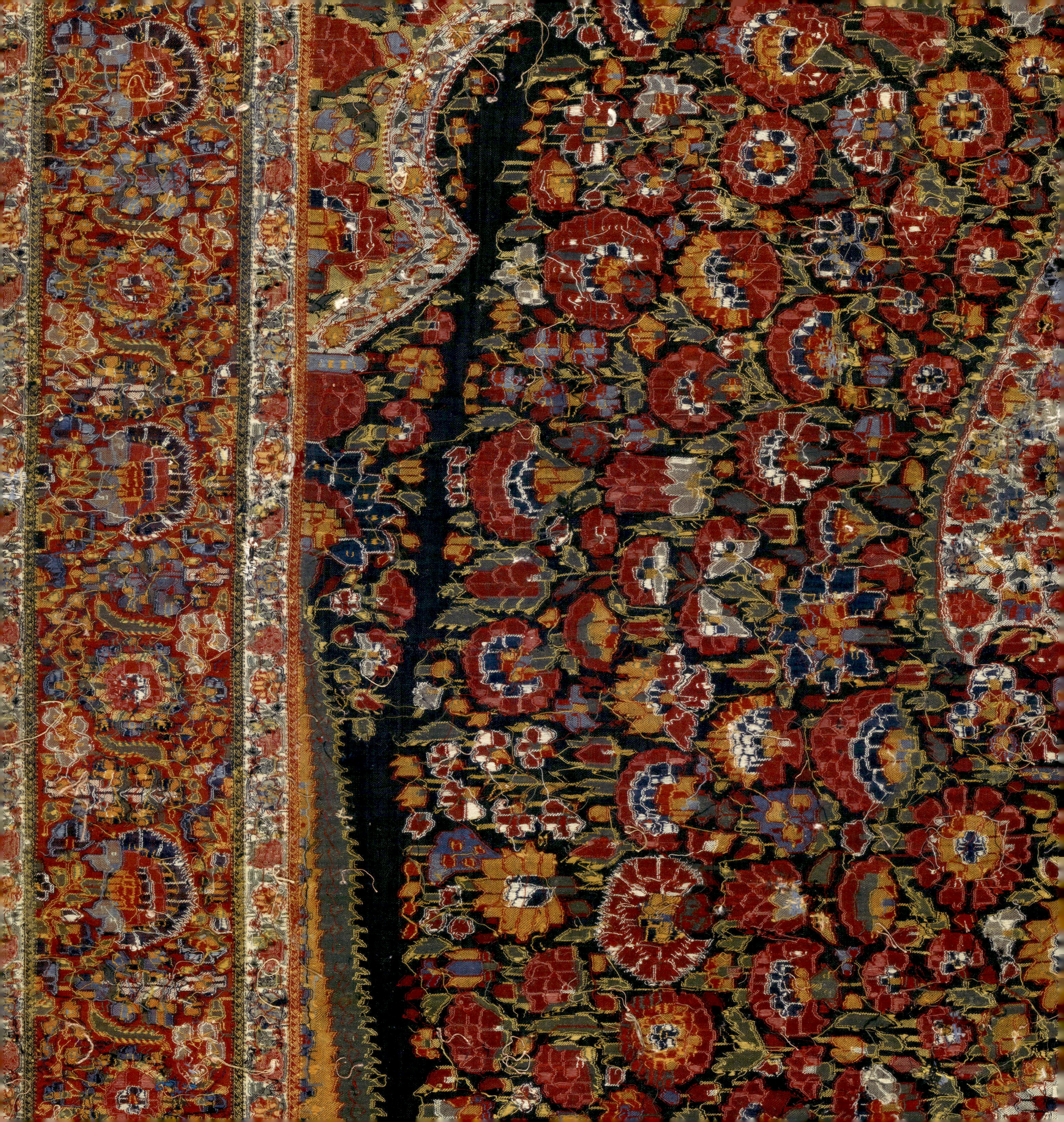

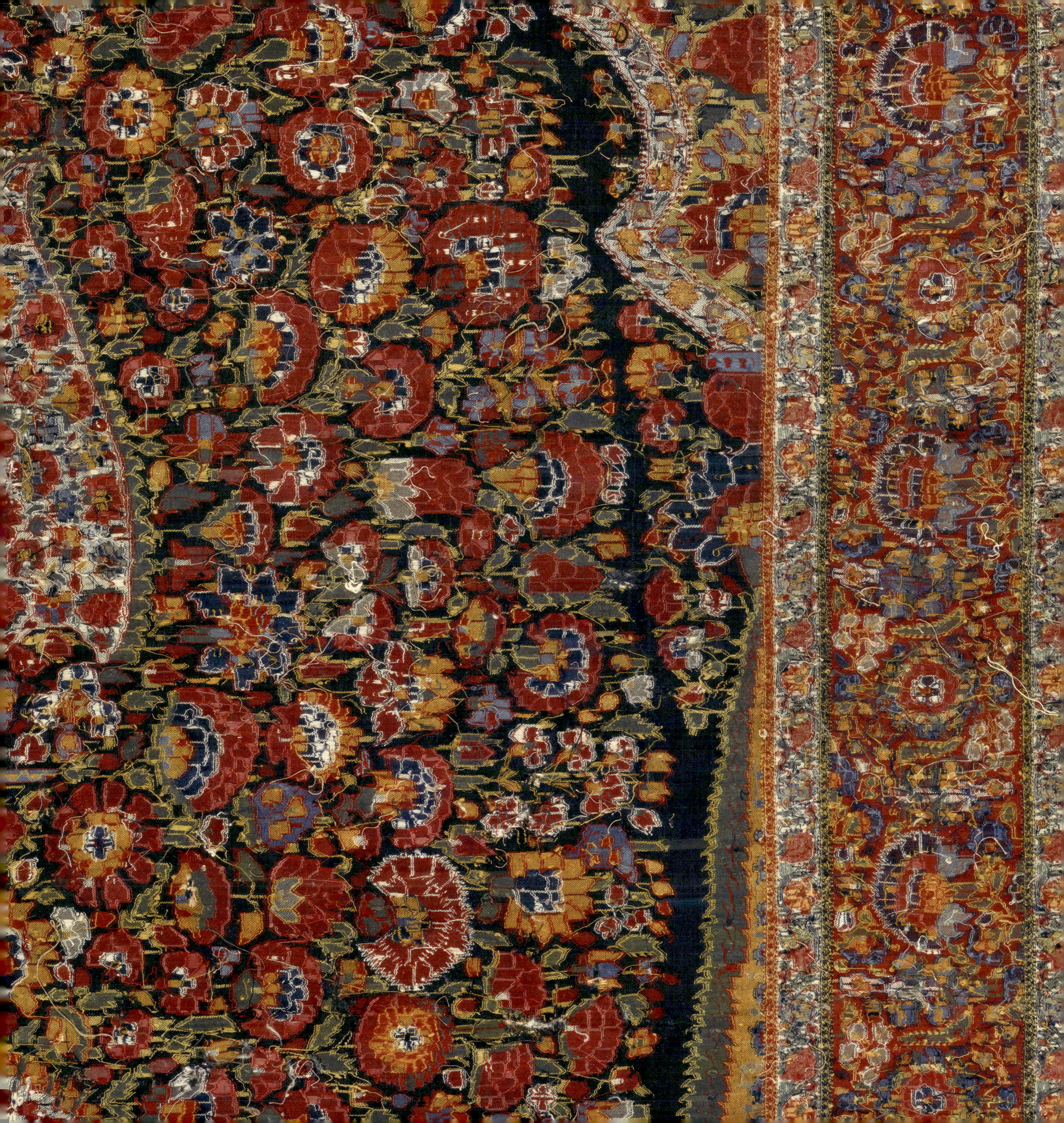

Dated 1911
India, Rajasthan, Dungarpur
Sisodia dynasty at Dungarpur (1358–1947)
Silver wrapped over wood, with velvet upholstery
PURCHASE: William Rockhill Nelson Trust through the
George H. and Elizabeth O. Davis Fund, 2013-10.1-2

The word maharaja *conjures up* images of elegant rulers in luxurious Indian palaces. The title is synonymous with wealth, opulence, and power. These qualities are evident in this pair of silver-clad thrones, which were created for the ruler of the Rajput kingdom of Dungarpur in the early twentieth century, the height of British colonial power in India. Their syncretic combination of Indian imagery and European forms demonstrates how Indian artists in the colonial era created new symbols of power using both traditional and foreign models.

The thrones are large, elaborately decorated Rococo-style chairs, nearly equal in size. Each chair is accompanied by a matching footrest. The royal chairs are further complemented by two objects of regalia, an umbrella (*chhatri*) and a fly-whisk (*chauri*). The thrones have wooden chair-frames wrapped in molded and carved silver. Their seats and backrests have tufted cushions upholstered in dark red velvet, which is now heavily worn. Each chair is covered with identical imagery, including depictions of Hindu deities, animals, and lush repeating floral designs. The backrest on the front of each throne features a prominent central lozenge with a raised relief depiction of Hanuman, the Monkey God, one of the most famous and heroic of Hindu deities, holding his mace in one hand and a bunch of grapes in the other. A roundel depicting the face of the sun sits above him, at the top of the seat back. Moving around the chairs to the back, one encounters a large central peacock with tail feathers fanned out, projecting from each of the seat backs in deeply molded relief. Above each peacock is another depiction of Hanuman and a small roundel featuring a gazelle. Perhaps the most striking features of the thrones are the elaborate sculpted lions that

form the legs of the thrones and footrests and support the armrests of each chair. These regal lions are wonderfully detailed and are cloaked in a repeating pattern of incised, curving stripes, combining their identity with the Indian tiger, also an emblem of power and royalty in South Asia. The striped lions stand with their mouths open, revealing a separate plate of inserted metal that forms each of their tongues.

The regalia that accompany the thrones appear to date roughly to the same era as the chairs. The *chhatri* consists of pale blue silk with silver embroidery and silver thread, suspended on a metal frame. The *chauri* has a gilt-silver handle that appears stylistically to date to the late nineteenth or early twentieth century. The silky, now yellowing, hair mounted on the handle comes from a horse or ox tail. These objects are symbols traditionally associated with Indian royalty and authority. The *chhatri* would have been placed above the head of a ruler or religious leader. A *chauri* is used to fan away insects from a political or religious leader, and has been depicted in the hands of attendants in sculptures dating back to the third century BCE.

These silver-clad thrones were created for the kingdom of Dungarpur, a small rural kingdom in southwest Rajasthan. The somewhat provincial style of the silverwork on the thrones suggests that they are of local manufacture. Indeed, there is a long history of silvermaking in the nearby city of Udaipur, capital of the Mewar kingdom. The king of Mewar, Maharana Fateh Singh, is illustrated in a handbook of the Delhi Durbar of 1911 seated on a very similar throne.[73] This suggests that the Mewar and Dungarpur thrones were commissioned from the same workshop, which may have been located in Udaipur itself.

The imagery found on the thrones is directly associated with the heraldry of the kingdom of Dungarpur. As a branch of the Sisodia Rajput family, which founded its own dynasty in 1170,[74] the kings of Dungarpur were believed to be part of a large group of royal families descended from the Sun. Thus, the disc bearing the face of Surya, the sun god, is part of

the Dungarpur kingdom's royal iconography. Other imagery found on the thrones relates to their specific familial and regional identities. The royal *achievement*, which includes the crest and its bearers, depicts a horned gazelle at its apex, while Hanuman resides in the center of the family crest. These European-style crests of the Indian royal families were developed only in 1877 for the Proclamation Durbar,[75] which supports an early-twentieth-century date for the thrones. The peacock that figures so prominently on the back of each chair is not found in the royal iconography of Dungarpur. It may allude to the Hindu god Krishna, with whom the kings may be associated, or more generally to the broader symbolism of the peacock as representing majesty, love, regeneration, and the coming of the life-giving monsoons.

While the imagery on the thrones derives from local sources, the shape and approach to the decoration of the thrones exemplify the hybrid nature of Indian art produced during the British Colonial era. The thrones are created to resemble grand European chairs and are accompanied by matching, almost baroque, footrests. Traditional Indian thrones were low benches upon which the ruler sat, perhaps supported by a small backboard and bolster cushions. Throughout the nineteenth century, royal houses in India adopted European-style chairs, replacing the low thrones used since ancient times. European elements in the decoration of the thrones also give evidence as to when they were created. Notice the way the royal symbols stand out against busy fields of low-relief floral decoration. Rather than depicting compositions where iconography and decoration are intertwined and fully integrated, the heraldic figures appear to float like a series of motifs upon an endless sea of petals and leaves. This accords with stylistic approaches to European decorative arts in the late nineteenth and early twentieth century.[76] Even the technique for molding the silver may date to this era, as the repetitive decoration looks as if it might have been rendered through stamp molding on a press.

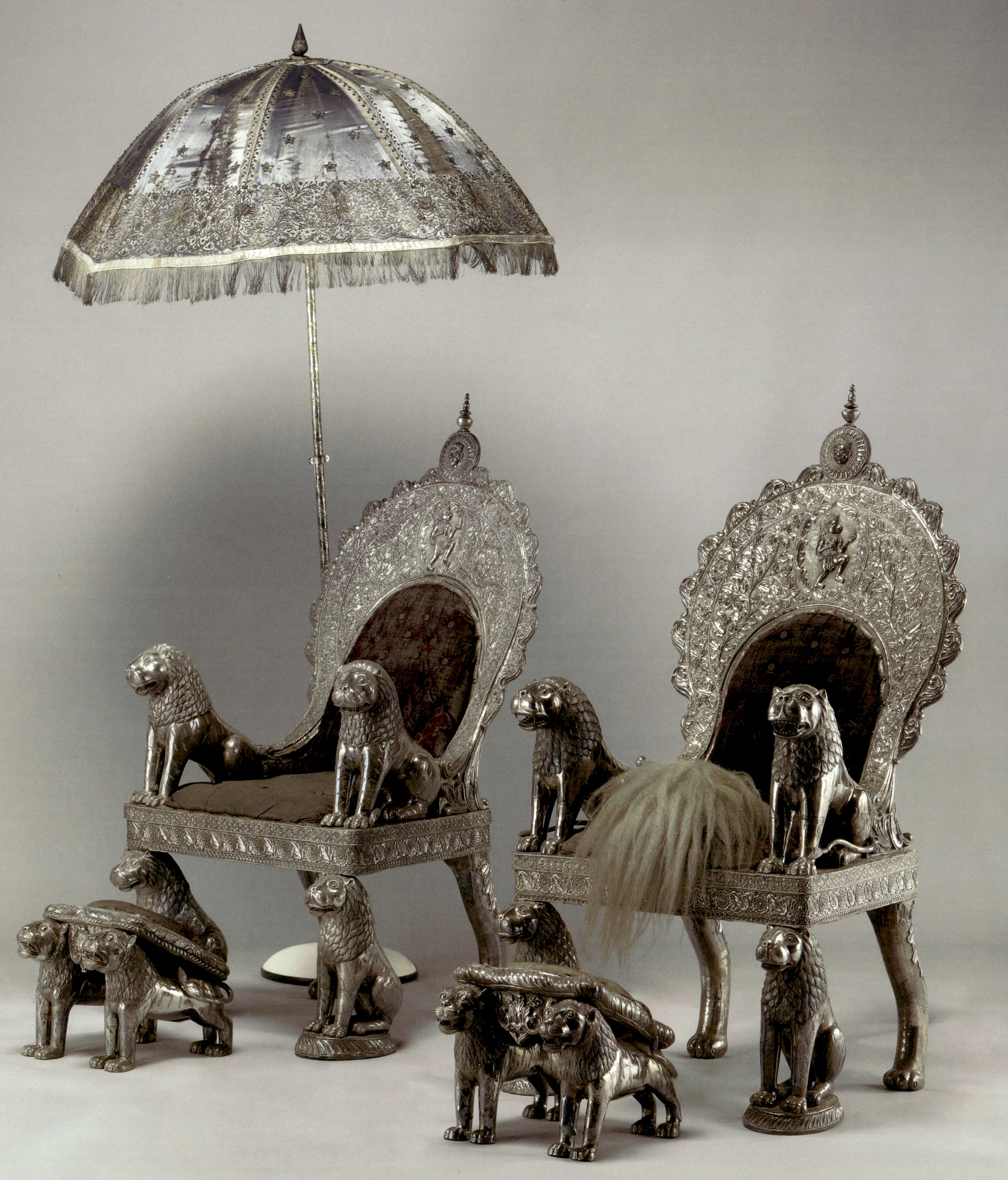

This technique was commonly used in European art only in the nineteenth century and imported to India later.

Two key questions regarding the thrones are why a new throne was needed and why two identical thrones were produced. To answer these questions, we must consider the date of their creation and their function at the time. The date inscribed in Devanagari on the thrones, ". . . san 1911," translated "in the year of 1911," provides a clue. From 1304 until the late nineteenth century, the kings of Dungarpur ruled from Juna Mahal, an elaborate, towering palace complex that was continually added to over the centuries. The backrest of the original Dungarpur throne at Juna Mahal was believed to be home to the lineage's guardian deity, who is the source of the king's power.[77] Legend dictates that to move that throne, which is still *in situ* in the Durbar Hall of the old palace, would be inauspicious for the kingdom. Beginning in 1883, work began on the creation of a new royal residence, the Udai Bilas on Gaip Sagar lake. Most of this structure was completed by the end of the first decade of the twentieth century, and certainly the new palace was in need of a new throne. These new silver thrones were commissioned in what was the current European-influenced style.

1911 was a supremely important year in modern Indian political history. It was the year that King George V of England travelled to India to be crowned Emperor at the great Delhi Durbar. During this grand celebration, the northern neighborhoods of Delhi were transformed into a vast encampment and parade grounds. Royal families from across India were invited to attend the ceremonies, and the Dungarpur entourage had a camp prominently located at the Durbar. It would not be surprising for royal patrons to have commissioned new furniture and artwork that year to take to the encampment and for receiving dignitaries at their new palace afterward. It is therefore possible that the new Dungarpur thrones were used for both purposes: to provide a proper throne for the new palace and to be taken to the Imperial Durbar of George V in Delhi.

Why were two thrones made? When they were acquired by the Nelson-Atkins, it was assumed that the two thrones had been intended for the king and the queen. However, the *maharani* would not have been seated on a throne during a royal durbar at this time, as she would have likely had to attend a public audience from behind a screen in *purdah*. So, if not for the queen, for whom was the second throne made? One possibility is that they were intended for multiple locations. Another theory is that the second throne was intended to be used by the second-highest ranking member of the family, the crown prince (*raj kumar*). In the early twentieth century, however, the highest-ranking official in colonial India was the Emperor or Empress, whose authority was embodied in India by the British Viceroy. Curator Michael Hall has suggested that one chair may have been intended to be used by the highest-ranking official in attendance at a royal audience, which in 1911 would have been the Viceroy, Lord Hardinge, or George V himself.[78] This audience configuration would require two thrones, and this scenario is evident in photographs of other durbar scenes from the late colonial era, as in the photograph in an album in the Royal Collection featuring two durbar thrones in Jaipur, taken during the tour of the Prince of Wales in 1875–76.[79] In this interpretation, the ruling *maharawal* of Dungarpur would have sat next to the British ruler, in an identical chair, a scene that seems charged with political meaning in our current, post-colonial world. The Dungarpur Thrones thus tell us multiple stories, as iconography and design from Rajput and European traditions fused together to create luxurious furniture that signify both Hindu kingship and colonial power.

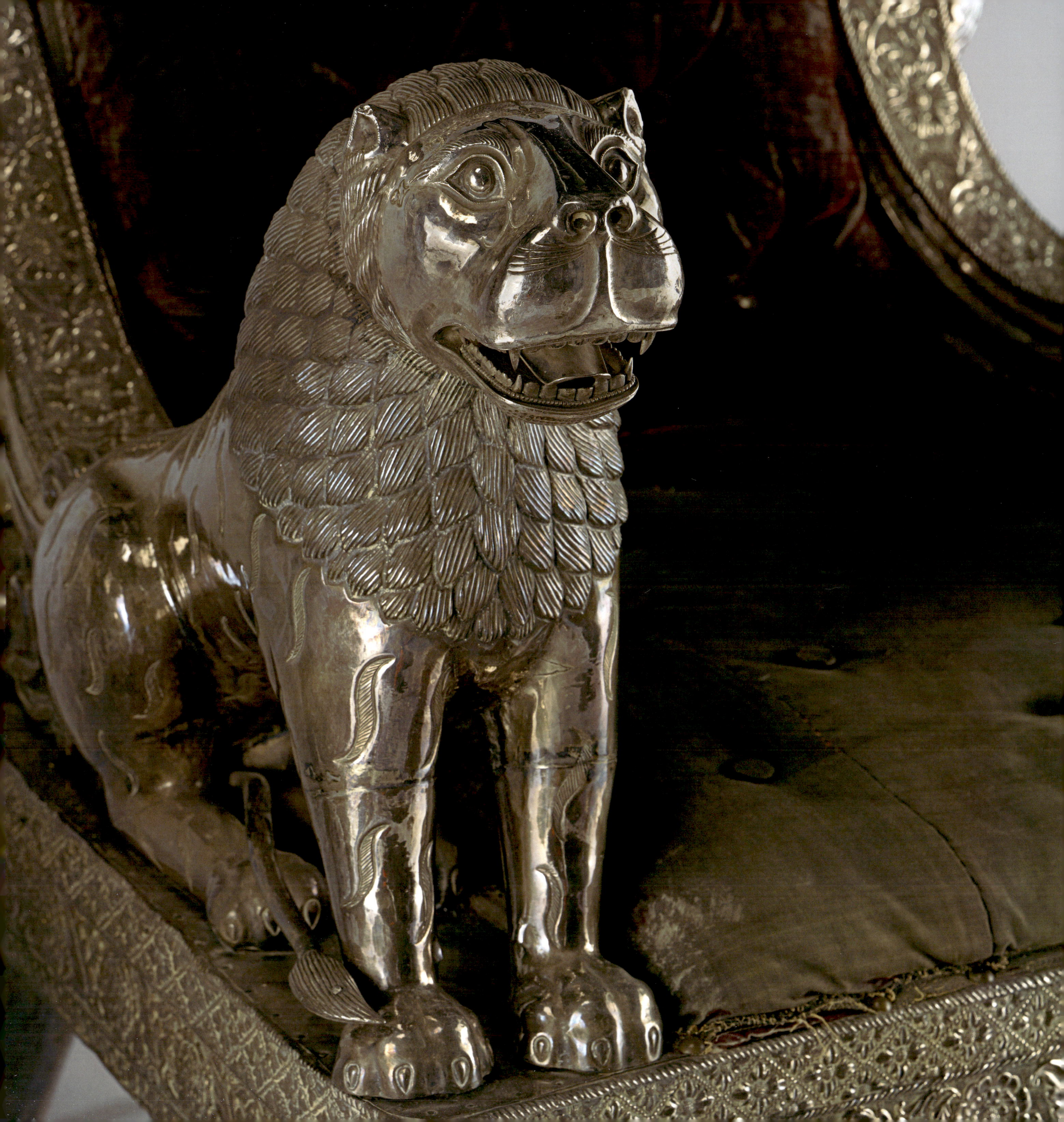

NOTES

1. Kurt A. Behrendt, *The Art of Gandhara in The Metropolitan Museum of Art* (New York: The Metropolitan Museum of Art, 2007), 35. The Hadda stupa of Megha is mentioned in the records of Xuanzang.

2. Relief of the Dipankara Jataka, accession number 1998.491. The relief is discussed in Behrendt, *The Art of Gandhara*, cat. 31, 34–35.

3. British Museum accession numbers: 1880.68, 1880.74, 1880. 208, 1899.0715.11, 1980.0225.1. Collections Online, accessed 10-20-2015.

4. Rafi U. Samad, *The Grandeur of Gandhara: The Ancient Buddhist Civilization of the Swat, Peshawar, Kabul and Indus Valleys* (New York: Algora Publishing, 2011), 186.

5. Nelson-Atkins Museum of Art, Department Files. Acquisition Proposal Form, December 18, 1988.

6. Angela Falco Howard and Giuseppe Vignato, *Archaeological and Visual Sources of Meditation in the Ancient Monasteries of Kuča, Studies in Asian Art and Archaeology*, vol. 28 (Leiden: Brill Publishers, 2015), 112–13.

7. Robert Linrothe, Christian Luczanits, and Melissa R. Kerin, *Collecting Paradise: Buddhist Art of Kashmir and its Legacies* (Illinois: Mary and Leigh Block Museum of Art, Northwestern University, 2014), 63.

8. Referenced from Fâ-hsien [Faxian], *A Record of Buddhistic Kingdoms: Being an Account by the Chinese Monk Fâ-Hsien of his Travels in India and Ceylon (A.D. 399–414) in Search of the Buddhist Books of Discipline*, trans. James Legge, chapter 16, Ebook edition: https://ebooks.adelaide.edu.au/f/fa-hien/f15l/chapter16.html.

9. This sculpture is illustrated and discussed in Joanna Gottfried Williams, *The Art of Gupta India: Empire and Province* (Princeton, NJ: Princeton University Press, 1982), plate 18, 29–30.

10. Laurence Sickman, "Stone Sculpture of India and South-East Asia," in *William Rockhill Nelson Gallery, Atkins Museum of Fine Art, Apollo Magazine* 97 (1973), 83.

11. Williams, *The Art of Gupta India*, 78.

12. Xuanzang, *Si-Yu-Ki: Buddhist Records of the Western World*, trans. Samuel Beal (London: Kegan Paul, Trench, Trubner and Co. Ltd., 1906), 2:45ff, op. cit.; Susan L. Huntington and John C. Huntington, *The Art of Ancient India: Buddhist, Hindu, Jain* (New York and Tokyo: Weatherhill, Inc., 1985), 201.

13. Frequently illustrated, including in Williams, *The Art of Gupta India*, plate 64; James C. Harle, *Gupta Sculpture: Indian Sculpture from the Fourth to Sixth Centuries A.D.* (London: Oxford University Press, 1974), plate 47; Huntington and Huntington, *The Art of Ancient India*, fig. 10.18, 200.

14. For discussions and attributions of the date of this sculpture, see Stanislaw J. Czuma and Rekha Morris, *Kushan Sculpture:*

Images from Early India (Cleveland: The Cleveland Museum of Art, 1985), cat. 117, 210; Pratapaditya Pal, *Bronzes of Kashmir* (New York: Hacker Art Books, 1975), cat. 72, 192; Dorothy H. Fickle, "An Early Gupta Bronze Buddha," *Lalit Kala* 28 (1997): 15–23; and Sheila E. Hoey Middleton, "The Quest for the Third Buddha: A Sequel," *South Asian Studies* 26, no. 2, (September 2010): 119–24. For a discussion regarding the supposed lack of bronze sculptures made in central and eastern India during the Gupta period, see Frederick M. Asher, *The Art of Eastern India: 300-800* (Minneapolis: University of Minnesota Press, 1980), 59.

15. Pal, *Bronzes of Kashmir*, 192.

16. The translation of the inscription reads: "This is the pious gift of the lay-woman Bedika [or Bodika?]. Whatever merit there may be in this, let it be for the attainment of ultimate wisdom by (my) mother and father (and) by all sentient beings." Translated by Richard Salomon in 1990 for the Nelson-Atkins Museum of Art, Department Object File and collections notebook.

17. For a recent illustration and discussion of this sculpture in the National Museum, Bangkok, see John Guy et al., *Lost Kingdoms: Hindu-Buddhist Sculpture of Early Southeast Asia* (New York: The Metropolitan Museum of Art, 2014), cat. 117, 206–09.

18. Huntington and Huntington, *The Art of Ancient India*, 395–96, and Susan L. Huntington and John C. Huntington, *Leaves from the Bodhi Tree: The Art of Pala India (8th–12th centuries) and Its International Legacy* (Dayton, Seattle, and London: Dayton Art Institute in Association with the University of Washington Press, 1990), 103–105, 136–37.

19. For a discussion of *andagu* and their iconography, see Sylvia Fraser-Lu, *Burmese Crafts: Past and Present* (Kuala Lumpur, Oxford, Singapore, and New York: Oxford University Press, 1994), plate 35, 59–60, and Huntington and Huntington, *Leaves from the Bodhi Tree*, cat. 62, 221–22.

20. Huntington and Huntington, *Leaves from the Bodhi Tree*, cat. 62, 221–22.

21. Ibid., 221–22.

22. Robert Linrothe et al., *Collecting Paradise*, 34.

23. Ibid., 33–34; Phyllis Granoff, "A Portable Shrine from Central Asia," *Archives of Asian Art*, vol. 22 (1968–69): 80–95; and Pratapaditya Pal, "Prologemena to the Study of a Portable Buddhist Shrine," *Bulletin of the Asia Institute*, vol. 18 (2004): 1–19.

24. Granoff, "A Portable Shrine from Central Asia," 82–84.

25. Pal, "Prologemena to the Study of a Portable Buddhist Shrine," 8–16.

26. Linrothe et al., *Collecting Paradise*, 33–35.

27. For the identification of the individual Bodhisattvas and their connection to the *astamahabodhisattva*s, see Phyllis Granoff, "A Portable Shrine from Central Asia," 90–94, and Dorothy Fickle, object essay and research materials, The Nelson-Atkins Museum of Art, Department Object File and Object Notebook.

28. R.E. Emmerick, *Tibetan Texts concerning Khotan*, London Oriental Series, vol. 19 (London: Oxford University Press, 1967), 12–15.

29. Robert Linrothe proposes that this could represent the bestowal of blessings like health, protection, and safety on the figure, see Linrothe et al., *Collecting Paradise*, 31–32.

30. Ibid., 31.

31. For a discussion of Ganesha in the program of Cave 6 at Udayagiri, see Huntington, *The Art of Ancient India*, 190–91.

32. For a recent essay on processional bronzes, see Richard H. Davis, "Chola Bronzes in Procession," in Vidya Dehejia, *The Sensuous and the Sacred: Chola Bronzes from South India* (New York, Seattle, and London: American Federation of Arts in association with University of Washington Press, 2002), 46–63.

33. For information on the discovery, see Lindsay Murdoch, "Lost Horizons: Mediaeval City Uncovered," *The Sydney Morning Herald*, June 15, 2013, http://www.smh.com.au/world/lost-horizons-mediaeval-city-uncovered-20130614-209p3.html. For early analysis of the hydro engineering of the site, see Dan Penny, Jean-Baptiste Chevance, David Tang, and Stephanie De Greef, "The Environmental Impact of Cambodia's Ancient City of Mahendraparvata (Phnom Kulen)," *PLOS ONE*: January 8, 2014, DOI: 10: 1371/ journal.pone.0084252.

34. For an attribution of this relief to the Banteay Srei style, see Sherman E. Lee, *Ancient Cambodian Sculpture* (New York: The Asia Society, Inc., 1969), cat. 18, 104–05.

35. Sherman E. Lee, *Ancient Cambodian Sculpture*, cat. 23, 105.

36. Op. cit. in Martin Lerner, "Some Unpublished Sculpture from Harshagiri," in *The Bulletin of the Cleveland Museum of Art* 56, no. 10 (Dec. 1969): 354–65, 355.

37. Ibid., 355.

38. Pratapaditya Pal, *Indian Sculpture*, vol. 2 (Los Angeles, Berkeley, and London: The Los Angeles County Museum of Art in association with University of California Press, 1988), cat. 53, 128.

39. This portion of the inscription is discussed in *Gods, Guardians and Lovers: Temple Sculptures from North India A.D. 700-1200*, ed. Vishakha N. Desai and Darielle Mason (New York and Ahmedabad: Asia Society Galleries in association with Mapin Publishing, 1993), cat. 12, 158.

40. Ramacandra Mahapatra Kaula Bhattaraka, *Shilpa Prakasha: Medieval Orissan Sanskrit Text on Temple Architecture*, trans. Alice Boner and Sadas'iva Rath S'aarma (New Delhi and Delhi: Indira Gandhi National Centre for the Arts and Motilal Banarsidass Publishers Pvt., Ltd., 1966), 165, lines 455 and 458. See also a reference to a similar sculpture by the 12th-century monk Ramacandragani (20–21), note 30 (24).

41. See Sherman E. Lee, *Ancient Cambodian Sculpture*, cat. 60, 113.

42. See, for example, the use of the terms in Michael D. Coe, *Angkor and the Khmer Civilization* (New York: Thames and Hudson, 2003).

43. For a discussion of *yoginis* and the potential powers offered through their worship, see Padma Audrey Kaimal, *Scattered Goddesses: Travels with the Yoginis* (Ann Arbor: Asia Past and Present, No. 8, Association of Asian Studies, Inc., 2012), 81–108; David Gordon White, *Kiss of the Yogini: "Tantric Sex" in its South Asian Contexts* (Chicago and London: The University of Chicago Press, 2003), chapters 5 and 6, 123–87; Devangana Desai, *The Religious Imagery of Khajuraho* (Mumbai: Project for Indian Cultural Studies, No. 9, Franco-Indian Research Pvt., Ltd., 1996), chapter 4, 81–98; and Vidya Dehejia, *Yogini Cult and Temples: A Tantric Tradition* (New Delhi: The National Museum, Janpath, New Delhi, 1986).

44. For a discussion of this group and their original context, see Kaimal, *Scattered Goddesses,* 2012.

45. Karaikkal Ammaiyar, *Tiruvaalankattu Mutta Tiruppatikam*, verse 1, translated and analyzed in Elaine Craddock, *Siva's Demon Devotee: Karaikkal Ammaiyar* (Albany: State University of New York Press, 2010), 38, 138–39.

46. "Karaikkal Ammaiyar," from the *Arputat Tiruvantaati*, verse 98. Translated in Craddock, *Siva's Demon Devotee*, 2010, 133.

47. Ananda K. Coomaraswamy, "The Dance of Shiva" (1918), in *The Dance of Shiva: Fourteen Indian Essays*, 2nd ed. (New Delhi: Munshiram Manoharlal, 1982), 83–95. Coomaraswamy's interpretation is questioned in Padma Audrey Kaimal, "Shiva Nataraja: Shifting Meanings of an Icon," *Art Bulletin*, no. 81:3 (1999): 393–94.

48. For a detailed analysis of the Nataraja form and its meaning and political use throughout history, see Kaimal: "Shiva Nataraja," 1999: 390–419.

49. Ibid., 395–96.

50. For a discussion of the differences between images of dancing Krishna and Sambandar, see Dehejia, *The Sensuous and the Sacred*, cat. 28, 154.

51. For a discussion of the *Devi Mahatmya* and an attribution of its date, see David Kinsley, "The Portrait of the Goddess in the Devi-Mahatmya," *Journal of the American Academy of Religion*, vol. 46:4 (December 1978), 489–506, 490.

52. For a description of Paryushan practices, see John E. Cort, *Jains in the World: Religious Values and Ideology in India* (New York: Oxford University Press, 2001), 159.

53. For an analysis of the relationship between the two texts and the festival, see John E. Cort, "Fistfights in the Monastery: Calendars, Conflict and Karma among the Jains," *Approaches to Jaina Studies: Philosophy, Logic, Rituals and Symbols*, Narendra K. Wagle and Olle Qvarnstrom, eds. (Toronto: University of Toronto, Centre for South Asian Studies, 1999), 36–59.

54. For a full discussion of this section of the manuscript, see Robert J. Del Bonta, "A Kalakacaryakatha in the Nelson-Atkins Museum," *Exemplar: The Journal of South Asian Studies*, 2:2 (Fall 2014), 50–56.

55. See Robert J. Del Bonta, "A Kalakacaryakantha in the Nelson-Atkins Museum," 52–54. For a larger discussion of the influence of Islamic art on Jain painting, see Saryu Doshi, "Colour, Motif and Arabesque," *Marg*, 45:2 (December 1993), 42–65, also published in *India and Egypt: Influences and Interactions*, ed. Saryu Doshi (Mumbai: Marg Publications, 1993), 112–35.

56. For a discussion of the Jain practices, including image veneration, see John E. Cort, "Bhakti in the Early Jain Tradition: Understanding Devotional Religion in South Asia," in *History of Religions*, 42:1 (2002), 59–86, 79.

57. See scientific report prepared for The Nelson-Atkins Museum of Art, John Twilley, "Polychrome Materials from a 16th Century Jain Shrine (#32-137)," April 10, 2012.

58. Jahangir, "The Jahangirnama," *The Jahangirenama: Memoirs of Jahangir*, ed. Wheeler M. Thackston (Washington, D.C., New York, and Oxford: Freer Gallery of Art, Smithsonian Institution, and Oxford University Press, 1999), 268.

59. For discussions about the Gulshan Album, including the Nelson-Atkins folios, see Susan Stronge, "The Gulshan Album, c. 1600–1618"; in Elaine Wright and Susan Stronge, *Muraqqa': Imperial Mughal Albums from the Chester Beatty Library*, (Alexandria, VA: Art Services International, 2008), 76–81, Fig. 32, 78; and Milo Cleveland Beach, *The Grand Mogul: Imperial Painting in India 1600-1660* (Williamstown, MA: Sterling and Francine Clark Art Institute, 1978), nos. 6–7, 26, 46–51. Current research by John Seyller, Milo Beach, and an upcoming thesis by Hamama Bushra should shed further light on the Nelson-Atkins folios in future publications.

60. Abul Fazl Allami, *Ain-I Akbari*, trans. H. Blochmann (1927) (Delhi: Low Price Publications and DK Fine Art Press, Ltd., 2008), vol. 1, 294. This description is given in a section on tiger hunting, but the technique appears to be the same one illustrated in this drawing.

61. The translations of both verses were provided by Sheila S. Blair in 1983 for The Nelson-Atkins Museum of Art, Department object files.

62. The fifth painting of Hindola Raga was formerly in the collection of Stuart Cary Welch, Jr. It was auctioned at Sotheby's, London, The Stuart Cary Welch Collection, Part II, May 31, 2011, Lot 10.

63. Mark Zebrowski, *Deccani Painting* (London, Berkeley, and Los Angeles: Sotheby Publications and the University of California Press, 1983), figs. 199–202, 226–33.

64. Ibid., 226–33.

65. Dorothy Fickle, object essay and research materials, The Nelson-Atkins Museum of Art, Department object file.

66. Translated by Richard J. Cohen in 1988 for The Nelson-Atkins Museum of Art, Department object file.

67. Andrew Topsfield, *Paintings from Rajasthan in the National Gallery of Victoria* (Melbourne: National Gallery of Victoria, 1980), cat. 223.

68. For a discussion of the *millefleur* type in carpets and woven shawls and hangings, see Dan Walker, *Flowers Underfoot: Indian Carpets of the Mughal Era* (New York: The Metropolitan Museum of Art and Harry N. Abrams, Inc., 1997), 119–29.

69. This number was reported in 1783 to the British traveler George Forster, referenced in Frank Ames, *The Kashmir Shawl and its Indo-French Influence* (Woodbridge, Suffolk: Antique Collector's Club Ltd., 1986), 20.

70. The Metropolitan Museum of Art, accession no. 1970.302.7.

71. Ames, *The Kashmir Shawl*, plate 161a, 248.

72. An observation by Victor Jacquemont, cited in Ames, *The Kashmir Shawl*, fn. 5, 66.

73. This photograph is a royal portrait of the Maharao of Jaipur that was supplied to the publication. The Maharao did not travel to Delhi to attend the Durbar. See *The Historical Record of the Imperial Visit to India: Compiled from the Official Records under the Orders of the Viceroy and Governor-General of India* (London: Published for the Government of India, 1914) by John Murray, plate 1.

74. For a history of the Dungarpur Kingdom, see Klaus Imig and Mahesh C. Purohit, *Juna Mahal Dungarpur: Ein Rajputen-Palast in Rajasthan/Indien* (Zurich: Museum Rietberg, 2006), 20, and www.royalark.net/India/dungarpur.htm.

75. For a discussion of the Durbar and the state achievements assigned there, see David F. Phillips, *Emblems of the Indian States*, The Flag Heritage Foundation Monograph and Translation Series, No. 2 (Winchester, MA: Flag Heritage Foundation, 2011), 11.

76. The attribution of this style to the turn of the twentieth century is suggested by Wynyard Wilkinson, personal conversation, November 2, 2012, and email correspondence, January 14, 2013.

77. Imig and Purohit, *Juna Mahal Dungarpur*, 107–108, and historical information provided on didactic panels at Juna Mahal, visited in September 2014.

78. Michael Hall refuted the identification of a "maharani's" throne in the court and suggested a link to paired thrones in colonial durbars, personal conversation, October 9, 2014.

79. Bourne and Shepherd, *Durbar Thrones*, Jaipur, 1875–76, albumen print, RCIN 27011963, in *Prince of Wales Tour of India 1875–76*, vol. 6.

BIBLIOGRAPHY

Abū al-Faẓl. *The Āʾīn-i Akbarī*. Translated by H. Blochmann and edited by D.C. Phillott. Delhi: Low Price Publications, 2008.

Ames, Frank. *The Kashmir Shawl and its Indo-French Influence*. Woodbridge, Suffolk: Antique Collectors' Club, 1986.

The Art Institute of Chicago. "Dhanasri Ragini." Accessed March 11, 2016. http://www.artic.edu/aic/collections/artwork /49229.

Asher, Frederick M. *The Art of Eastern India, 300–800*. Minneapolis: University of Minnesota Press, 1980.

Basham, A. L., *The Wonder that was India: A Survey of the Culture of the Indian Sub-Continent Before the Coming of the Muslims*. London: Sidwick and Jackson, 1954.

Beach, Milo Cleveland, Stuart Cary Welch, and Glenn D. Lowry. *The Grand Mogul: Imperial Painting in India, 1600–1660*. Williamstown, MA: Sterling and Francine Clark Art Institute, 1978.

Behrendt, Kurt A. *The Art of Gandhara in The Metropolitan Museum of Art*. New York: The Metropolitan Museum of Art, 2007.

The British Museum. "Dhanasri Ragini." Accessed March 11, 2016. http://www.britishmuseum.org/research/collection_online /collection_object_details.aspx?objectId=1607792&partId =1&searchText=Dhanasri+Ragini&page=1.

The British Museum. "The Dīpaṃkara jātaka." Accessed October 20, 2015. http://www.britishmuseum.org/research/ collection_online/collection_object_details.aspx?objectId=1823 06&partId=1&searchText=1880.68&page=1.

The British Museum. "The Dīpaṃkara jātaka." Accessed October 20, 2015. http://www.britishmuseum.org/research/ collection_online/collection_object_details.aspx?objectId=1821 69&partId=1&searchText=1880.208&page=1.

The British Museum. "The Dīpaṃkara jātaka." Accessed October 20, 2015. http://www.britishmuseum.org/research/ collection_online/collection_object_details.aspx?objectId=2253 80&partId=1&searchText=1899,0715.11&page=1.

The British Museum. "The Dīpaṃkara jātaka." Accessed October 20, 2015. http://www.britishmuseum.org/research/ collection_online/collection_object_details.aspx?objectId=1835 64&partId=1&searchText=1980,0225.1&page=1

The British Museum. "Panel." Accessed October 20, 2015. http://www.britishmseum.org/research/collection_online/ collection_object_details.aspx?objectId=182300&partId=1& searchText=1880.74&page=1.

Coe, Michael D. *Angkor and the Khmer Civilization*. Ancient Peoples and Places. New York: Thames & Hudson, 2003.

Coedès, George. *The Indianized States of Southeast Asia*, original French edition. Paris: Editions E. de Boccard, 1964.

Coomaraswamy, Ananda K. *The Dance of Shiva: Fourteen Indian Essays*. 2nd ed. New Delhi: Munshiram Manoharlal, 1982.

Cort, John E. "Bhakti in the Early Jain Tradition: Understanding Devotional Religion in South Asia." *History of Religions* 42, no. 1 (August 2002): 59–86.

Cort, John E. "Fistfights in the Monastery: Calendars, Conflict and Karma among the Jains." In *Approaches to Jaina Studies: Philosophy, Logic, Rituals and Symbols*, edited by Narendra K. Wagle and Olle Qvarnström, 36–59. South Asian Studies Papers 11. Toronto: University of Toronto Centre for South Asian Studies, 1999.

Cort, John E. *Jains in the World: Religious Values and Ideology in India*. New York: Oxford University Press, 2001.

Craddock, Elaine, and Kāraikkālammayar. *Siva's Demon Devotee: Kāraikkāl Ammaiyār*. Albany: State University of New York Press, 2010.

Czuma, Stanislaw J., and Rekha Morris. *Kushan Sculpture: Images from Early India*. Cleveland: Cleveland Museum of Art in cooperation with Indiana University Press, 1985.

Dehejia, Vidya. *Discourse in Early Buddhist Art: Visual Narratives in India*. New Delhi: Munshiran Monharlal Publishers Pvt. Ltd., 1997.

Dehejia, Vidya. *Yoginī, Cult and Temples: a Tantric Tradition*. New Delhi: National Museum, 1986.

Dehejia, Vidya, Richard H. Davis, Irā Nākacāmi, and Karen Pechilis. *The Sensuous and the Sacred: Chola Bronzes from South India*. New York: American Federation of Arts in association with University of Washington Press, 2002.

Del Bontà, Robert J. "A Kālakācāryakathā in the Nelson-Atkins Museum." *Exemplar: The Journal of South Asian Studies* 2, no. 2 (Fall 2014): 50–57.

Desai, Devangana. *The Religious Imagery of Khajuraho*. Project for Indian Cultural Studies 4. Mumbai: Franco-Indian Research, 1996.

Desai, Vishakha N., and Darielle Mason, eds. *Gods, Guardians, and Lovers: Temple Sculptures from North India, A.D. 700-1200*. New York: Asia Society Galleries in association with Mapin Publishing, Ahmedabad, 1993.

Doshi, Saryu. "Colour, Motif and Arabesque." *Marg* 45, no. 2 (December 1993): 42–65. Also published in *India and Egypt: Influences and Interactions*, edited by Saryu Doshi and Mostafa El-Abbadi, 112–135. Bombay: Marg Publications, 1993.

"Dungarpur." Accessed December 3, 2015. http://www.royalark .net/India/dungarpur.htm.

Emmerick, R. E. *Tibetan Texts Concerning Khotan*. London Oriental Series 19. London: Oxford University Press, 1967.

Fâ-hien [Faxian]. *A Record of Buddhistic Kingdoms: Being an Account by the Chinese Monk Fâ-Hien of his Travels in India and Ceylon (A.D. 399–414) in Search of the Buddhist Books of Discipline*. Translated by James Legge. E-book edition. Accessed November 30, 2015. https://ebooks.adelaide.edu.au/f/fa-hien/ f15l/chapter16.html.

Fickle, Dorothy H. "An Early Gupta Bronze Buddha." *Lalit Kala* 28 (1997): 15–23.

Fraser-Lu, Sylvia. *Burmese Crafts: Past and Present*. Kuala Lumpur: Oxford University Press, 1994.

Goswamy, B. N., and Eberhard Fischer. *Pahari Masters: Court Painters of Northern India*. Zurich: Artibus Asiae Publishers, 1992.

Granoff, Phyllis. "A Portable Shrine from Central Asia." *Archives of Asian Art* 22 (1968–69): 80–95.

Guy, John, Pierre Baptiste, Lawrence Becker, Berenice Bellina, Robert L. Brown, Federico Carò, M.L. Pattaratorn Chirapravati, Janet G. Douglas, Arlo Griffiths, Agustijanto Indradjaya, Thi Liên Lê, Pierre-Yves Manguin, Stephen A. Murphy, Ariel O'Connor, Peter Skilling, Janice Stargardt, Donna K. Strahan, U Thein Lwin, Geoff Wade, U Win Kyaing, Hiram W. Woodward, Thierry Zephir. *Lost Kingdoms: Hindu-Buddhist Sculpture of Early Southeast Asia*. New York: The Metropolitan Museum of Art, 2014.

Harle, James C. *Gupta Sculpture: Indian Sculpture of the Fourth to the Sixth Centuries A.D.* Oxford: Clarendon Press, 1974.

The Historical Record of the Imperial Visit to India, 1911: Compiled from the Official Records Under the Orders of the Viceroy and Governor-General of India. London: Published for the Government of India by John Murray, 1914.

Howard, Angela Falco, and Giuseppe Vignato. *Archaeological and Visual Sources of Meditation in the Ancient Monasteries of Kuča*. Studies in Asian Art and Archaeology 28. Leiden: Brill Publishers, 2015.

Huntington, Susan L., and John C. Huntington. *The Art of Ancient India: Buddhist, Hindu, Jain*. New York: Weatherhill, 1985.

Huntington, Susan L., and John C. Huntington. *Leaves from the Bodhi Tree: the Art of Pāla India (8th-12th centuries) and Its International Legacy*. Dayton, OH: Dayton Art Institute in association with the University of Washington Press, 1990.

Imig, Klaus, and Mahesh C. Purohit. *Juna Mahal Dungarpur: ein Rajputen-Palast in Rajasthan/Indien*. Zürich: Museum Rietberg, 2006.

Jahangir, and W. M. Thackston. *The Jahangirnama: Memoirs of Jahangir, Emperor of India*. New York: Freer Gallery of Art, Arthur M. Sackler Gallery in association with Oxford University Press, 1999.

Kaimal, Padma Audrey. *Scattered Goddesses: Travels with the Yoginis*. Asia Past and Present 8. Ann Arbor, MI: Association for Asian Studies, Inc., 2012.

Kaimal, Padma Audrey. "Shiva Nataraja: Shifting Meanings of an Icon." *Art Bulletin* 81, no. 3 (September 1999): 390–419.

Kimball Art Museum. "Ragamala Painting of Dhanasri Ragini." Accessed March 11, 2016. https://www.kimbellart.org/collection-object/ragamala-painting-dhanasri-ragini.

Kinsley, David. "The Portrait of the Goddess in the Devī-Māhātmya." *Journal of the American Academy of Religion* 46, no. 4 (December 1978): 489–506.

Lee, Sherman E. *Ancient Cambodian Sculpture*. New York: Asia Society; distributed by New York Graphic Society, 1969.

Lerner, Martin. "Some Unpublished Sculpture from Harshagiri." *The Bulletin of the Cleveland Museum of Art* 56, no. 10 (December 1969): 354–364.

Linrothe, Robert N., Christian Luczanits, and Melissa R. Kerin. *Collecting Paradise: Buddhist Art of Kashmir and its Legacies*. New York: Rubin Museum of Art, 2014. Exhibition catalog.

Lyons, Tryna. *The Artists of Nathadwara: the Practice of Painting in Rajasthan*. Bloomington, IN: University of Indiana Press, 2004.

The Metropolitan Museum of Art. "Pashmina Carpet with Gateway-and-Millefleur Pattern." Accessed December 2, 2015. http://www.metmuseum.org/collection/the-collection-online/search/452192?rpp=30&pg=1&ft=1970.302.7&pos=1.

Middleton, Sheila E. Hoey. "The Quest for the 'Third Buddha': A Sequel." *South Asian Studies* 26, no. 2 (September 2010): 119–124.

Murdoch, Lindsay. "Lost Horizons: Mediaeval City Uncovered." *The Sydney Morning Herald*, June 15, 2013. Accessed December 1, 2015. http://www.smh.com.au/world/lost-horizons-mediaeval-city-uncovered-20130614-209p3.html.

Pal, Pratapaditya. *Bronzes of Kashmir*. New York: Hacker Art Books, 1975.

Pal, Pratapaditya. *Indian Sculpture: A Catalogue of the Los Angeles County Museum of Art Collection*, Vol. 2. Los Angeles: Los Angeles County Museum of Art in association with University of California Press, Berkeley, 1986-88.

Pal, Pratapaditya. "Prologemena to the Study of a Portable Buddhist Shrine." *Bulletin of the Asia Institute*, New Series, 18 (2004): 1–17.

Penny, Dan, Jean-Baptiste Chevance, David Tang, and Stéphanie De Greef. "The Environmental Impact of Cambodia's Ancient City of Mahendraparvata (Phnom Kulen)." *PLOS ONE*, January 8, 2014. Accessed December 1, 2015, DOI: 10.1371/journal.pone.0084252.

Phillips, David F. *Emblems of the Indian States*. Flag Heritage Foundation Monograph and Translation Series 2. Winchester, MA: Flag Heritage Foundation, 2011.

Rāmacandra Kaulācāra. *Silpa Prakāsa: Medieval Orissan Sanskrit Text on Temple Architecture*. Translated by Alice Boner and Sadashiva Rath Sharma. Leiden: E. J. Brill, 1966.

Russell, William Howard, Sydney Prior Hall, and Edward, King of Great Britain. *The Prince of Wales' Tour: A Diary in India; with Some Accounts of the Visits of His Royal Highness to the Courts of Greece, Egypt, Spain and Portugal . . . with Illustrations by S. P. Hall*. Vol. 6. London, 1877.

Samad, Rafi U. *The Grandeur of Gandhara: The Ancient Buddhist Civilization of the Swat, Peshawar, Kabul and Indus Valleys*. New York: Algora Publishing, 2011.

Schlievert, Chelsea, and Jason Steuber, "Collecting Asian Art, Defining Gender Roles: World War II, Women Curators and the Politics of Asian Art Collections in the United States." *Journal of the History of Collections* 20, no. 2 (2008): 291–303.

Sickman, Laurence. "Stone Sculpture of India and South-East Asia," in "William Rockhill Nelson Gallery, Atkins Museum of Fine Arts, Kansas City," ed. Denys Sutton, special issue, *Apollo Magazine* 97 (1973): 82–87.

Sotheby's (Firm). *The Stuart Cary Welch Collection: Part Two, Arts of India: Including Art of the Himalayas*. Date of Sale: May 31, 2011. London: Sotheby's, 2011.

Srinivasan, Doris Meth. "Monumental Nāginīs from Mathura," in *On the Cusp of an Era: Art in the Pre-Kuṣāṇa World*, Brill's Inner Asian Library 18. Leiden: Konninklijke, 2007.

Topsfield, Andrew. *Paintings from Rajasthan in the National Gallery of Victoria: A Collection Acquired Through the Felton Bequests' Committee*. Melbourne: National Gallery of Victoria, 1980.

Twilley, John. "Polychrome Materials from a 16th Century Jain Shrine (#32-136)." Scientific report prepared for The Nelson-Atkins Museum of Art, April 10, 2012.

Walker, Daniel S. *Flowers Underfoot: Indian Carpets of the Mughal Era*. New York: Metropolitan Museum of Art, 1997.

White, David Gordon. *Kiss of the Yoginī: "Tantric Sex" in its South Asian Contexts*. Chicago: University of Chicago Press, 2003.

The William Rockhill Nelson Gallery of Art and Mary Atkins Museum of Fine Arts, Handbook of the William Rockhill Nelson Gallery of Art. Kansas City, MO: William Rockhill Nelson Gallery of Art and Mary Atkins Museum of Fine Arts, 1933.

Williams, Joanna Gottfried. *The Art of Gupta India: Empire and Province*. Princeton, NJ: Princeton University Press, 1982.

Wright, Elaine Julia, and Susan Stronge. *Muraqqa' Imperial Mughal Albums from the Chester Beatty Library, Dublin*. Alexandria, VA: Art Services International, 2008.

Xuanzang. *Si-Yu-Ki: Buddhist Records of the Western World*. Translated by Samuel Beal. London: Kegan Paul, Trench, Trubner and Co. Ltd., 1906.

Yale University Art Gallery. "Ragini Dhanasri, an Illustration from the Ragamala Series." Accessed March 11, 2016. http://artgallery.yale.edu/collections/objects/83943.

Zebrowski, Mark. *Deccani Painting*. England: Sotheby Publications, 1983.

112

114

Notes on style and transliteration:

For ease of reading, foreign words that are not in common English usage are transliterated phonetically, without diacritical marks, and remain italicized throughout the text. In this volume, the term 'buddha' is used in lower case when discussing multiple buddhas or an unidentified buddha. 'Buddha' is capitalized when it refers to a specific being, like Shakyamuni Buddha, or when it refers to the title of a work of art.

Funding was provided by the Estelle S. and Robert A. Long Ellis Foundation

Library of Congress Cataloging-in-Publication Data
Names: Nelson-Atkins Museum of Art, author. | Masteller, Kimberly, author.
Title: Masterworks from India and Southeast Asia: the Nelson-Atkins Museum of Art / Kimberly Masteller.
Description: Kansas City, Missouri; Seattle and London: The Nelson-Atkins Museum of Art, In association with the University of Washington Press, 2016. | Includes bibliographical references and index.
Identifiers: LCCN 2016022312 | ISBN 9780997249293 (hardcover: alk. paper)
Subjects: LCSH: Art, Indic—Catalogs. | Art, Southeast Asian—Catalogs. | Art—Missouri—Kansas City—Catalogs. | Nelson-Atkins Museum of Art—Catalogs.
Classification: LCC N7301 .N45 2016 | DDC 700.95—dc23
LC record available at https://lccn.loc.gov/2016022312

Published by the Nelson-Atkins Museum of Art,
Kansas City, Missouri
in association with University of Washington Press,
Seattle and London
www.nelson-atkins.org
www.washington.edu/uwpress/

Produced by Lucia | Marquand, Seattle
www.luciamarquand.com

Edited by John Stevenson
Designed by Zach Hooker
Typeset in Minion Pro by Maggie Lee
Proofread by Barbara Bowen
Indexed by Candace Hyatt
Color management by iocolor, Seattle
Printed and bound in China by Artron Art Group

Jacket: (front) *Shiva Nataragia* (cat. 22);
(back) *Celestial Nymph* (cat. 18)
Page 2: *Domestic Jain Shrine* (cat. 26)
Page 4: *Folio from the Muraqqa Gulshan* (cat. 29)
Page 26: *Indra's Visit to the Buddha* (cat. 2)
Page 107: *Royal Throne* (armrest) (cat. 37)

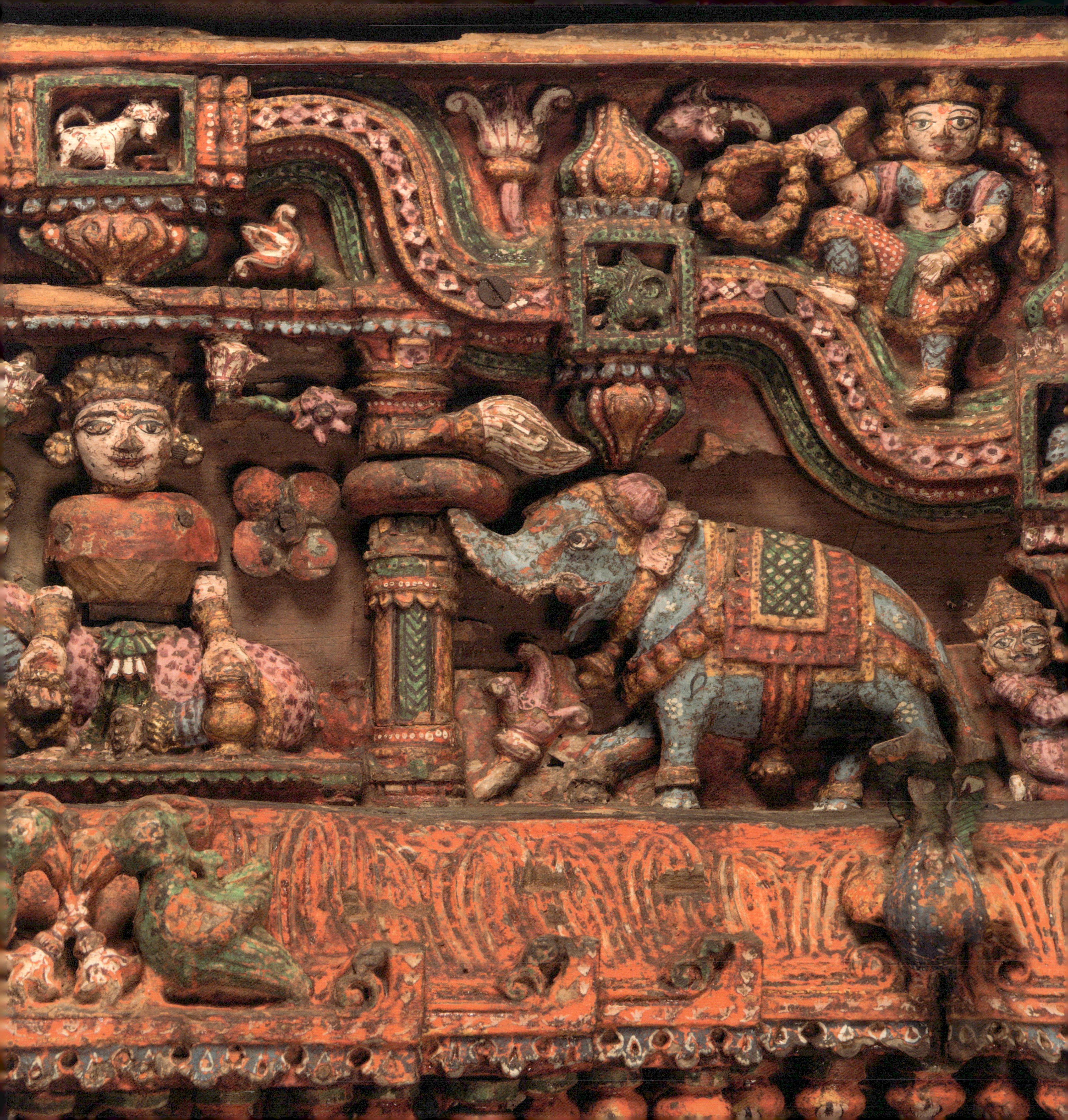